A
FOXHOLE
VIEW

To SFC Laura Wheeler.

Many thanks for supporting
Korean War Veterans and
the Sales of this book.
Hope you find this
book to your liking.

Mahalo and Best Wishes
Louis Baldovi.

A
FOXHOLE
VIEW

Personal Accounts of Hawaii's
Korean War Veterans

EDITED BY
LOUIS BALDOVI

A Latitude 20 Book
University of Hawai'i
Honolulu

© 2002 University of Hawai'i Press
All rights reserved ·
Printed in the United States of America
07 06 05 04 03 02   6 5 4 3 2 1

Library of Congress Cataloging-in-Publication Data

A foxhole view : personal accounts of Hawaii's Korean War veterans / edited by Louis Baldovi.
    p. cm.
"A Latitude 20 Book."
Includes bibliographical references and index.
ISBN 0-8248-2588-8 (cloth : alk. paper) – ISBN 0-8248-2610-8 (pbk. : alk. paper)
    1. Korean War, 1950–1953—Regimental histories—United States.   2. United States.
Army. Regimental Combat Team. 5th.   3. Korean War, 1950–1953—Personal narratives,
American.   4. Korean War, 1950–1953—Veterans—Hawaii.   5. Hawaii.   I .
Baldovi, Louis.

DS919 .F68 20002
951.904'28—dc21   2002018078

Frontispiece: Old Baldy after weeks of fighting (July 1952). Courtesy of Glenn E. White.

University of Hawai'i Press books are printed on acid-free
paper and meet the guidelines for permanence and durability
of the Council on Library Resources.

Designed by Bookcomp, Inc.
Printed by The Maple-Vail Book Manufacturing Group

A SOLDIER'S STORY

The rifleman fights without promise of either reward or relief. Behind every river there's another hill—and behind that hill, another river.

After weeks or months in the line only a wound can offer him the comfort of safety, shelter or bed.

Those who are left to fight, fight on, evading death but knowing that with each day of evasion they have exhausted one more chance for survival. Sooner or later, unless victory comes, this chase must end on the litter or in the grave.

General of the Army
Omar N. Bradley

CONTENTS

PREFACE

On the north lawn of the state capitol in Honolulu, beneath a canopy of native Hawaiian trees are two serpentine walls 5 feet high, one much longer than the other. The walls are made of polished black granite and are pedestaled, each pedestal bearing the name of a Hawaii soldier killed in the Vietnam or Korean War. The longer of the two walls, about 80 feet in length, honors 456 of Hawaii's men who died in the Korean War. On July 24, 1994, forty-two years after the Korean War cease fire took place, the State of Hawaii dedicated this monument to honor all its gallant sons.

In comparison to the overall population of the United States, Hawaii suffered three times as many wounded and three and a half times the total number of casualties. Of the sixteen nations, excluding the United States, that sent ground combat units to Korea, only Turkey and the United Kingdom had more men killed in action than Hawaii.

In spite of the sacrifices by Hawaii soldiers, little had been told about them following the war and, at the same time, very little was heard from its veterans. Perhaps people were just tired of hearing about wars. For whatever reasons, Korea became known as the "Forgotten War."

On July 27, 1995, the Korean War Memorial in the nation's capital was dedicated, giving notice to the country that the Korean War was not a "Forgotten War" after all. In his address at the dedication, President Clinton declared that July 27, 1996, through July 27, 2003, shall be known as "National Korean War Veterans Armistice Day." In 1997, the Defense Department announced that June 25, 2000, to November 11, 2003, would be recognized as the "50th Anniversary of the Korean War Commemoration." In 1999, Hawaii's governor appointed a commission comprised of Korean War veterans to conduct events related to the commemoration.

However, even with their newly found identity, very little has been written about Hawaii's Korean War veterans. This was the primary reason for my interviewing and compiling the experiences of the Korean War veterans of Hawaii.

Seventy Korean War combat veterans, from various units, were invited to share their accounts of the war. Of the seventy, fifty agreed to be interviewed. However, when informed of the interview requirements and format of the book, fifteen had a change of heart and withdrew from the interviews.

The main reasons for veterans declining to be part of this writing project were that they thought readers would not believe what they had experienced, they did not want to be branded as someone fabricating stories, and they could not remember what unit they served with and the details of their experiences.

For those who consented to be interviewed, their cooperation exceeded my expectations. Interviews were conducted in their homes, in my home, and in public places in Honolulu and the neighbor islands. Most were able to recall the details of their ordeals. In fact, the more harrowing the incident, the more detailed the description.

These veterans remembered the unit they served with, from squad to division level. Some, who initially had difficulty recalling their experiences, talked freely when prompted with key words. But recalling specific names, dates, and places was most difficult for the veterans, for the years that separated them from the conflict have dimmed their collective memory.

Consequently, the approximate time in months was used unless the exact dates were recalled by the veteran. Places where the events took place were equally difficult to determine so a general vicinity or area was used for location. More often, people were remembered by first or last names, not by full names. Whenever possible, statements have been checked against official sources to validate places, dates, units, and names. But the accuracy of places, dates, and names is not critical in this book. What happened is.

All the experiences are woven together in chronological order, starting with the year 1950, rather than presenting thirty separate accounts or short stories of each veteran. This format allows the reader to read a veteran's experience in Korea and, at the same time, know what was happening elsewhere, either in Korea or in Hawaii.

There are times when the experiences recounted here will seem unreal to those who were not in combat and would dispute the story. And because the stories are based on individual recollections years after the war, validating them would be difficult.

Yet for many veterans telling their story was a matter of a "cleansing" experience. They were able to vent what was kept hidden in their minds for years and years and, finally, were able to make public for the first time their war experiences.

For their families and friends, this would be their first encounter with what their husband, brother, or close friend had experienced in the Korean War.

ACKNOWLEDGMENTS

As in any work of this nature, a host of people have contributed to its publication. First and foremost are the Korean War veterans who consented to be interviewed for the book. At the risk of opening old wounds, they were willing to make public their memories, thoughts, and fears so that others might relate to those experiences. Without their input this narrative would not have been written.

My thanks also to the people of the University of Hawai'i Press, particularly the anonymous reviewers of the original manuscript, for recommending publication of the book. I am also grateful to Masako Ikeda, who believed that my manuscript was worthy of publication and worked with me, a neophyte in this field, to get the book published. I have found that it takes a lot of hard work to publish a book.

I am indebted to the *Honolulu Advertiser*, the *Honolulu Star Bulletin*, and the *Maui News*, who generously allowed me reproduce articles and photos for the book.

A great deal of thanks goes to Glenn E. White, David Lindroth, David Hackworth, and Theodore Savas of the Savas Publishing Company. All, without hesitation, granted me access to their materials.

I want to recognize Lt. Col. Lee Dong Koo (Ret.), Korean Veterans Association of the Republic of Korea, for providing the reference that authenticated questionable material in these memoirs.

Grateful acknowledgment is made to former combat photographer Al Chang for sharing his priceless collection of photographs of the Korean War.

Equally important and deserving recognition are many veterans, friends, and family members whose names do not appear in the book but who made significant contributions.

OVERVIEW OF
THE KOREAN WAR

Prior to World War II, Korea had been occupied by Japan for thirty-five years. Following World War II, the United States and the Union of Soviet Socialist Russia divided Korea in half at the 38th parallel. Russian forces occupied the northern half and U.S. troops the southern half, resulting in the birth of the two Koreas. South Korea chose a democratic form of government, and North Korea, a Soviet-style communist form of government. But both sides wanted the right to rule all of Korea.

At 4:00 A.M. on a rainy Sunday morning, the North Korean People's Army, numbering over 90,000 men and supported by Russian-built T-34 tanks, crossed the 38th parallel. The North Koreans quickly overran the South Korean defenses and, on June 28, entered Seoul, the capital of South Korea.

The Republic of Korea had 95,000 men, but less than half were on the border when the invasion began. Further, it had no tanks and its artillery was limited to a few battalions of 105mm howitzers.

After receiving news of the invasion, the United States requested a meeting of the UN Security Council. At the meeting a resolution was adopted demanding an immediate halt of hostilities and a withdrawal of North Korean forces to the 38th parallel. North Korea ignored UN demands.

Taking independent action, President Harry S. Truman authorized Gen. Douglas MacArthur to use U.S. sea, air, and ground forces against the invading North Koreans. Ground forces were terribly under strength in personnel, weapons, and equipment and physically not ready for combat. The United States Navy and Air Force operating in the Far East faced similar problems, but played an important role in delaying North Korean forces early in the war.

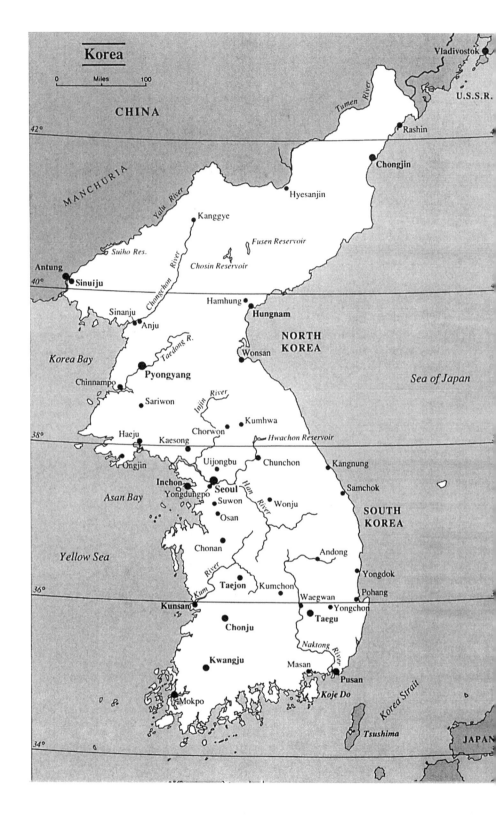

As the North Korean army steamrolled south past Seoul, an American task force from the 24th Infantry Division in Japan was quickly dispatched to South Korea by air. The task force was dubbed "Task Force Smith," named after its commander, Lt. Col. Charles Bradley Smith. The task force, numbering about 500 men, was quickly overwhelmed north of Osan on July 5 and forced into a disorganized retreat.

The rest of the 24th Infantry Division arrived shortly after and engaged the enemy at the Kum River and at Taejon, halting the North Korean drive temporarily for a few days. But facing the threat of encirclement, the division was forced to retreat south. The newly arrived 25th Infantry Division and 1st Cavalry Division were also forced to withdraw.

The Eighth Army Commander, Lt. Gen. Walton Walker, deployed his forces, which included Republic of Korea units, in the southeast corner of South Korea. Roughly 60 to 80 miles in size, the defensive perimeter was called the Pusan Perimeter.

The month of August saw the arrival of additional U.S. ground units. From Okinawa came two battalions of the 29th Infantry Regiment that fought with the 25th Infantry Division. From the United States came the 2d Infantry Division, the 1st Provisional Marine Brigade, and the 5th Regimental Combat Team (from Hawaii). The 7th Infantry Division, which was also stationed in Japan when the Korean War began, was slowly being brought to strength after being cannibalized by the 24th, 25th, and 1st Cavalry Divisions. The 3d Infantry Division arrived in Japan from stateside in October, where it was augmented by South Korean troops. It later landed at Iwon on the east coast as part of the 10th Corps in its drive north. The defense of the Pusan Perimeter was bolstered by the arrival of other UN ground forces and newly formed army divisions of the Republic of Korea.

On September 15, U.S. and Republic of Korea marines made an amphibious landing at Inchon, a port city 30 miles west of Seoul, hoping to trap the North Korean army south of Seoul. The 7th Infantry Division followed a day later. The combined forces drove inland and by September 26 had liberated Seoul. On September 16, UN forces broke out of the Pusan Perimeter and linked up with U.S. forces south of Seoul. Of the 90,000 North Koreans that invaded South Korea, only 30,000 escaped north.

In October UN forces started their drive to the Yalu River, the northern boundary of North Korea. Advance elements of two units, one American and one Republic of Korea, reached the Yalu River. China warned the advancing UN forces not to cross the 38th parallel, but the warning was ignored by General MacArthur. On October 25, Chinese forces entered the war. In the drive north friendly units captured Chinese soldiers. Intelligence sources viewed the soldiers as Chinese volunteers and maintained that China would not dare send regular troops into Korea.

On November 25, the Chinese attacked in force all across North Korea and drove UN forces south beyond the 38th parallel. This was the worst defeat of U.S. ground forces in U.S. military history. The 1st Marine Division and units of the 7th Infantry Division took a severe beating at the Changjin Reservoir on the eastern front. In the west the 8th Cavalry Regiment of the 1st Cavalry Division was manhandled by the Chinese at Unsan. The 2d Infantry Division in their retreat south of Kunuri suffered nearly 6,000 casualties.

On New Year's Eve the Chinese launched an offensive that drove UN forces 40 miles below the 38th parallel and captured Seoul for the second time. From January to May 1951, the Chinese mounted three offensives while the UN countered with several of their own. In one offensive the Chinese sent nearly 500,000 men against UN forces. All were beaten back with tremendous losses to the Chinese. The war continued for months below the 38th parallel. In March 1951, the allies finally drove the Chinese north of the 38th parallel and liberated Seoul for the second time.

In July peace talks started and the conflict settled down to a war of the outposts, terrain critical to both sides. Bitterly contested hills at the time were Old Baldy, Pork Chop, T-Bone, Heartbreak Ridge, Bloody Ridge, Jane Russell, Bunker Hill, and Triangle Hill.

In April 1953, the first exchange of prisoners, called "Little Switch," took place, at which time only the badly wounded were repatriated. Susumu Shinagawa of Kauai was the first Hawaii soldier to be freed from captivity.

On July 27, 1953, at 10:00 A.M. the cease fire was signed at Panmunjom and at 10:00 P.M. that night, after three years, one month, and two days, all fighting stopped. In the weeks following the cease fire, the final exchange of prisoners of war took place.

CHRONOLOGY OF THE KOREAN WAR

1950

June 25—North Korean People's Army (NKPA) invades South Korea.

June 28—Seoul falls to NKPA.

June 30—President Truman orders U.S. ground forces into Korea.

July 4–5—Task Force Smith of 24th Division in delaying action north of Osan.

July 9—President Truman names General MacArthur supreme commander in Korea.

July 10—Arrival of 24th Division in Korea. Fifth Air Force destroys large number of NKPA tanks and troops at Pyongtaek.

July 18—1st Calvary Division lands at Pohang-dong.

July 19—Battle for Taejon. 24th Division retreats south.

July 24—Arrival in Korea of 29th RCT from Okinawa.

July 31—Arrival in Korea of 5th RCT from Hawaii and 2d Division from stateside.

August 21—1st Provisional Marine Brigade, reinforced, arrives in Pusan.

August 4—Defense of Pusan Perimeter in southeastern Korea begins.

September 15—Inchon landing by 1st Marine Division and 7th Infantry Division.

September 16–18—UN forces break out of the Pusan Perimeter. NKPA forces retreat north.

September 19–29—Attack and capture of Seoul by UN troops.

October 1—UN troops cross 38th parallel.

October 19—Pyongyang, the North Korean capital, is captured.

October 25—Chinese Communist Forces (CCF) intervene in Korean War.

October 26—X Corps troops land at Wonsan on east coast.

November 1—CCF attack in force near Unsan. 1st Cavalry Division retreats.

November 3—Arrival in Korea of 3d Division.

November 21—U.S. and ROK units advance to the Yalu River.

November 26—U.S. 2d and 25th Divisions battle Chinese at Chongchon River. 5th RCT fights delaying action.

December 8—1st Marine Division and one regiment of 7th Division trapped at Changjin Reservoir fight way toward port of Hungnam.

December 12–24—Evacuation of Hungnam.

December 30—U.S. Air Force's first encounter with Red Chinese MIGS.

1951

January 4—Reds retake Seoul.

January 24—UN forces resume offensive.

March 15—Seoul retaken by UN forces.

April 22—CCF begins their spring offensive.

May 23—UN forces drive north again and dig in on the 38th parallel.

June 11—Eighth Army repulses two Red drives and penetrates "Iron Triangle."

July 10—Truce talks begin at Kaesong.

August 18—U.S. 2d Division and 5th ROK Division battle for "Bloody Ridge."

August 23—Reds break off truce talks.

September 13—U.S. 2d Division and French battalion take "Heartbreak Ridge."

October 25—Peace talks resume at Panmunjom.

November 1—Trench warfare stalemate along 38th parallel.

December 18—Exchange of POW lists between UN and CCF.

December 31—Arrival of 45th Division in Korea. 1st Cavalry Division returns to Japan.

1952

January 1—40th Division arrives in Korea. 24th Division returns to Japan.

February 18—Riots begin in Koje-do Prison.

March 1—Trench warfare continues along 38th parallel.

May 7—Koje-do prisoners seize General Dodd.

May 12—General Dodd released in return for concessions.

June 6–16—Operation Counter. Last major offensive by a division. Two regiments of 45th Division capture eleven hills in Yokkok-chon Valley.

October 8—General Clark calls off armistice talks because of deadlock of POW exchange.

December 5—President-elect Eisenhower winds up three-day Korean tour.

1953

January 1—Continuation of static war with numerous hill battles.

January 12—Sinanju hit by 440 planes.

April 11—General Clark asks Chinese Reds to exchange sick and wounded POWs before truce talks resume.

April 20–26—Operation Little Switch. Exchange of sick and wounded POWs.

May 31—South Korea vows it will fight alone if truce term leaves nation divided.

June 18—President Rhee releases 27,000 anti-Red prisoners.

June 25—CCF launches massive attacks against ROK troops in east-central front.

June 30—Sabre jets set air combat record by shooting down fifteen MIGs without loss of a Sabre.

July 6–11—Battles for Pork Chop and Arrowhead.

July 10—Truce delegates resume secret meetings.

July 13—80,000 Reds drive back ROK troops in central Korea.

July 18—ROK forces gain back ground lost earlier.

July 27—In Panmunjom cease fire signed at 10:00 A.M. Fighting ends 24 hours later at 10:00 P.M.

August 15–September 6—Operation Big Switch. Final exchange of prisoners.

MILITARY TERMS
AND EXPRESSIONS

As an aid to readers who may not be familiar with technical military terms, the following definitions may be helpful in following the stories in this book.

Ammo	Ammunition
BAR	Browning automatic rifle
Brah	Brother
CCF	Chinese Communist Forces
Chink	Chinese soldier
Chogie bearer	Korean porter
Commie	Chinese or North Korean soldier
Commo	Communication
CO	Commanding officer
CP	Command post
FECOM	Far East Command
EUCOM	European Command
GI	Government Issue. Also used to identify an American soldier.
Haole	Caucasian soldier from the mainland United States
HE	High explosive
HITC	Hawaiian Infantry Training Center
Hootchie	Bunker
KATUSA	Korean Augmentation to the U.S. Army. South Korean soldiers who were integrated into the U.S. Army.
KIA	Killed in action
KSC	Korean Service Corps

Local boy	A soldier from Hawaii
LP	Listening post
MIA	Missing in action
MG	Machine gun
MLR	Main line of resistance
MSR	Main supply route
NK	North Korean
NKPA	North Korea People's Army
OP	Outpost
OPLR	Outpost line of resistance
Pineapple	Hand grenade or soldier from Hawaii
P-38	A very tiny can opener
POW	Prisoner of war
RCT	Regimental Combat Team
Recon	Reconnaissance
ROK	Republic of Korea. South Korean soldiers were also referred to as ROKs.
R&R	Rest and Recuperation
UN	United Nations
WIA	Wounded in action
WP	White phosphorous
Yobo	A Korean
ZI	Zone of Interior, United States

PART I

1950 | The Cold War Turns Hot

On Sunday, June 25, 1950, at 4:00 a.m., the North Korean People's Army (NKPA) forces, numbering approximately 90,000 men and supported by Russian-built T-34 tanks, attacked across the 38th parallel into South Korea. The South Korean army was quickly overwhelmed by the communist juggernaut. In three days, Seoul, the capital city of South Korea, fell to the NKPA.

The United States 24th Infantry Division was rushed to Korea from Japan and was the first American unit to do battle with the NKPA. It was quickly followed by the United States 25th Infantry Division and 1st Cavalry Division, also from Japan.

Initially, American and Republic of Korea forces were no match for the NKPA and were forced into a defensive perimeter in southeast Korea known as the Pusan Perimeter.

The defense was bolstered in August by the arrival of two battalions of the 29th Regimental Combat Team from Okinawa, the 5th Regimental Combat Team from Hawaii, and the 1st Marine Brigade and the 2d Infantry Division from the United States. UN forces also arrived to reinforce American units.

From August to the middle of September, fierce battles raged in the perimeter, with friendly forces inflicting heavy casualties on the North Koreans.

JUNE 1950
SGT. CLARENCE YOUNG
Fort Shafter, Territory of Hawaii

I already had put in four years in the army and was married, with a four-year-old son and a six-year-old daughter. I was an auto mechanic at Fort Shafter with the Hawaiian Ordnance Depot. When I heard about the invasion of South Korea, my first thought was, *Heck, I'm safe,* thinking that only those men in infantry units would be sent to Korea if the United States decided to become involved in the war. I also thought that it was only five years before that World War II had ended and, surely, the United States would not even think of getting involved in another war so soon. Was I ever wrong!

JUNE 1950
CPL. HARRISON LEE
Charlie Company, 34th Infantry
Camp Mower, Japan

I was the company clerk. Our unit had been on field maneuvers for several weeks. Shortly after midnight, we were abruptly awakened and ordered to strike tents in the rain and return to Camp Cower. Once in camp, we received word about the situation in South Korea and the possibility of our unit being sent there.

"We will be back in Japan in thirty days," an officer told us, giving us the impression that we would handily whip the North Koreans' asses. So it was no big deal.

JUNE 1950
PFC. NICK NISHIMOTO
Baker Company, 35th Infantry
Camp Otsu, Japan

I was a gunner on the light .30 caliber machine gun in the weapons squad. Our regiment had just completed an amphibious training exercise and was on a ship on our way back to camp just a day out of Yokohama when over the public address system came the announcement that North Korea had invaded South Korea.

SGT. LUCIO SANICO
Baker Company, 35th Infantry
Camp Otsu, Japan

I was a World War II veteran. The Korean War came too fast to suit me. I was enjoying occupation duty in Japan as the 1st cook in the kitchen of Baker Company.

Duty was fun in Japan, especially when there were other Hawaii men in the company. With me were Nick Nishimoto, Henry Higa, Tadao Murakami, Al Chang, William Kim, and Wilfred Chun.

PFC. SUSUMU SHINAGAWA
Service Company, 34th Infantry
Camp Cower, Japan

I was on a five-day pass in Hiroshima having a great time when the war began so I knew nothing about the invasion of South Korea. I was a teletype operator on temporary duty from my regiment to the Composite Service Company, which provided services to rear echelon units. When my pass was over, I reported back to camp and was told of the situation in Korea. I was instructed by the sergeant in charge of quarters (CQ) to call my sergeant at regimental headquarters as soon as possible. He said it was important that I call him. I told the CQ that I would call the sergeant first thing in the morning.

Early the next morning, word came down through the public address system that all men on temporary duty with the Composite Service Company were to return to their respective regiments. When I arrived at my regiment, I called my sergeant's office but was told that he wasn't available so I walked over to regimental headquarters to find him, but no one seemed to know where he was.

The army sure can screw a guy up. An officer, not knowing what to do with me, told me to report to Able Company of the 34th Infantry Regiment. Able Company was an infantry company.

At Able Company we packed our gear and boarded a train for the port of Sasebo. At the dock a personnel officer read the names of those boarding. The personnel officer called everyone's name but mine. He looked at me and asked for my name and what company I was from. I gave him my name and told him most emphatically that I was a teletype operator on temporary duty to the Composite Service Company and not an infantryman. He looked at me with a quizzical smile and said, "Huh?" Again, I said, "I'm a teletype operator."

"Sorry, son. You are now in the infantry. Get your ass on board!"

Talk about being shanghaied. I learned later that the phone call I did not make would have kept me in Japan.

JUNE 1950

CPL. JAY HIDANO
Yokohama, Japan

Having reenlisted in the summer of 1949, I was in my fourth hitch in the United States Army stationed in Japan when the Korean War broke out.

I met my wife, Carol, in Tokyo in 1947 and we became the proud parents of two children, Susan and George. They were only babies when I left for Korea.

JUNE 1950

PFC. PEDRO BEHASA
Military Police Detachment
Schofield Barracks, Territory of Hawaii

I was with the military police detachment at Schofield Barracks, Wahiawa, pushing paper and pencil when the Korean War started. But that soon ended in July when the 5th Regimental Combat Team (RCT), stationed at Schofield Barracks, was alerted for overseas duty and was recruiting men to fill its ranks. I thought of volunteering, but decided against it and to just wait the alert out.

After a couple of weeks the regiment was still desperately looking for men so the army transferred men from various other units to the regiment. The military police detachment was no exception. It was overstaffed and, since I was the lowest-ranking enlisted personnel, I was the first in the detachment to be transferred to the regiment.

JUNE 1950

2D LT. HERBERT IKEDA
Schofield Barracks, Territory of Hawaii

When the war broke out I was an instructor with a military reserve unit on Oahu. I found out that the 5th RCT at Schofield Barracks was alerted and would soon be deployed overseas, probably to Korea. I went to S-1 (personnel section) at battalion headquarters and asked if I could volunteer to serve with the regiment. I was flatly refused. I asked S-1 to submit my request by telephone to the army adjutant general in Washington, D.C. The next day S-1 called me and said that the army adjutant general had approved my request and the army would accept volunteers who wanted to serve with the 5th RCT. With this information I sought out other men to volunteer with me.

JUNE 1950

CLAYTON MURAKAMI
Naalehu, Territory of Hawaii

There wasn't any excitement at Pahala High and Elementary School when North Korea invaded South Korea. I was a senior at the Kau High School when it happened. I remember reading about the war in the newspaper and always read the Korean War casualty list when it appeared. At the time, I never realized that someday I, too, would be on such a list.

JUNE 1950

LOUIS BALDOVI
Maui, Territory of Hawaii

I didn't know a war had begun in Korea until several of my classmates enlisted in the army in July. At the time I was employed by Libby McNeil and Libby, a pineapple company, in my hometown of Kuiaha, Maui. I had just completed my first year at Maui Technical School, where I was studying to be an auto mechanic and had one more year to go before graduating.

JUNE 1950

PVT. ARSANIO VENDIOLA
Schofield Barracks, Territory of Hawaii

After completing basic training at Schofield Barracks in May, my orders read to report to Fort Shafter. Because all my buddies I took basic training with were assigned to the 5th RCT at Schofield Barracks, I decided to try and have my orders changed. I went to personnel headquarters

after my furlough and requested a transfer to the 5th RCT. No problem.
My request was granted immediately.

JUNE 1950

SGT. MARCELLO VENDIOLA
Post Engineer Detachment
Schofield Barracks, Territory of Hawaii

I was a plumber with the post engineers at Schofield Barracks when the
fighting started in Korea. I was ordered to report to the 5th RCT and
was assigned to Charlie Company of the 1st Battalion. Charlie Company was an infantry and rifle company. Now, what good can a plumber
be in an infantry outfit?

But luck was with me because of my background as a plumber. A
sergeant was needed to be in charge of the battalion's water supply so I
volunteered for the job and got it. I was now with the 1st Battalion, and
in charge of the water supply. I was given a jeep and a water tank trailer.
All I had to do was to see that the companies in the battalion had enough
water when we were out in the field.

JUNE 1950

PFC. ROBERT ALIP
How Company, 19th Infantry
Taegu, South Korea

Our unit was on amphibious training off Yokohama on that memorable
Sunday morning of June 25. On June 28, we prepared ourselves for our
shipment to Korea and on June 30, sailed for Pusan, South Korea. We
arrived there on July 1. The division's two other regiments got to Korea
ahead of us.

We never stayed long in Pusan. We got on trucks and went north to
the city of Taegu, where we stayed for a couple of days camping on a
South Korean hospital ground. It was there that I caught my first look
at a dead American. The body was on a jeep, wrapped up in a poncho.
That brought me down to earth, for now I realized that I could be killed,
too, because fighting was taking place a few miles to the north.

I was with How Company, a heavy weapons company, of the 2d Battalion. I was a gunner on a heavy .30 caliber, water-cooled machine gun.
Not only did I have a machine gun, but I had a pistol and a rifle as well.

PFC. IRWIN COCKETT
5th Regimental Combat Team
Schofield Barracks, Territory of Hawaii

I enlisted in the army in November 1949 and took my basic training with the 5th RCT at Schofield Barracks. My platoon sergeant was M. Sgt. Alfred Los Banos, who left a lasting imprint on my backside throughout my military career.

When the war broke out in Korea, I was nineteen years old, married, and had a five-month-old daughter. Rumors were that we were going to the Philippines, where we would pick up replacements and receive additional training. I was concerned for my family and sent them to live with my parents on the island of Kauai.

We were restricted to the post. When orders came for our departure, Schofield Barracks hummed with activity. We worked long into the night crating and preparing our equipment for shipment. We were lined up for vaccinations and were given, not one, but several shots at a time. Many of the men got sick because of that. We had a final dental examination. The dentists never bothered filling cavities. That took too long so they simply pulled out the bad teeth.

We were allowed to take with us one duffle bag, a combat pack, and web gear. We boarded trucks and departed for Pier 40 in Honolulu. My wife had heard of our pending departure and flew to Honolulu hoping to see me. She stood along Kamehameha Highway with hundreds of other families hoping to get a glimpse of their loved ones. We never saw each other, and it sure was a sad, sad day for me. I worried about her and my daughter.

At Pier 40 my battalion loaded on the USNS *General W. A. Mann.* We were herded below to the bottom of the hold in very cramped quarters, where I was assigned a lower bunk. It was miserable. Men above me vomited and the stench was unbearable. Whenever I could, I would make my way up to the deck to gulp in fresh ocean air.

SGT. CLARENCE YOUNG
Schofield Barracks, Territory of Hawaii

Orders came down to every unit in every army installation in Hawaii to send all available men to Schofield Barracks in Wahiawa to build up the

FIGURE I. Hawaii's 5th Regimental Combat Team prepares to leave Schofield Barracks for Pier 40 for shipment overseas. July 20, 1950. Courtesy of Al Chang.

5th RCT to combat strength. Lifeguards, cooks, clerks, maintenance personnel, and others who were not in infantry units at the time found themselves in the 5th RCT. I was assigned to George Company, 2d Battalion.

We spent a couple of weeks training, familiarizing ourselves with our new "occupation," and trying to get in physical condition because the soft duty we had enjoyed had left us in poor shape. Many of us were potbellied. Two weeks was not enough time to get ourselves into any semblance of physical condition.

Before leaving the house for Schofield Barracks one morning, I told my family I would see them later that evening. When I got to Schofield Barracks, trucks were already waiting for us to load up. It took us several hours to pack and get squared away. We finally boarded the trucks and headed for Pier 39 at Kapalama. There was no fanfare, no band, and only the wives of the officers were permitted to see their husbands off. I would not see my family again until August 1953.

Several days out at sea, our battalion commander, Col. John L. Throckmorton Jr., informed us that we were headed for Sasebo, Japan. I was disappointed that we were headed for Japan instead of Korea because I wanted to see combat and earn myself a few medals. My disappointment was only short-lived because a few days later on the bitch box [public address system] came the announcement that our destination was now Korea.

JULY 1950

SGT. MARTIN PESTANA
Schofield Barracks, Territory of Hawaii

I was told to report to "C" Battery, 555 (Triple Nickel) Field Artillery Battalion. I was made the motor sergeant in charge of all the battery's vehicles.

All the talk about the regiment being deployed to Korea made me more anxious to get married, so I wrangled a few days of furlough from the battery commander and went home to Maui and got married.

JULY 1950

PFC. SUSUMU SHINAGAWA
Able Company, 34th Infantry
Pusan, South Korea

We sailed from the port city of Sasebo in the evening. Once we left the harbor area we were issued weapons and ammunition. I was issued an M-1 rifle, which I had not seen since basic training some time before. I was not issued a poncho and combat boots. What I had on were low quarters or dress shoes for the Class A uniform, so I requested a pair of combat boots from the supply sergeant. But because of my small feet he could not find a pair that would fit me. Fortunately, one of the men had an extra pair of boots, which he gave me. They were one size too large so I stuffed them with toilet paper. They were better than the dress shoes I had on.

Pusan, South Korea

It was pitch-dark in the early morning hours when we docked at Pusan. After getting off the ship, we were trucked to an assembly area near a rail yard on the outskirts of Pusan. We stayed there for a couple of days as we checked out our combat gear and waited for transportation. We were told that this was strictly a "police action," not a war, so there was little to worry about.

After loading onto several Korean trains in the afternoon, our regiment headed north. Several hours into our journey we saw train load after train load of South Korean troops, all headed south. We were going north and the South Korean troops were headed south? It didn't make sense. We passed through the city of Taejon without stopping and saw many South Korean soldiers milling around, some with weapons, many without weapons. They appeared confused and disorganized.

Vicinity of Pyongtaek, South Korea

The train chugged to a stop just before daylight at Pyongtaek. There was a light, steady drizzle as we got off the train and waited in the muddy streets for our orders. Without a poncho, I was soaked to the skin. When the orders came, Able and Baker Companies were to set up blocking positions on two hills about 2 miles north of the town. Charlie Company was designated the reserve company somewhere behind us.

The rain stopped when we started the 2-mile hike to our objective. When we got to the hills Able Company veered left and occupied the hill to the left of the road and Baker Company peeled off to the right of the road. Separating us were rice paddies, a rail line, and the road. I could see a small bridge several hundred yards farther north. Five hundred yards separated our company from Baker Company.

We paired off and dug our foxholes. I can't remember who my foxhole buddy was at the time. About this time we were sloshing around on the hillside, slipping and falling, which made it difficult to dig our holes.

The 3d Platoon was on our left and the 1st Platoon was in the rice paddies to our right. My platoon, the 2d, was in the middle. There were no friendly units to the left of the 3d Platoon.

From my position I could see refugees moving south on a road to the left of the 3d Platoon. My squad leader came by and told my buddy and me to camouflage our position with some branches and leaves. Then it began to rain. It rained for about an hour. I was already soaking wet from the earlier rainfall when we first arrived at Pyongtaek.

Nothing happened that night except that it rained all night. My steel helmet kept my head dry—the only part of my body that wasn't wet. Within a couple of hours there was more than a foot of water in our foxhole. My feet were sloshing in my oversize boots. In July the weather was very, very warm and, despite being soaking wet, I wasn't cold. I got out of the foxhole and sat on the edge of the foxhole. My buddy was asleep, curled up in over a foot of water. When I gazed north into the darkness I asked myself, *What am I doing here? How can events turn so drastically in such a short time from one of ease and comfort to this miserable situation that I am now in?*

Sometime after midnight I was startled by several explosions coming from the north. I didn't know what caused them but later someone explained that a patrol from one of the other companies had gone to destroy the small bridge just north of our positions.

Just before daylight, a light morning fog settled on the hill but did not affect our visibility. Then I heard a loud bang. I peered through the fog and saw three tanks making their way toward us on the road near the blown-up bridge. We knew that Task Force Smith, which was north of us, didn't have tanks so we knew the tanks were North Korean. Then puffs of smoke appeared from the enemy tanks and a split second later we could hear the sharp blast of their guns.

To the back and left of the tanks I could see more tanks, followed by North Korean infantry. Then another line of tanks and more infantry came into view on the right side of the road. Our mortars located in the rear started firing and I could see the rounds exploding among the North Korean tanks and infantry. Our mortars had no effect on the tanks. When the line of tanks was about 300 yards away, a few of the men opened fire. I fired my M-1 rifle for the first time in more than a year. My right shoulder got sore after emptying a few clips at the North Koreans.

Then enemy tanks turned their big guns on our hill, the bursting shells showering the area with shrapnel, dirt, and rocks. The fog had now dissipated and I could clearly see the North Korean infantrymen as they ran past the blown-up bridge and fanned out on both flanks. We were in danger of being surrounded.

"Pull out! Pull out!" came frantic shouts from the top of the hill. I was only too damn happy to obey the order. I grabbed my gear and hauled ass with several other men to the top of the hill and down the reverse slope. We headed for the village behind the hill. There were no officers around to give us any instructions.

While we were retreating, several shots rang out. No one knew where the shots came from but this meant the North Koreans were probably very close. Before we got to the village, we were fired on by North Koreans who somehow got abreast of us on our left about 200 yards away. Not only were they behind us, but they were in a position to surround us. We dove to the ground and fired back. I emptied a clip, firing blindly, when my rifle jammed. I tried kicking the bolt free but it wouldn't budge. The North Koreans stopped firing, so we decided to move again.

We came to a granary that was just outside the village and stopped to rest. While we were deciding what to do, a Korean civilian ran toward us and told us the North Korean soldiers were coming. We hurried inside the granary and hid behind some bundled rice straws.

The North Koreans knew where we were and threw hand grenades into the granary. They also just shot it full of holes with their burp guns. Wood splinters and rice straws filled the air above us. My rifle was still jammed so I couldn't return fire. All of a sudden, I felt my right arm being thrown back. I tried to move it but could not feel a thing. I thought, *Good God, my right arm is blown off!* I turned my head and reached out with my left arm to find out what was wrong and saw my right arm bent back in an awkward position. Instinctively, I pulled my right arm back in place. Through all of this I don't remember feeling any pain. I was relieved to know that I had not lost my arm and stuck it in my shirt like a sling. We didn't have a chance to fire back. Someone yelled, "We may as well surrender or we'll all be killed. Okay?"

For a brief moment no one said anything. Finally, during a lull in the firing, one of the guys yelled, "We surrender! We surrender!" The firing from the outside stopped, and he got up and walked to the door. We all followed him out of the granary.

For the first time I came face to face with North Korean soldiers. Man, they looked mean. One had a uniform different from the others and I guessed he must have been an officer because he had red epaulets on his uniform. Gesturing with their weapons and blabbering in Korean, which none of us understood, they herded us in a single file on the road and pointed north.

I really felt terrible having to surrender and I thought this day would be the last day of my life.

As we were walking out, I realized that I was also shot in the thigh just above the right knee. It was a clean wound where the bullet passed through and I felt little pain. With wounds on my right arm and right leg, I wondered what was going to happen to me. But both wounds bled very little so I was lucky in a way. While our captors were deciding what to do with us, one of our guys opened up my first aid kit and helped me apply sulfur and bandages to my wounds. For the next five or six days, that was all the treatment I had.

We were taken to a village, where we joined about a dozen captured Americans, including a couple of ROK soldiers and a lieutenant from our company. There were now a couple dozen of us and about a dozen North Korean soldiers.

They questioned us and wanted to know why we had come to Korea and all that bull. After they were done, we were marched to the rail line, where we thought we were going to be shot. At this point I really didn't care much and accepted whatever they were going to do with us. No one cried or complained. I guess we were too numb to realize the seriousness of the situation. Instead, they lined us up by the color of our hair. Those with red, blond, and brown hair were put in one column and those with black hair in another column. "You are all Japanese," a North Korean said, pointing to us with black hair, "and you are all Americans," he said, pointing to the light-color-haired men. No one tried to explain we were all Americans. It wasn't funny then, but recalling that incident later in the prison camps made me laugh.

Except for me, because of my injured right arm, all the prisoners' hands were tied behind their backs with commo wire. I was allowed to keep my hands under my shirt to support my injured arm. We were then marched north along the rail line. It was dark when we arrived at a small village after about four hours of walking. We were all crowded into a jail house that had wooden bars, just like the ones I saw in Japanese movies back home. My arm and leg didn't hurt too much that night and I was grateful for that.

Vicinity of Osan, South Korea

I was able to get a little sleep. When morning came I found my injured leg stiff and painful. There was very little pain in my arm, but it was beginning to swell and turn black and blue.

At mid-morning we were hustled out of the jail house without any breakfast and headed north again. It was already very hot and humid and we were very thirsty. The guards never offered us any water to drink. Being wounded, I was doubly thirsty. We found out later the farmers used human waste to fertilize their rice crops. No wonder the guards didn't allow us to drink the rice paddy water.

But much later an American plane buzzed the column and made the guards jump into the rice paddy. We followed them into the water and drank it, quenching our thirst, not fearing the consequences of the polluted water. When the plane didn't return, the guards rounded us up.

We moved out again in two small groups of eleven prisoners each. I was in the middle of the second group with a lieutenant in front of me. For no apparent reason, one of the guards shoved the lieutenant out of line. Like the others, his hands were tied behind his back. The same guard, who was only a few feet from me, fired a burst from his burp gun and simply riddled the officer with bullets. It just stunned and terrified all of us. We stood there, shocked, and watched him die. We couldn't do anything for him. The guard told us that if any of us lagged behind, he would shoot us like he did the lieutenant.

It was now about noon and very, very hot. Now my leg was hurting with every step I took and my arm was also beginning to hurt very badly. Being treated this way, suicide was definitely an option. All I had to do was fall behind, and hadn't the guard promised to shoot anyone who fell behind?

I couldn't keep up with the pace and fell behind. I could see that the others were putting distance between us and I anticipated a bullet in the back of my head. It would relieve me of my suffering. I heard a shot, and to my surprise, I was still standing. I looked back and saw a South Korean soldier on the ground. I thought, *That could have been me,* and suddenly, something in my mind made me want to live again. I don't know where I got the strength, but somehow I caught up with the rest of the group.

It was early evening when we reached the town of Osan, which was about 20 miles north from where I had been captured. We were marched in a column of twos down the middle of the street in the center of the town. People were lined up on both sides of the street to see us. They jeered us and spat at us. Mind you, this was a town in South Korea, a town we were supposed to liberate from the North Koreans. One young North Korean soldier came up to me and said in Japanese, "I'm going to shoot you." Feeling miserable and having nothing to lose, I mocked him and said, "Go ahead, shoot me." He laughed.

By this time, the polluted water I had drunk from the rice paddy was beginning to take its effect on me. Here I was, in the center of a town and people lined up to see us, and I had this urgent need to take a crap. If I left the column I would be shot. But damned if I was going to crap in my pants. I still had my pride. Not caring about the consequences, I broke away from the column, expecting to be shot. I went down an embankment and took a crap while hundreds of Koreans watched and jeered. For some reason the column had halted, whether for me or for some other reason, I don't know, and I was able to catch up to it. We stayed in Osan for three days.

This time we were put on trucks and headed north again to Yong-dong-po, a town west of Seoul across the Han River. I was very relieved when we were told to board the trucks because my leg was really hurting. I didn't think I could have kept up with the group if we had continued walking. My arm had swollen and turned purple and I was afraid gangrene might set in. To make things worse, I was coming down with a fever.

It took most of the day to reach Yongdong-po because of the North Korean southbound military traffic. Tanks and trucks laden with soldiers along with civilian refugees slowly made their way south. The thing that amazed me was the endless stream of North Korean infantrymen moving south.

At Yongdong-po we were joined by a larger group of prisoners, which brought the total to about 150. Included in this group was another prisoner from Hawaii. Prisoners couldn't talk to each other so we only made eye contact and acknowledged each other by moving our chins up and down like saying, "Howzit, brother." I never got to know his name.

Pyongyang, North Korea

We left Yongdong-po by train and arrived at the North Korean capital of Pyongyang. Once off the train we were marched four abreast through the city, having to pass through angry crowds of North Koreans. Those in the lead were forced to carry banners denouncing the United States.

It was still hot and humid and, worse, I had yet to be treated for my wounds. Pain shot up my leg with every step I took. I kept up for about a quarter of a mile. Finally, I just gave up and dropped to the ground. The other prisoners could not do anything for me and passed by me. I prayed that whoever was going to shoot me would step up from behind and shoot me in the back of the head without telling me. My morale at the time was at the lowest and, most of all, my pride was broken. I had pissed in my pants.

Then out of nowhere, another Hawaii soldier from Maui, whose name I can't remember, came to my aid. I told him to leave me alone, to go with rest of the guys or the guards would kill him, too. "Nah, they won't," he said. I broke into tears and begged him to leave me alone, but he stayed with me. All this time, there was a guard near him, but he never threatened me or gave any indication he was going to shoot me. Then an officer in a jeep came by and spoke to the guard. The guard must have told him of my condition. He looked at me, and I must have been a pathetic sight to him. He then motioned to the Maui GI and me to get into the jeep. I would like to believe that the reason we were not shot was because we were Orientals.

We rode for several hours until we came to what looked like a school. It was a big two-story building with a large yard. A group of American prisoners was already there. The guys who were captured with me on July 6 helped me to the second floor. I just sat on the floor, curled up into a ball, and cried like a baby.

Word got around that there was an American doctor whom the North Koreans permitted to check on injured prisoners. After the American doctor looked at my wounds I was taken to a nearby hospital.

In the operating room I was put to sleep with ether, and when I awoke my injured arm and leg were heavily bandaged. My bandages were not changed for four days. Soon, I noticed a lot of wiggly worms on my bed and felt something moving under the bandages. With my left hand I lifted the bandages from my right arm for a peek. Much to my horror, worms came out of the bandages. I yelled for the doctor and when he came he asked what was the matter. I said, "There's a million worms in my wound."

He took off the bandages from my arm and I was shocked to see so many worms all over the wound. I could see three cuts on my arm filled with worms. The largest cut was about an inch wide, 5 inches long, and a half inch deep. To my surprise the doctor said, "Very good." He explained the worms were maggots that ate the pus and cleaned the wound. With a knife he scraped off the maggots and, sure enough, the wound was clean. He stuffed the wound with gauze and bandaged it. That was it. No stitches.

As for my leg, the bullet had gone through the fleshy part of my thigh. The doctor stuffed gauze in each of the openings until the two pieces of gauze met somewhere in the middle of my thigh and bandaged it. When I told the nurse that bandages were changed every day in America, she said, "That method is old-fashioned. Here, we change bandages every fifth day." My arm was not put in a cast, although I had a compound fracture. I was sent back to the prison compound after spending two and a half weeks in the hospital.

JULY 1950

CPL. HARRISON LEE
Charlie Company, 34th Infantry
Camp Mower, Japan

July 1 was my birthday and my friends and I were going to celebrate it with a tea house party that evening in town. We were going to sneak off base despite the confined to camp order.

But my birthday party had to be scrapped because we received orders in the afternoon to get our gear together.

Pusan, South Korea

After a train ride we arrived at the port of Sasebo and sailed for Pusan, which is on the southern tip of South Korea. After we disembarked we were put on a train and headed north without any briefing whatsoever.

I suppose the officers knew what the situation was all about in Korea, but a plain GI Joe like me did not know what the hell was going on.

Butterflies flapped their wings in my stomach and my mouth became dry. I could see by the faces of the others that they were experiencing the same things I was. Would we measure up in combat?

Vicinity of Pyongtaek, South Korea

We got off the train somewhere above Taejon, got on trucks, and headed north to Pyongtaek. We were kept in reserve while Able and Baker Companies were dug in north of the town.

As the company clerk, I stayed with the first sergeant a couple of hundred yards behind our company's line of defense. We dug a large foxhole, set up the radio equipment, and waited.

It rained on the morning of July 5, and soon our foxholes became muddy. As the water began to rise, we bailed out our foxholes using our steel helmets. We were told that a battalion named Task Force Smith from the 21st Regiment, 24th Division, was much farther north and had probably already engaged the North Koreans.

In the afternoon, our company commander got word from the battalion that Task Force Smith had been overrun by the North Koreans, who were now attacking Able and Baker Companies 2 miles north of us. We were in danger of being outflanked and surrounded. Our battalion commander ordered the entire battalion to withdraw to the town of Chonan to the south.

There were no trucks to transport us so we walked. Halfway to Chonan we had to stop to take a break. The long walk tired everyone and most of the guys just flopped on the side of the road or propped themselves against the walls of huts, not even preparing some semblance of a defensive perimeter.

Vicinity of Chonan, South Korea

All of us were worried, but our company commander told us not to because a South Korean division was on our right and an American division, the 1st Cavalry, was supposedly on our left. It wasn't, and our left flank was open. We felt more secure because there were now trucks to take us south if need be.

When night came no one bothered to post security because we thought we had left the North Koreans far behind and felt pretty safe. The communication sergeant and I bedded down on the right side of a raised roadway. A large, dry rice paddy was on the other side of the road.

In the middle of the night I was awakened by the sound of a heavy engine. I raised myself up so I could look across the road. In the rice paddy about 100 yards away I could make out the outline of a tank as it made its away across the rice paddy in our direction. It churned up the slight embankment of the road and parked between two trucks about 20 or 30 yards from us. Someone said, "Great, we got a tank with us." I felt good because the only weapons we had were rifles and light machine guns. The driver of the tank cut the engine off, and all was quiet again so I went back to sleep.

It was nearly light the next morning when the tank engine again woke us up. The dark was turning into early morning gray with a light fog settling down, so things looked just a little hazy. I sat up, my eyes level with the road, and looked at the tank, which looked awfully huge and less than a stone's throw from where I was. I cussed the driver out loud for waking me up. The tank's engine ran idle for a few seconds, then revved up just a little as if not to wake up those who were still asleep. Then the tank slowly backed up off the road into the rice paddy. It seemed like it was trying to sneak away. I am sure that others heard and saw the tank, but no one paid it much attention or got excited over it. Anyway, it started backing up quite a ways when I saw the puff of smoke from the tank's gun. Wham! Almost instantly, the truck nearest me blew up and burst into flames. There was debris flying all over the area, some small pieces falling where we were huddled.

Those who were bedded down on the other side of the road scrambled across the road to our side. By this time the column came alive and began firing at the tank with rifles and machine guns but with no effect. I blasted away with my rifle until I realized that it was a stupid thing to do. The tank then disappeared in the light fog, heading north.

We later learned that the tank was a North Korean T-34 without any markings on it. We tried to piece together what had happened and we all agreed that the driver of the tank mistook us for North Koreans in the dark and joined us. They must have immediately realized their mistake but played it cool, hoping no one would try to contact them during the night. We were too damn tired to talk to anyone. What pissed me off was that the truck that the tank blew up was the company's headquarters truck that contained my typewriter.

Taejon, South Korea

We arrived in Taejon before noon and found the 34th Infantry headquarters located on the second floor of a two-story building. Several of us climbed the stairs to the second floor to get a better view of what was happening in the city.

All we could see were rooftops and smoke, so I just flopped against the wall next to a window where someone was standing, looking out with a pair of binoculars. Then I noticed that there were lots of high-ranking officers. They didn't pay any attention to us. Besides, we were too damn hungry and tired to obey orders. I then decided to eat my breakfast. I broke open the box of C-rations that I had carried in my shirt. There was a can of frankfurters and beans, hamburger patties, and other stuff. There was a can of peaches, which I decided to eat first. I dug into my pocket for my P-38, but couldn't find it. Now, the P-38 was the most important piece of equipment the foot soldier had because without it, he couldn't open his cans of food. Without looking up, I tapped the leg of the guy with binoculars standing by the window and asked if he had a P-38. "Sure thing, soldier," he remarked. I raised my hand, palm up, and felt the P-38 drop into my hand. I proceeded to open the cans of peaches and frankfurters. When I was through I tapped the same soldier on the leg, looked up, and said, "Here you go, buddy, thanks," and handed him the P-38. The soldier turned to face me, stooped down a little, and took the can opener from my hand. "Don't mention it," he replied. When he stooped down I saw two stars on his helmet. Shit! It was Maj. Gen. William Dean, commander of the 24th Infantry Division. I started to stammer an apology, but he put one hand on my shoulder and said, "Keep your seat and finish your breakfast."

"Yes, sir," I blurted out, and sat down to finish my breakfast. While I was eating General Dean called all the commanders he could find and told them that the North Koreans were closing in and already had road blocks south of the city. He said he wasn't ordering anyone to stay and fight, but those who did, were doing so voluntarily. Those who decided to leave should try to make it to the 1st Cavalry Division, which was dug in farther south beyond the North Korean road blocks. He wished everyone good luck and dismissed us. Although the 24th Infantry Division command post was farther south, General Dean had remained in Taejon to gain firsthand information on what was happening in the city.

A colonel began to organize the men who wanted to leave Taejon so I joined his group. There must have been about twenty of us at the start. The colonel pointed to some distant hills to the east and said that we must strike out in that direction to avoid North Korean soldiers. He also said that enemy infantry and tanks were all over the city and we had to find a route through the city not yet controlled by the North Koreans. We left the building and headed up a street.

As we moved through the street we saw other friendly units also making their way out of the city, all trying to find an escape route. Some men left their groups and joined us, which made our group quite large. The colonel took us through narrow streets and alleys, but we had to backtrack several times because we ran into dead ends.

We finally made it to the outskirts of the city and headed up a draw to the hills beyond. I have to believe that Taejon was not completely surrounded or we were just plain lucky because we never ran into any North Korean soldiers while threading our way through the city and into the hills.

We got to the top of a ridge and looked down on the city of Taejon. A light haze hung over it and plumes of smoke rose above the haze from different points of the city. We could hear the now faint sounds of explosions, which indicated that fighting was still going on. I wondered if our division commander, General Dean, had escaped.

Finally, about 0800 hours, the second day after we left Taejon, we stumbled upon a road held by friendly troops. We were safe, at least for the time being. We continued down the road until we came to a town about 40 miles southeast of Taejon, where it became the assembly point for the retreating men of the 34th Infantry.

JULY 1950

CPL. JAY HIDANO
Easy Company, 8th Cavalry
Vicinity of Taegu, South Korea

Easy Company was already on line and dug in a few miles north of Taegu when I joined the company and reported to the company commander, 1st Lt. William McClain. I expected to be assigned to one of the rifle platoons, but I was surprised when McClain assigned me to his headquarters staff.

JULY 1950

PFC. MOSES PAKAKI
4.2 Inch Mortar Company, 35th Infantry
Vicinity of Hamchang, South Korea

I was a squad leader with the 4.2 Inch Mortar Company, 35th Infantry Regiment.

My unit stayed in this location for about a week. A lot of fighting took place in this area. We were warned by men of other units to be especially alert because North Koreans dressed in U.S. Army uniforms were getting through our line and harassing our rear echelon units. It was impossible to tell a North Korean from a South Korean if they both were wearing American uniforms.

JULY 1950

SGT. ROBERT JAMIESON
Headquarters Company, 1st Battalion, 5th RCT
Schofield Barracks, Territory of Hawaii

I had been in the army since 1945 and was stationed at Fort Shafter, assigned to the Criminal Investigation Division. I was the provost sergeant with the military police detachment.

After the outbreak of the Korean War I was declared surplus and was transferred to Headquarters Company, 1st Battalion, 5th RCT. My new assignment was assistant platoon sergeant of the communications platoon. My platoon sergeant was M. Sgt. Jean Labarre.

JULY 1950

PFC. ROBERT ALIP
How Company, 19th Infantry
Taepyong-ni, South Korea

Our journey by train and truck finally ended just before dark in the vicinity of Taepyong-ni, which was about 13 miles north of Taejon on the south bank of the Kum River.

My heavy machine gun crew was attached to George Company, which was in reserve about 2 miles below the Kum River. On the south bank of the river ahead of us were the companies of the 1st Battalion.

On the morning of July 15, enemy troops attempted to cross the river between Baker and Able Companies but were thrown back. George Company was ordered to reinforce Baker and Able Companies.

I set my gun on a hill looking down on the Kum River, which was a couple of hundred yards ahead. About noon North Korean tanks came out of hiding and poured fire into Baker Company to our left. I could see them clearly with binoculars. Pieces of equipment would be blown into the air and sometimes a body could be seen be hurtling through the air. Their tanks were less than a mile beyond the river. I could see the puffs of smoke from their guns and, within a second or two, their shells would impact into Baker Company's positions.

At about 0200 hours our flares revealed small groups of enemy troops in the water at several points along the river. The distance from the north bank to my position was about 300 yards. While I fired, my assistant gunner kept yelling at me to pour it on. He spotted a small enemy force taking cover in the wreckage of a bridge that had been blown up a couple of days earlier and pointed them out to me. Adjusting my gun, I took them under fire, using more than two cans of ammunition. Our combined fire along the front chased the enemy back to the north bank.

As the evening of July 15 approached, we were alerted for an enemy night crossing. As soon as it got dark enemy artillery and tanks pounded the entire length of the 1st Battalion front. Then, as flares from our mortars and artillery began to light up the banks of the Kum River, I could see groups of North Koreans forming and starting to cross the river. As the North Koreans tried to cross the river, our fire cut them down. I could see my red tracer rounds plunging into the water. The river seemed to erupt into many geysers of water from our concentrated fire. Then the small geysers were dwarfed by the larger geysers from our artillery and mortars. Not many North Koreans reached our side of the river; those who did were cut down by the small arms fire or were driven back across the river. The NKs tried two more times that night, but both attempts failed. We took a breather and I sent my ammo bearers down the hill for more ammunition. I thought that the enemy was through for the night.

At about 0300 hours a single North Korean plane flew above our positions and dropped a flare. Instantly, all hell broke loose from the opposite river bank. Again, our flares lit up the night. The enemy was crossing everywhere in front of us. They used boats and rafts or waded and swam and in every possible way were trying to cross the river. Our mortars and artillery began pounding the river area just a few hundred yards ahead of us. From my position I had a clear view of the river, so I began firing my machine gun into the mass of bodies in the water. They looked like an army of rats.

What happened next almost made me shit in my pants. One by one our flares began to die out until our area was plunged into darkness. We couldn't see the river or what the enemy was doing. Then the hillside and river to the left of us were lit by our flares. The guns that provided us with flares earlier had shifted their concentration to our left in support of Baker Company. Having failed to cross the river in front of us, the enemy was attempting to cross in front of Baker Company.

All we could do was to fire blindly at gun flashes in front of us. And finally, I ran out of ammo. I could hear a lot of small arms fire coming from Able Company to my right This meant that the NKs had probably broken through and were attempting to get to the rear and cut us off. There now was firing in back of us and it appeared that we were surrounded. I took my last hand grenade, pulled the pin, placed it under the water jacket of the machine gun, and took off. With my rifle I ran about 20 yards and dove into a small shell crater when the grenade went off. I only hoped the grenade did the job.

It was now every man for himself! By this time other men were making their way to the back of the hill. The enemy was now all around us and was taking potshots at us in the dark. We were also snap shooting at them, at least where we thought they were. I had only one eight-round clip for my M-1 rifle so I had to be sure of what I was firing at. It was a confused situation. I ran, stumbled, rolled, and slid on my ass down the hill and made it to the base of the hill. Others joined me.

My platoon sergeant joined us and told us that we had to get back up the hill again. We all looked up at him with the kind of look that said, "What? You must be nuts!" He gave us his plan of attack and told us to scrounge up some ammo and hand grenades.

It must have been about 0500 hours when the sergeant led us back up the hill. When we were halfway up automatic rifle fire poured down on us. Like everybody else I threw myself to the ground. I could hear bullets striking the ground and cutting the air above me so I didn't dare raise my head to see where all the firing was coming from. I finally raised my head and looked up the hill. I could the flashes of fire from the enemy.

The platoon sergeant had a brilliant idea. He said, "Alip, find out where that fire is coming from." Shit, the fire was coming from all over the hill. Any damn fool could see that. But like a good soldier, I slowly raised myself to a half crouch position. I was instantly jerked around and knocked on my ass. I took a bullet in the left shoulder. With my right hand I tried to find out how badly injured I was. My hand got wet and sticky when I touched the injury.

The platoon sergeant saw me go down and immediately yelled for a medic, but there was no medic with us. There was a medic, but he was at the bottom of the hill. Heavy enemy fire was still coming from the top of the hill, so I told the sergeant not to let the medic come up the hill or he'd be killed.

It was easier for me to crawl downhill than for the medic to climb up. I threw my rifle to the platoon sergeant since I couldn't fire it with one good arm. I still had the .45 caliber pistol strapped to my right side. Using my one good arm, I belly surfed and barreled my way down the hill over brush and rocks. I covered a distance of nearly 200 yards on my belly slide and found the medic, who was cowering behind a boulder.

The medic took off my bloody and dirty shirt to see how badly injured I was. I was lucky. The bullet had gone right through my shoulder without touching a bone. The funny thing was that I hardly felt any pain at all. He patched the wound the best he could. He said my shoulder wound was serious and he had to get me to the nearest aid station, but he didn't how far away it was or where it was located.

The medic told me that he would help me to the aid station, but I said I could find the aid station by myself. He insisted on escorting me. I didn't blame him for wanting to get out of there. I was so eager to leave that I left behind my helmet and my dirty shirt. I was half naked. The heel of my right boot was missing.

We stumbled in the hills, walking west, then south, then west again, hoping to avoid the enemy and picking up more men along the way. We were a sorry-ass-looking bunch. Never in my life did I expect to find myself in a situation like this, me, an American soldier, helpless and running away from the enemy.

When night came, a chaplain who had joined us assembled all the wounded. I hadn't realized there were so many wounded, some so severely that they couldn't be moved. There was someone in charge but I couldn't get his name or his rank. He probably was an officer. He said that the North Koreans knew where we were and were closing in fast, trying to cut us off. The wounded prevented us from putting distance between them and us. He told all the walking wounded, including me, to get off their butts, and to get the hell out of there. The badly wounded had to be left behind. A chaplain, whose name I can't remember, volunteered to remain with the badly wounded.

There must have been close to 200 walking wounded. I don't know how many badly wounded were left behind, but there were quite a few. Taking the advice, we started walking southeast. We must have been about half a mile from where we'd left the badly wounded when we heard small arms fire coming from that direction. We assumed that our men back there were captured by the North Koreans. Later, we were told that the chaplain and wounded were massacred by the North Koreans.

We came out of the hills to see many trucks parked on the MSR facing south. Those were our trucks! We had lucked out! Tired as we were, we hustled out of the hills to the waiting trucks. They were waiting for the survivors of the 19th and 34th Infantry Regiments. We got on the trucks, which took us to the city of Taejon.

When we arrived at the Taejon train station, we saw that the station was being used as a collecting point for the wounded. It was packed with wounded. There were many dead bodies, covered with ponchos and shelter halves, lined up in rows.

One of my buddies, who was once assigned to Special Services in Japan where I boxed for the regiment, recognized me and immediately had me put me on a stretcher and loaded on the train. However, we didn't leave until the following day. All night long the wounded and the dead were put on the train while I lay on a stretcher on the floor of a box car. Finally, the train pulled out and we were taken to the division hospital south of Taejon.

When the train arrived at the division hospital, I met an old friend, Yamato, from Kakaako, who was a medic, and with whom I took basic training. I could not remember his first name. He looked at my wound and changed the bandages. It was then that I realized I was pretty much shot up. The left side of my upper body was numb and I couldn't feel anything.

Later, while I was lying on the stretcher, a chaplain knelt down beside me and prayed. It was my last rites! I was shocked! I didn't feel that I was dying! But perhaps Yamato thought that he was doing me a favor by not telling me that I was going to die. When the chaplain had finished his prayers, I propped myself up on my elbows and yelled for Yamato, who came running. I think he tried to stifle a laugh when I asked if I was going to die. He calmed me down and told me that the chaplain had mistaken me for another soldier. I flopped back in relief.

JULY 1950

1st Lt. Herbert Ikeda
Charlie Company, 5th RCT
Schofield Barracks, Territory of Hawaii

Thomas Ebato, William Coleman, Edward Ikeda, Vernon Jernigan, Oliver King, Carl Noblock, Vance McWhorter, Roy Nakashima, Leonard Werner, and Antonio Ventura volunteered with me and we were sworn into active duty with the 5th RCT on July 16.

When I got home I told my seven months' pregnant wife what I had done. She thought I was just kidding her. When I finally convinced her what I had told her was true, and I was leaving soon, she clutched her stomach and cried.

I spoke to my dad and told him to take care of my wife and the baby to be born if I didn't make it back. I told him that I would not bring shame to the family. He only nodded his head in response.

JULY 1950

Pfc. Nick Nishimoto
Baker Company, 35th Infantry
Vicinity of Pusan, South Korea

After six hours on a small Japanese transport ship, we arrived about noon at Pusan and camped in a rail yard without putting up our tents. The next morning we got on trucks and headed north.

My first combat action took place just south of Taejon, when our battalion was ordered to cover the withdrawal of the 24th Infantry Division.

C-ration Hill, South Korea

Baker Company was on C-ration Hill for over a month in the Pusan Perimeter. Constant artillery and mortar fire prevented the kitchen from making daily trips to the top of the hill with hot food, so we lugged boxes and boxes of C-rations whenever we could to our positions. The supply would last us four or five days at a time. Hence the name C-ration Hill. The hillside was just littered with empty boxes, cans, paper, and other kinds of rubbish.

We were always short of water and ammo because of the continuous fighting. On one occasion we were supplied by air. A small piper cub airplane flew just a few feet above the crest of the hill and dropped several cases of .30 caliber ammunition. No parachute was used because of the possibility of the air drop drifting into the hands of the enemy, who were less than 300 yards away.

When the cases hit the ground they shattered, scattering thousands of rounds of ammunition all over the hillside. We were like kids going after candy, disregarding long-range sniper fire.

During this period two Hawaii men became casualties. While we were withdrawing, Wilfred Chun became exhausted and fell behind. I went back to help him, but he told me to go ahead and he would catch up with me. We both didn't realize realize the NKs were just a couple of hundred yards away. Reluctantly, I left him behind. He never caught up with us and was listed as Missing in Action. I should have dragged him with me.

After we had regrouped I found out that another local boy, Charles Kim, never made it back.

JULY 1950

PVT. WALTER OGASAWARA
Item Company, 5th RCT
Aboard the USNS General Mann

I had just completed basic training at Schofield Barracks, Wahiawa, and found myself on a ship with the 3d Battalion of the 5th Regimental Combat Team. Rumor was that we might be headed for Japan and then to Korea.

While on board the ship I was told that I was now the gunner of a 57mm recoilless rifle team. I knew shit about firing a 57mm recoilless rifle, which really was a small cannon fired from the shoulder or tripod. The damn thing weighed about 45 pounds and one round weighed about 6 pounds. Although we had simulated firing on the ship, we never fired live ammunition.

JULY 1950

PFC. PEDRO BEHASA
Item Company, 5th RCT
Aboard the USNS General Mann

It was hard to believe that only a couple of weeks ago I had been a military policeman stationed at Schofield Barracks, and now I was the second gunner on a 60mm mortar squad on my way to Korea on a troop transport. As the second gunner, my job was to drop the mortar round into the mortar tube. I had never fired a 60mm mortar before except in basic training, which was some time ago.

After many "dry" fire missions, we were given eight rounds for "live" practice. We were also given one clip of rifle ammo to fire into the sea. That was the extent of my combat training.

JULY 29, 1950

SGT. ROBERT JAMIESON
Headquarters Company, 1st Battalion, 5th RCT
Aboard the USNS General Mann
Letter Home

Dearest Mom & Pop,
    How are you two swell people coming along? Everything O.K.? Not working too hard I hope. Especially you, dad, you're always falling off a ladder or hitting your thumb with the hammer or some fool stunt (some

joke). Mom, you've got to take good care of dad (boy, this tub is sure pitching and rocking).

Well, there isn't much to say except that we left on the USNS *General Mann* in the afternoon and went directly to Pearl Harbor to take on fuel. We left about 10:00 P.M. the same night. This ship is good riding but has poor ventilation. I couldn't have expected a smoother trip. Today is the first day that the ship really pitched and rocked. In fact, I might say it is getting rough.

I wasn't fortunate enough to get a stateroom like a lot of other sergeants but I did manage to make the most of this trip because it may be my last. I sure hope not.

Sergeant La Barre and I play a lot of pinochle and some poker. There is also a movie every night. I'm surprised to see such confidence and high morale among the troops. It's one hundred percent. We've got a very good fighting team and all we need is a little more training. Most of us have been training daily on radios and various weapons.

We were informed the other day that we were going to dock at the port of Pusan, South Korea, and I sure hope there is time for us to get there before it's too late. We keep a daily progress of the war in our lounge and it doesn't look too good. I can tell you one thing when we get there, those goddamn red sons of a b——s will know that they've been in a fight.

This is the hottest ship I've been on. Why, even the old USS *Blatchford* was cooler than this when I came home from Saipan.

We've also been setting our watches back a half an hour every night plus a day that we lost somewhere along the line. We crossed the 180th meridian so I guess that was it.

I'm doing my best during this trip to learn every type of weapon thoroughly. We have a good Platoon Leader, Lieutenant Brewster. He is usually my pinochle partner. Our mess (kitchen boss) sergeant brought along nine half-pints of whiskey and he seemed to be having himself quite a time.

I don't have much more to write but please take care of yourselves. I went to church last Sunday and I felt a lot better. I intend to go again this Sunday.

I have one request. If I don't survive, please don't leave me to rot in Korea. When the Army permits, let me come home to rest.

Say hello to the Haynes' and my love to Barbara and the rest of you.

Love, Bob

AUGUST 1950

PFC. ARSANIO VENDIOLA
George Company, 5th RCT
Pusan, South Korea

We were welcomed by a South Korean band when we arrived in Pusan.
We off-loaded and marched to a warehouse, where we were separated
from our duffel bags and other personal items. We kept our combat packs,
ponchos, and sleeping bags and were issued ammo and grenades. We then
walked to a staging area foul with the stench of manure and spent the night
there. The next morning we found out that the staging area was a collection point for human waste, which was used by the farmers.

AUGUST 1950

PFC. IRWIN COCKETT
Dog Company, 5th RCT
Masan, Korea

When our ship finally docked in Pusan Harbor we were loaded onto cat-
tle cars and made our way west to the town of Masan. It was already dark
when the column of trucks halted near the front lines. A dark hill mass
loomed in front of us. Someone dropped the tailgate of the truck and
said, "This is it. Unload the mortars."
   Incoming rounds burst from quite a distance away and intermittent
flares lit the night. As we made our way to the hill, troops came stum-
bling down the trail in complete disarray, anxious to get off the hill.
Someone grabbed me by the arm and said, "Don't go up there. Don't go
up there."
   Before we had a chance to feast on our C-rations for breakfast in the
morning, orders came to pack up and assemble on the road. The battalion was moving forward again.

Sobuk-san, South Korea

Sobuk-san was a large hill complex with many secondary ridges. While
in support of the infantry, our 81mm mortar platoon fired hundreds of
rounds on enemy positions.
   My foxhole buddy was Herbert Kalino, an experienced combat veteran, who had fought on Guadalcanal in the South Pacific during World

War II. He was my mentor and was always on my case because he wanted to keep me alive, at least that's what he told me.

One night the North Koreans attacked Charlie Company, which was positioned directly in front of our mortar platoon. It was overrun, forcing Charlie Company's survivors back nearly into our positions. There was a lot of confusion, and I felt frustrated because we couldn't fire our mortar. Kalino kept telling me to keep my head down.

I didn't want to be killed in the foxhole so I told Kalino that I was going to join the men of Charlie Company. Before he could react I jumped out of the hole and dashed forward to where I thought Charlie Company was. Kalino screamed at me to get back to the foxhole. I never reached Charlie Company but instead ended up in a small draw with a couple of other men fighting off North Koreans.

As soon as the sky began to lighten up, I ran to Kalino to see if he was okay. He was slumped in the hole without his helmet, a bullet hole in his forehead. He died on my birthday, August 24.

There was a lull in the fighting one afternoon, so we all sat down to eat C-rations. Scattered around us were dead North Koreans. Derek Hara, a unit medic, sat with Ino Alo, who had been a wrestling champion at Schofield Barracks. Alo was big and Hara was one of the smallest guys around, maybe 5 feet tall standing in his combat boots.

In front of the two, about 5 yards away, was a shallow foxhole we dumped our rubbish in. I heard the distant sound of enemy artillery and, within seconds, enemy shells burst in our positions. We dumped whatever we were eating and ran for the nearest cover we could find.

Hara, who was faster than Ino, dashed for the hole in front of him and tumbled into it, rubbish and all. Alo was a couple of steps behind and took a flying leap into the hole, landing on top of Hara. I was in a hole about 20 yards away and watched the damndest thing unfold in front of my eyes. The two had a wrestling match to see who would get the bottom of the hole. Naturally, Alo, being bigger, won the match.

AUGUST 1950

PFC. SUSUMU SHINAGAWA
Able Company, 34th Infantry
POW camp, somewhere in North Korea

At the prison camp, I felt much better. For the first time since my capture I felt that I had a decent chance of staying alive. Meeting other prisoners from Hawaii also boosted my morale. There was Goichi Tamaye and Henry Arakaki from Honolulu. And I finally met up again with the Hawaii soldier who had risked his life trying to help me on our march north. His name was Tomio Tadaki from Maui. There was also a Japanese national, whom we only knew as Mike, who was captured the same time as Tamaye and Arakaki. Because Mike could also speak English, he was used as a translator. There were at least a dozen men in the camp from Hawaii. Half of them made it back home after the war. Mike also survived the ordeal.

My fever came back again and it left me weak and listless. Someone called the American doctor. When he saw me he knew what was causing it. He talked to the camp commander and told him that I had to go the hospital again because my arm was getting infected. I could barely move my fingers. The commander ordered one of the officers to take me to the hospital and have my arm amputated. It had come to this and I realized that I was going to lose one arm or die from the infection.

When we reached the hospital the officer told the doctor what the camp commander had told him. The doctor examined my arm and told me to move my fingers, which I could barely do. He said there was no need to amputate my arm and that he could save it. The officer argued with the doctor and reminded him that it was an order from the camp commander. Reluctantly, the doctor said he would but only if the officer would go back to the camp commander and tell him how he felt. The officer returned and told the doctor to try and save my arm. That was one doctor I really respected, enemy or not. After the successful operation a cast without padding was put on my arm.

AUGUST 1950

SGT. CLARENCE YOUNG
Item Company, 5th RCT
Pusan, South Korea

After spending only a night in Pusan, our battalion moved out and occupied a hill several miles west of Masan. This was the front lines and I was anxious to see my first combat action. My foxhole was near the top of the crest so I had a good view to the front. There were other foxholes staggered below me occupied by other men from my platoon.

At noon the next day, our company was relieved by another company. We marched to an assembly area below the hill and were told that our company was going to attack another hill.

CPL. LARRY ACOSTA
Item Company, 5th RCT
Vicinity of Sobuk-san, South Korea

Item Company was ordered to attack through rugged terrain just south of the Sobuk-san hill mass in the Masan sector.

I was a BAR gunner in the 2d Platoon and my platoon sergeant was M. Sgt. Alfred Los Banos, also from Hawaii. Before we assaulted this hill, Los Banos told our young platoon leader to remove his gold bars if he didn't want to be the first one shot by the NKs. Los Banos reminded the lieutenant that officers were often marked by enemy snipers. The lieutenant took off his bars and gave them to Los Banos, who put them in his shirt pocket. In actuality, Los Banos ran the platoon because the lieutenant was a recent replacement and did not have combat experience. Los Banos had been a combat veteran in World War II.

With our platoon and Los Banos leading the way, our company started the climb up the hill, which was supposedly unoccupied, based from an earlier reconnaissance patrol report. It seemed that way as we neared the top of the hill. About 50 yards from the crest, we were driven to the ground by rifle and burp gun fire and hand grenades. Then a machine gun opened up on the platoon.

Los Banos, who was about 6 feet to my left, told me to take the enemy machine gun under fire with my BAR. My BAR assistant gunner and I were on our bellies and couldn't see where the enemy gun was located, so I asked Los Banos where in the hell it was. He pointed uphill and to the right and said to fire in that direction. I let loose with two magazines and the NK gun stopped firing. I assumed that I had put the enemy gun out of action. So did Los Banos, as he raised himself to one knee and tossed a hand grenade up the hill. The enemy gun fired again, kicking up dirt where we lay. "I'm hit," Los Banos called out. He fell to the ground toward me. I yelled several times for the medic and stayed with Los Banos until a medic arrived. I couldn't tell how badly Los Banos was hit.

After Los Banos was evacuated from the hill, I moved my BAR to another position to get a better shot at the North Korean gun. Before we got up to move, I told my assistant to keep his ass down because I didn't want to see another buddy get cut down. I pointed to a spot for us to set up and said, "Go!" He took about five steps and fell down. He was on one knee, his head on the ground and his butt in the air. "You hit?" I shouted.

"No, just tripped," he said without looking at me.

"Get going," I yelled.

He got up and fell down again. "Clumsy bastard," I said to myself. I grabbed him by the leg to urge him forward but he didn't move. His helmet had fallen off his head when I got to him. "Move," I yelled again, but he just laid there. I turned him over and saw a bullet hole in his forehead just below the hairline. Blood had just started to ooze slowly out of the bullet hole. He was dead. Shit! In a couple of minutes my platoon sergeant was wounded, probably killed, and my assistant gunner was dead. You talk about someone shaking. I couldn't control the trembling of my hands until I heard shouts to move up the hill.

We finally chased the NKs off the hill and were relieved by another company.

AUGUST 1, 1950

SGT. MARTIN PESTANA
C Battery, 555 FAB
Vicinity of Munchon-ni, South Korea

Our battalion was ordered to halt for the night, so I prepared to bed down in the cab of the truck. But before I got into my bedroll, I took a last look at the hillside. I saw movement in the hills to the left of us about 200 yards away. The other guys saw it too. There were hundreds of people, many dressed in white. I thought they were civilians.

I was on the passenger side of a three-quarter-ton truck at the time. I got out of the truck to get a better look when I saw flashes coming from the hillside. The next thing I knew bullets were zapping overhead and striking the vehicles. Everyone took cover, some under and behind the vehicles, while others dove into holes on the side of the road. I sought cover on the opposite side of the truck behind the spare tire. To the right of road was a rice paddy and I saw the bullets that overshot us kicking up water. There was an ambulance 20 yards behind my truck so I decided to get cover there instead. I sprinted the 20 yards and ducked behind it, keeping the vehicle between the NKs and me. A voice rang out, "Keep your ass down!" No sooner after the warning came then a volley of bullets struck the ground between my truck and the ambulance.

By this time our quad fifties mounted on half-tracks returned the fire and literally blasted the hillside with .50 caliber bullets. I could see the tracer bullets sweeping the entire hillside until the firing from the hillside stopped completely.

I went back to my truck and found several bullet holes in it. Several vehicles had their engines and tires shot up and had to be abandoned. Later that night when I unrolled my sleeping bag, I found bullet holes in the bag.

AUGUST 1950

CPL. ARSANIO VENDIOLA
George Company, 5th RCT
Vicinity of Masan, South Korea

Early in the morning we boarded trucks and headed for the front. As we got close to the front lines I could hear sounds of artillery firing. I couldn't tell if they were ours or the enemy's. After a couple of hours we stopped, got off the truck, and took up defensive positions on a hill. The hill was a high point on a finger ridge that reached down from a higher hill mass called Sobuk-san peak, which was about 3 or 4 miles higher up the ridge. Slightly higher up above our hill was another hill called Fox Hill.

I was one of the ammo bearers for the 57mm recoilless rifle in the weapons platoon although I had been trained on the 60mm mortar.

The first thing the crew did was to dig a firing position for the 57mm recoilless rifle on the crest of the hill. After we had finished, we quickly set up the gun to zero it in. The gunner sighted on an enemy bunker about 400 yards away. We fired one round. It was wide to the left by about 50 yards but the yardage was correct. The back blast of the gun kicked up a dust storm, giving away our position. The gunner quickly made a slight adjustment and the second round was perfect, blowing up the bunker. We considered the gun zeroed in. No sooner than the second round had been fired, then I heard the sounds of enemy mortars firing. The firing sounded like someone coughing, only in rapid succession. Enemy mortar rounds began falling in our area, one round bursting only 30 yards from us. We picked up the gun and hustled to our holes on the reverse slope of the hill.

When the barrage finally lifted, I looked up the slope and saw our guys leaving their positions and running past me to the bottom of the hill. Some were yelling, "There's too many of them!" The North Koreans had walked right through their mortar fire and were upon us while we took cover.

As more of our men came bounding over the crest and some were running past me, I took off too, with the gun crew following me, without the 57mm recoilless rifle. At the bottom of the hill our platoon leader pulled us together and chewed us out for bugging out, especially our crew for abandoning the 57mm recoilless rifle. The lieutenant said that we were going to take back the hill because there were some dead and wounded men from our company up there.

I must say this for the lieutenant—he had guts. He led us up the hill, and when we got to within 50 yards of the crest, we ran charging, making a lot of noise and expecting to be met with a barrage of hand grenades and bullets. Nothing of the sort happened. The hill had been abandoned by the North Koreans. We found the 57mm recoilless rifle intact, right where we had left it.

We took care of our dead and wounded and dug in again, this time with more confidence.

AUGUST 1950

SGT. MARCELO VENDIOLA
Item Company, 5th RCT
Vicinity of Masan, South Korea

It was dark when we left Pusan by truck. But this time I wasn't driving a jeep pulling a water tank trailer. Somebody must have pulled rank on me and took my job. I was reassigned to Item Company, an infantry unit.

Finally at about 2300 hours, the trucks stopped. We got off and were told that we were at the Masan front, 3 miles from the sea and west of Pusan. Our platoon leader led us off the road and up a trail to a hill. It was warm, even at that hour near midnight. We huffed and puffed our way up. No one was in physical shape. The garrison duty in Hawaii made us unfit for combat. When we got to the top we immediately dug foxholes facing west and north. The platoon leader told us that whatever happened we had to hold the hill at all cost; otherwise, we would be pushed into the sea. I couldn't believe we were on the front lines! It gave me a spooky feeling.

It was dark, except for the occasional artillery flashes a couple of miles to the north. I couldn't see anything looking down the hill and couldn't tell if there were other hills in front of us. I asked myself, *Where in the hell is the front line?*

I blistered my hands digging my foxhole. The nearest friendly foxhole was about 20 yards to my right and slightly up the hill from me. I can't remember who was in it, but whoever it was kept calling me, "Mark, you there? Mark, you there?"

"Yeah! Yeah!" not wanting to say more because if the North Koreans were at the bottom of the hill they would know where I was.

At about 0200 hours green flares shot up into the sky. A few seconds later I could see red tracers from enemy machine guns in the air streaking toward us. There was a hill after all, in front of us, occupied by NKs. Then our hill seemed to explode. Enemy heavy mortar shells fell on us with great accuracy. Some shells burst so close to my hole they created a rush of air that took my breath away. The air was filled with shell fragments, dust, and the smell of powder. Then the hill was lit up from our flares thrown up by our own mortars. There was some scattered rifle fire from some of our positions so I started firing down the hill, too, not seeing anything. Some yelled, "They're down there!" And sure enough, I could see shadowy figures moving up the hill in front of us about 200 yards away, made visible by our flares. The firing from our own guns increased in intensity as our machine guns laid grazing fire down the slope, their spent tracer rounds ricocheting into the night.

To get to us they had to get through rolls of concertina barbed wire that was laid about 50 yards below our positions. The barbed wire didn't stop them. When they got to it, some of the North Koreans simply threw themselves on the wire, flattening it, allowing those following to step on them to get past the wire.

Now they were less than 50 yards from where I was. Someone yelled, "Get the hell out of there!" I emptied a clip at the charging North Koreans and threw one hand grenade. I hauled my butt out the hole, ran to the reverse slope, and then tore down the hill.

In the dark it was difficult to distinguish friendly troops from the enemy, but the jabbering of Korean voices told me that the North Koreans had broken through and were already among us and moving down the reverse slope with us. There was scattered rifle fire. I ran into the rice paddy and hunkered down in knee-deep water against the paddy dike and waited. I couldn't tell what was going on and I was afraid to call out in case North Koreans were in the vicinity. Others soon joined me and we took the hill under fire, firing blindly, hoping that none of our guys were still on the hill. After a few minutes we moved back to the road, dug in, and waited for morning.

At first light, our planes strafed the hill and drove off the North Koreans. We were then ordered back on the hill to retrieve our dead and wounded. Several of our men were missing and presumed captured. We went into reserve for three days following this action to take in replacements.

FIGURE 2   U.S. Army photographer M. Sgt. Al Chang, with camera in hand, waits for orders to move out with the 5th RCT. August 1950. Courtesy of Al Chang.

AUGUST 1950

PFC. PETE BEHASA
Item Company, 5th RCT
Vicinity of Taejong-ni, South Korea

I was transferred to the light machine gun squad. That was like a punishment because the mortar positions were on the reverse slope, not subject to direct enemy fire, unlike the machine guns, normally dug in on line with the riflemen.

We must have lost a lot of men because my gun crew was made up of a former truck driver and the company's first sergeant. Of the three of us I had the most experience with weapons so I was elected gunner. The first sergeant was the assistant gunner and the truck driver was the ammo bearer.

Our machine gun was in a flat area overlooking dry rice paddies. We were flanked by riflemen on both sides. However, we were spaced widely

FIGURE 3　Religious service in the field. August 1950. Courtesy of Al Chang.

FIGURE 4　While in reserve, Hawaii's men catch up on the news about Hawaii from the *Honolulu Star-Bulletin.* September 1950. Courtesy of Al Chang.

FIGURE 5   5th RCT soldiers of Hawaii prepare for another battle. *Left to right*, S. Sgt. Julian Haleamau, Cpl. Harold Vierra, and M. Sgt. David Broad. September 1950. Courtesy of Al Chang.

apart and I did not have visual contact with them. Of some consolation, barbed wire and mines had been placed in front of our positions by combat engineers.

Just before dark one of our tanks rumbled into position about 30 yards to the left of me. It made me feel just a bit safer. Nothing happened that night, but just before daybreak some screaming and shouting in Korean could be heard ahead of us. We couldn't see anything. It sounded like a mob making all that noise. Then I heard the tank engine start up and when I looked toward the tank, it backed up, pivoted, and took off for the rear. The truck driver yelled, "Come back here, you son-of-a-bitch," but the tank disappeared from view. Mortar rounds began falling in on our positions while the screaming and yelling continued until daylight.

At first light the yelling and screaming stopped and I could see on the hills about 500 yards away people milling around and moving down to the valley floor in our direction. I looked at the first sergeant and said, "Shit, we've had it!" While we braced ourselves for the mass attack,

FIGURE 6   1st Sergeant Frank L. Chandler of Massachu-
setts comforts a soldier who lost a buddy. Medic Cpl. Joseph
Villaflor of Eleele, Kauai, is on the left. August 1950.
Courtesy of Al Chang.

intense small arms fire broke out from the hills to our left and right
where other friendly units were dug in. I fired my gun in long bursts even
though the range was still great and saw my tracer rounds arcing high
and disappearing. Above the din of gunfire I didn't hear or see the flight
of navy Corsairs flying in until I saw the yellow flame and black smoke
from the napalm bombs dropped by the Corsairs. I wanted to jump up
and cheer! The air strike broke up the mass attack. Not one North
Korean got to our lines.

AUGUST 1950

1ST LT. HERBERT IKEDA
Charlie Company, 5th RCT
Vicinity of Masan, South Korea

Our company was ordered to take a hill that was steep on all sides, rocky,
and dry, with very little vegetation. We had to cross a stretch of dry rice

paddies for about half a mile before we reached the base of the hill. To make things worse, the day was humid and hot. The temperature must have been over 100 degrees.

Our artillery pounded the hill first before my platoon, the lead platoon in the attack, started out in a skirmish line. Enemy mortar rounds began falling among our ranks as we started across the rice paddies. I yelled at my men to keep on moving to the base of the hill. Some of the men got hit and others fell to the ground, not wanting to go on. We had not received rifle and machine gun fire so I moved through the skirmish line and pressed my men on while mortar rounds kept bursting around us.

We finally got to the base of the hill, where I organized what was left of my platoon. I then waved my platoon forward in a skirmish but the skirmish line broke down when enemy mortar rounds again fell among the men. There was still no fire coming from the top of the hill. I thought maybe the North Koreans had given up the hill after our artillery barrage.

While moving up I bumped into Sgt. Reginald Nash from Hawaii, who was laying commo wire for the company. I told him to drop the roll of wire and to join me, which he did. Mortar rounds were still coming and more men were down from it and from the heat. As we neared the crest of the hill, we ran into a wall of hand grenades and automatic rifle fire. More of my men were hit and the attack stalled. I finally ordered my platoon to pull back halfway down the hill, where the rest of the company was dug in.

My radio man, Ben Terukina, grabbed me by the arm and told me he just received word from battalion that we were getting air support in a few minutes and for everyone to take cover. Minutes later, P-51 Mustangs appeared and made several strafing runs on the North Korean positions. Some of the Mustangs' spent cartridges fell on the hill, one hitting me on my helmet. The support was so close that some of my men ran farther down the hill to escape being strafed by our planes.

After the air strike the entire company resumed the attack, this time meeting only scattered small arms fire. The air attack must have taken its toll on the North Koreans because they were bugging out when we reached the top of the hill. I saw a dozen or so North Koreans about 50 yards away leaving their holes and running down the reverse slope. Some of my men took pot shots at them and got a couple of them. I finally ordered my men to quit firing so we could dig in and prepare for a counterattack. When I took a head count of my platoon, I counted only thirteen men left from the original thirty-six when we started the assault.

Before my platoon had a chance to rest and recover from the attack and heat, my company commander told me to take some men and clear the right ridge line that extended to the valley below. I told him that I had only thirteen men left in my platoon and asked if he could assign another platoon to that mission. He was furious. He said it was a direct order. Before he could say anything more, I pointed out to him a group of men in the valley some 500 yards away crossing the river and heading up the same ridge line that I was to clear. I told him that they were NKs. He said no, they were men from the 3d Battalion and for me to take my patrol out immediately and to link up with them. I said if they were men from the 3d Battalion coming up this way, then there was no need to send a patrol down the same ridge. He said to meet them halfway. I got my thirteen men together and told them of the assignment. Were they pissed!

We made better time going down the ridge than the men coming up. When we were halfway down the ridge and about 200 yards from the men climbing up, I recognized them as North Koreans. I had no radio to warn the company back on the hill, so I sent my runner to inform inform the CO that what we saw were not "friendlies" but North Koreans and that I was going to withdraw to the company's position. Then I told my men to keep their heads down and to make it back to the company.

We were about 100 yards from the company when I happened to glance at smaller ridge, which was only a shallow gully away from where we were. A small enemy force was moving up that ridge, apparently unseen by our company on the hill. The enemy force was about 100 yards from us and about 200 yards below our company's position on the hill. With my binoculars I saw some had American uniforms on.

What I did next must have shocked my men. I told them to get down and to wait for my orders to fire. I took off my steel helmet and wrapped my head with a green towel that I always carried. Then I stood up in plain sight and waved my hands to catch the enemy's attention. Some of the NKs stood up and waved their hands, apparently thinking that we were the NKs coming up the ridge behind us. I yelled, "Fire!" and dropped to the ground. My men were on their knees firing, emptying clip after clip of ammo into the NKs. The firing alerted our men on the hill and took the NKs under fire. It was a wipeout.

However, we were now receiving machine gun fire and rifle fire from the NKs below us so I turned the patrol to face that threat. In the exchange of fire, my BAR man got hit in the shoulder. His assistant took over the BAR, only to yell at me that it wouldn't fire. I grabbed the gun from him, tapped the magazine at the bottom, and pulled the trigger.

The gun fired! I gave it back to the assistant BAR man and rolled over to another position about 3 yards away. At this instant the BAR man got hit. I rolled back to the BAR man and found that he had been hit in the shoulder and stomach and was killed instantly. Two other men were killed in this action. With half my patrol killed or wounded, I decided that it was time to make it back to the company's position. Under cover of mortar and machine gun fire, we were able to make the last 100 yards back to our company.

AUGUST 1950

CPL. HARRISON LEE
Love Company, 19th Infantry
Pusan Perimeter, South Korea

After taking a terrible beating at Taejon, the 34th Infantry gathered itself to rebuild inside the Pusan Perimeter. We had walked all the way from Taejon while others reached Pusan by boat and hitched rides to assembly areas. More came by train and trucks. We spent about a week in the rear trying to build up our strength. Our regiment was so decimated that replacements in personnel and equipment were not enough to rebuild the regiment to even half its strength. The 34th Infantry Regiment was declared not up to combat strength and was ordered to the rear to reorganize. It existed only on paper. All personnel were transferred to the 19th Infantry or 21st Infantry of the 24th Division. I was transferred to Love Company, 19th Regiment. Later, the 5th Regimental Combat Team from Hawaii took the place of the 34th Infantry.

While in reserve we took advantage of the time to clean up and wash our clothes. Most of us had gone for three weeks without a change of clothing. I still had the same set of fatigues that I was wearing when I landed at Pusan. The only spare clothing I had were socks and underwear. No one carried an extra pair of fatigues in his combat pack.

I was at the stream bank doing my laundry in my undershorts when a haole guy from another company approached me with an armful of dirty laundry, dumped it in front of me, and said, "Boy-san, washee, washee."

I didn't know whether to laugh or get angry. I looked up at him and shot back, "Wash the goddamn things yourself!" You should have seen the look on his face.

From that time on I realized that I could be mistaken for a Korean or maybe even a North Korean and even be shot by one of our men.

Pusan Perimeter, South Korea

We loaded onto several trucks and relieved another company on line. One jeep led the column and another took up the rear. I was in the second truck with the first sergeant. The company we were to relieve was positioned in a valley beyond some low-lying hills. The only way we could get to the company was through a pass between two hills. It was a winding road because that part of South Korea was quite mountainous. The road was bad. After a couple of hours, the convoy reached the pass and began to make its way slowly down the winding road into the valley. On the left and to the front was the valley and on the right was a ridge line that paralleled the road.

When the last vehicle, a jeep, cleared the pass, the North Koreans opened fire with automatic weapons and grenades from the hillside to our right. We had run into an ambush! Then mortar rounds began to fall on the convoy. I was sitting on the bench seat near the tailgate and I could see what was happening behind me. The driver of the third truck sounded his horn and waved his hand at us, telling us to speed up. Our driver didn't need any encouragement. He stepped on the gas and we barreled down the road. It was about a mile from the pass to the valley floor. Our trucks did not have canvas tops so those who were able to maintain their balance in the bouncing trucks fired wildly into the hillside, hoping to hit something. But most of the guys tried to lay flat on the beds of the trucks. Later we found out that we had lost two trucks and all their occupants when the drivers were killed and the trucks plunged into the valley.

In a few minutes we were at the bottom of the hill, where the trucks came to a dusty, grinding stop. We were ambushed behind our lines and had not reached the company we were to relieve. The NKs were not through with us yet. They had followed us down into the valley and were spraying us with machine gun fire.

There was a dry river bed with large boulders. We scrambled out of our trucks with our wounded and took positions behind the boulders. Others took cover under the trucks. Now enemy fire came from all around us. The NKs had arranged a two-part ambush for us. The first part was at the pass and the second in the valley. I could see them on the hillside, milling around, and I could see the small puffs of smoke when they fired. Our guys were getting killed and wounded.

The first sergeant grabbed me by the arm, pointed to a shack about 100 yards from the river bed, and hollered, "Let's make it to the shack!" He went first and I followed. Two others who saw us leave followed us. Then others trickled in with some wounded and soon the shack, which measured about 20 feet by 20 feet, became quite crowded. A GI came in with a badly wounded soldier over his shoulder. The first sergeant and I picked up the injured man, laid him on the floor, and tried to dress his wounds. He was hit in the chest. Then an explosion on the outside rocked the shack and sent pieces of metal whizzing into the shack. There were other explosions outside. Someone yelled, "Tank!" I peeked out from one of the windows and, sure enough, there was a NK tank in the valley about 500 yards away, ripping away at the trucks.

What we didn't know at the time was that directly above us in the loft was a 55 gallon drum of fuel. Another explosion outside again sent shrapnel through the shack, one piece puncturing the 55 gallon drum and spilling oil all over us and on the wounds of the young GI. He gave a horrible scream and died in the arms of the first sergeant.

Soaked with fuel, the sergeant and I decided to get the hell out of there because another round could set off a fire or an explosion. But we changed our minds and decided to take our chances in the shack because enemy machine gun fire raked the open area outside the shack. Most of the trucks were destroyed or were on fire. I thought to myself, *We sure ain't going to ride back, that's for sure.* Surprisingly, the enemy tank did not get any closer but continued to pour fire into our positions.

Then we heard the roar of jets making strafing runs into the valley and the hillside. They napalmed the hillside and the valley and rocketed the tank. Man, did we jump up and down with joy! The old man must have called for air support and they came just in the nick of time. But the joy was only short-lived because the North Koreans still controlled the hillside and we were still surrounded. As long as there was daylight, we would have the support of our planes.

When night came the company formed a perimeter around the shack and we dug in for the night. We were told that we had been ambushed by a pretty large enemy force and had to stay put for the night. A rescue unit would be on its way first thing the next morning. That night we got very close artillery support, with rounds falling sometimes only a few yards from our positions. We beat back two separate attacks between 0300 and 0400 hours.

When daylight came the enemy had vanished from the hills and at noon the rescue party arrived. Our dead and wounded were put in trucks and taken to the rear. As the company clerk, I had to report all the casualties in the company's morning report. Love Company had suffered over 60 percent casualties.

AUGUST 1950

PFC. FRED ITO
Easy Company, 5th Cavalry
Pusan, South Korea

I was on my way to Korea on a Japanese ferry boat escorted by a British destroyer wondering what the heck I had gotten into.

When the Korean War started, I was twenty years old and stationed in Kobe Sannomiya with the Quarter Master branch. What easy duty! It was great while it lasted. The word came that a whole bunch of us were being transferred to the 1st Calvary Division in Korea.

Pusan, South Korea

When we arrived in Pusan in the morning we were given all the ammunition we could carry and put on a rickety Korean train that puffed and chugged its way north to Taegu. No one told us that the front lines were close to that city. We arrived in Taegu late in the afternoon and were given our specific assignments. I was assigned to Easy Company, 2d Battalion, 5th Cavalry, 1st Cavalry Division.

I was the only one from Hawaii assigned to Easy Company. But the next day when I went to the supply tent to draw some equipment, I met the supply sergeant, Sergeant Burgess, who was from the island of Kauai. He asked me if I was a local boy. When I told him I was, he pulled me to the side and gave me the low-down—the things that I needed to know to survive in Korea. I felt really good meeting someone from Hawaii. I never saw him after that, but it raised my morale quite a bit.

After we had our dinner, the last good one for a long time, we loaded onto trucks and began a blackout drive to our company. We detrucked and were told that was as far as the truck could take us and we would have to walk the rest of the way to the company, which was about 2 miles away. A sergeant, who guided us to meet up with our company, said that they had not had replacements for quite some time and were dug in on the east bank of the Naktong River. As we walked, we could see flares in the distance lighting up the night sky and the terrain ahead of us.

The sergeant took us to our respective platoons, where we were assigned to squads. I was put in the 2d Squad, 1st Platoon, and was paired off with a haole from the mainland. We were led to an empty foxhole and told to be quiet and listen for noises. Our position was just short of the river bank and I could hear the running water and see the river whenever an occasional flare lit the area in front of us.

AUGUST 1950

PFC. SUSUMU SHINAGAWA
Able Company, 34th Infantry
POW camp, somewhere in North Korea

I was in the hospital lying in bed when huge explosions rocked the far side of the camp. We were too far north so it couldn't have been our artillery. They were bombs dropped by our planes. We couldn't hear the whine of jet engines so the bombs must have been dropped from a high altitude. The guards didn't attempt to evacuate anyone, so I stayed in bed looking up at the ceiling. A bomb hit one end of the hospital and the whole building shook. The ceiling seemed to be moving up and down, and then a huge piece of plaster started to fall. I turned and dropped to the floor just as the plaster fell on the entire length of my bed. Before the air raid I was fed soup, rice, and a side dish. After the air raid, all I was given to eat was rice. The North Koreans were pissed off.

[Gen. Douglas MacArthur took North Korea by surprise with the invasion of Inchon deep behind enemy lines. On September 15, the 1st Marine Division, augmented by South Korean marines, landed at Inchon west of Seoul. The 7th Infantry Division followed a day later. By September 29, friendly forces had recaptured Seoul, the capital city of South Korea. On September 19, the 1st Cavalry Division, the 2d, 24th, and 25th Infantry Divisions, and other UN forces broke out of the Pusan Perimeter and routed North Korean forces after heavy fighting.]

SEPTEMBER 1950

PVT. HISASHI MORITA
Schofield Barracks, Territory of Hawaii

I was caught in the second draft call and was sent to Schofield Barracks for thirteen weeks of training.

My fiancée and I had planned to be married after I completed basic training, but she changed our plans. Her mother told her that I might be killed in Korea and that wouldn't be fair to her daughter. We postponed our marriage until my return.

SEPTEMBER 1950

1ST LT. HERBERT IKEDA
Charlie Company, 5th RCT
Vicinity of Sobuk-san Mountain

Our entire regiment moved south of Sobuk-san for some rest after being relieved by the 27th Wolfhound Regiment of the 25th Infantry Division. And it was during this time that the battalion ordered me to form a unit of volunteers to conduct special operations behind enemy lines. The unit was dubbed "Ikeda's Raiders," named after me. Quite a tribute, I thought.

But after several missions my platoon was bitching about the many times I had volunteered the platoon for dangerous missions and that I was jeopardizing the lives of the men. So for the next mission I decided to rest my men and asked for volunteers from KATUSAs who had been assigned to our company. There were so many volunteers that I had to turn away about a dozen. My special unit was now made up entirely of Koreans.

SEPTEMBER 1950

Honolulu, Territory of Hawaii

The *Honolulu Star Bulletin* reported the following story by Capt. Bert N. Nishimura, who was dispatched to Korea from the troop information and education division in Tokyo:

HONOLULU MAN COMMANDS GROUP
OPERATING BEHIND N. KOREANS.

With the 5th Regiment in Korea—The saga of "Ikeda's Raiders" is a page out of some of the thrilling episodes in the fighting here in Korea. Living those fantastic and often-times unbelievable feats are men of Lt. Herbert Ikeda's special patrol missions.

Lt. Ikeda, whose home is at 1025 Kikeke Ave., Honolulu, is almost shy. Asked about these escapades behind enemy lines, he pointed to his two squad leaders, Corporal Joseph S. Tupa and Corporal Homer K. Kuhns. "They're the guys who can tell you about those missions."

Lt. Ikeda is more interested in the baby boy which he expects to be added to the household. If he turns out to a girl, he will be happy also. . . .

On many occasions, this patrol has been dispatched through enemy lines to gain information. . . . They gathered important information and they have personally led the entire combat team in some of the bloodiest fighting seen anywhere at any time.

SEPTEMBER 1950

CPL. LARRY ACOSTA
Item Company, 5th RCT
Vicinity of Taegu

Our company was supposed to relieve a ROK unit on line, but when we got to their position they were gone. Normally, a unit being relieved will stay in position before the exchange is made. No one could account for their absence.

Our platoon was deployed on a small hill that overlooked a knoll about 100 yards away. That knoll was supposed to have been cleared by the ROK unit we relieved. Sgt. Santiago Piscusa and Sgt. Leonard Kaae, both from Hawaii, were on the same hill with me. Piscusa was standing about 20 feet to my left when a burst of machine gun fire from the knoll cut him down. I dove into a nearby hole, from where I could see the North Korean machine gun.

FIGURE 7   Preparing for a patrol mission are members of "Ikeda's Raiders." *Left to right,* Sgt. Joseph Tupa, Lt. Herbert Ikeda, and Cpl. Homer Kuhns. September 1950. Courtesy of Al Chang.

FIGURE 8   Lt. Herbert Ikeda *(center)* and members of "Ikeda's Raiders" display a North Korean trophy. October 1950. Courtesy of Al Chang.

Piscusa was on open ground. I could see he was still alive and was trying to back up into a nearby hole but wasn't making any progress. The North Korean gun was still sweeping the hill with fire, kicking up dirt. Lugging the heavy BAR, I sprinted the 20 feet to Piscusa and hit the ground beside him. He was conscious. That son-of-a-gun smiled at me! Maybe he was just happy to see me. With bullets zipping around and in the dirt, I grabbed Piscusa by the arm and dragged him about 10 feet into a shell crater.

A medic answered my call and joined us in the shell crater, which was too small for three men, so I ran back to my hole and found Leonard Kaae there, firing like mad at a couple of bunkers. Then our 60mm mortars dusted the hill for about ten minutes and silenced the enemy machine gun. Kaae and I leaped out of the shell crater and made our way up the hill, firing as we went. Others, seeing what Kaae and I had done, joined us in the final dash to the top. The last mortar barrage must have taken its toll because all we found in the bunkers were dazed and scared NKs.

Vicinity of Waegwan, South Korea

I was on a squad-size motorized patrol on four jeeps; each jeep was mounted with a light .30 caliber machine gun.

We were several miles ahead of the battalion when we approached

FIGURE 9   Sfc. David Broad of the 5th RCT takes a well-deserved rest after weeks of fighting. October 1950. Courtesy of Al Chang.

a small village of five thatched-roof houses. We were about 300 yards from the village when squad leader Sgt. Martin Ortegero stopped the patrol and told us to dismount. With his binoculars he carefully surveyed the village and noted that it appeared to be uninhabited, which he thought was rather odd. He then took each house under observation again and, lo and behold, he spotted a tank partially hidden behind one of the houses. No wonder there were no villagers. They must have fled into the hills.

He radioed our company commander and told him of the situation. Since there were no signs of NK troops in the vicinity, Ortegero told the CO that he was going to take a closer look at the village to determine if there were more hidden tanks. He pointed to me and two others to follow him over a small ridge that led to the back of the village. Before we set off, he told the jeep drivers to turn the vehicles around for a fast getaway.

The ridge offered great cover, enabling us to get to the top without being seen. The village was in front of us about 100 yards away. Ortegero again took another look at the village with his binoculars. After a minute he told us that he was certain that there was only one tank and no enemy troops in the area.

We cautiously approached the tank from the rear. The turret hatch was open and we could hear voices inside of the tank. This was my first close-up of a Russian-built T-34 tank and, man, that thing was *huge!*

About 5 yards from the tank Ortegero motioned us to hit the ground. He then surprised us when he took a running jump and landed on the deck of the tank, climbed to the open hatch, and dropped a grenade into the tank. He barely got off the tank before the grenade exploded. His timing was perfect. I could hear the crew screaming inside the tank.

The escape hatch at the bottom of the tank opened, so we fired at the hatch, preventing anyone from getting out. Ortegero did it again. He jumped on the tank and dropped another grenade into the open hatch, which started a fire inside the tank. We yelled at him to get away from the tank because the fire could set off the ammo in the tank. The entire action must have taken only a couple of minutes.

With Ortegero leading the way, we made a beeline directly to the jeeps. Halfway to the jeeps we could hear the tank's ammo exploding. When I looked back, the house that the tank had used for camouflage was on fire. The house next to it was smoking and then burst into flames.

Our drivers didn't spare any gas as we hauled ass back to the company—a patrol mission highly successful with an enemy tank to our credit.

Two miles before we reached the company, the lead jeep suddenly slid to a halt, kicking up dust and almost causing a pileup. The lead driver pointed to the bank of a stream about 30 feet from the road where two bodies lay, seemingly dead. We got off the jeeps to investigate and when we got closer, the bodies appeared to be North Korean. There were no visible wounds and the bodies appeared too clean, so one of the men prodded one of the bodies with his bayonet. The body flinched! Then I was startled by a couple of rifle shots fired from one of the men behind me. We all turned to see a North Korean soldier tumble from behind a bush about 30 yards away. It was a trick. The two "dead" North Koreans jumped up and raised their hands. Someone said, "Shoot the bastards," but Ortegero said no, we needed prisoners.

We had a good day. One tank and two prisoners.

SEPTEMBER 1950

PFC. ARSANIO VENDIOLA
Company G, 5th RCT
Naktong River Front

The 5th RCT was now the third regiment of the 24th Infantry Division replacing the 34th Infantry, which was attempting to recover from its terrible losses in July.

We now had the assignment to take a hill on the east side of the Naktong River below Taegu. Before we moved out I noticed one of our tanks was hidden behind some clumps of bushes.

We made good time but when we were several hundred yards from the base of the hill, an enemy recoilless rifle fired at the tank behind us. We scrambled and scurried around trying to find cover. I didn't have time to see what everybody else was doing and my natural instincts told me to find a hole. I saw a small crater and dove in, but it wasn't big enough to contain my entire body. I curled my body, trying to get every inch of it into the hole. Then the firing stopped. I got up and looked around and saw that our tank was not hit. Why the enemy gun stopped firing I didn't know. Maybe our tank knocked it out. But I couldn't tell whether or not our tank had returned fire. Just then, a jeep with three men came speeding up. All three got out of the jeep in a hurry and made a dash for my hole. Hell, there wasn't room for one man, much less room for four. I let them pile up on me, each trying to burrow under me. I felt safer under the human pile. Then an instant later the jeep blew up.

One of the guys from the jeep caught shrapnel on his backside. I guess he couldn't keep his ass down. There was a call for a medic.

One of our guys who had been crouching near the tank had caught shrapnel in his shoulder. The medic, who was from the Big Island, ran to the wounded man to give him aid. The enemy recoilless rifle fired again! I could hear the "whoosh" of the round as it passed over our heads and impacted beyond the tank. The enemy gun was firing quickly, about one round every ten seconds. I yelled for the medic to take cover, but I guess he didn't hear or didn't want to leave the injured man. He still worked on the wounded man as the enemy fire continued.

Our artillery was called in again and the hill took a pounding like I had never seen before. When it was over we walked up the hill without drawing any fire. Not all the North Koreans fled the hill. Many were still hunkered in their holes with dazed looks on their faces, the effects of the blistering artillery barrage. This was the first time I really saw shell-shocked men.

[After the battle for Waegwan, the North Koreans were bugging out in droves, hoping not to get trapped between the marines who had landed at Inchon and the UN forces that had broken out of the Pusan Perimeter.]

SEPTEMBER 1950

PFC. IRWIN COCKETT
Dog Company, 5th RCT
Vicinity of Waegwan, South Korea

With the 1st Cavalry Division on our right flank we managed to punch our way out from the river beachhead to the outskirts of Waegwan, which was the regiment's objective. But getting there was a bitch because the North Koreans fought bitterly for the hills surrounding the town before giving them up.

Before entering the town, we took a breather on a hill that overlooked the town. The rifle companies in front of us were expecting some tough street fighting in the town and were planning on the best way to take it. The next thing we knew, Waegwan and the surrounding area were engulfed in huge explosions, smoke, and dust. Without announcing their

arrival, air force B-29 bombers had bombed the town from a high altitude. It seemed that the town was completely leveled. It reminded me
of what the air force did to Germany in World War II when it applied
what was called carpet bombing, a technique used to lay waste a designated area. It was awesome. We entered Waegwan with very little opposition.

Vicinity of Kimchon, South Korea

I received word that one of my buddies, Homer Kuhns, had been killed.
Kuhns was a classmate of mine at the Kamehameha School for Boys and
a member of "Ikeda's Raiders," whose exploits were legendary in the regiment. I was told that Kuhns, who carried a burp gun he had taken off
a North Korean earlier, had fought his way up a hill. When he got to the
crest, he came face to face with a North Korean who also had a burp gun.
Both had fired at the same time. Kuhns lost the burp gun duel.

What was especially sad for me was that a couple of days later, while
moving forward along a road, we came across several dead bodies alongside the road by the graves registration people. The bodies were not covered. As I walked by I recognized my classmate, Homer Kuhns. There
was my classmate, lying there. It stuck with me for a long time.

SEPTEMBER 1950

1ST LT. HERBERT IKEDA
Charlie Company, 5th RCT
Vicinity of Taegu, South Korea

Our company halted on the top of a hill that overlooked a small village.
The battalion commander called to inform me that he was sending my
special unit to the village, where our intelligence reported NK antitank
weapons were known to be. He believed the village to be deserted and
felt my patrol would not have any trouble.

Our company on the hill observed our movements as we worked our
way down the hill to the village. We made it to the village square without any incident, and it appeared that the village was deserted. I positioned my men and went to the middle of the village square and shouted
in Japanese, "Come out and surrender!" Nothing happened.

Then my Koreans began to shout in Korean, "Come out and surrender!" About a dozen North Koreans came out from several houses
with their hands above their heads. We bound their hands and one of

my men escorted them to the bottom of the hill to wait for us. As we searched the village for more North Koreans, one ran out of a hut about 30 paces away from me and threw a concussion grenade, which burst several feet from me. I was showered with thin metal pieces from the grenade. I let off a short burst from my burp gun, which I had taken from a dead NK in an earlier battle, and killed him. An instant later we were met with automatic fire, which sent us scrambling for cover behind the houses we had already cleared.

I realized then that there was a sizable enemy force in the village and that my patrol was too small to win the fight. I yelled to my men to disengage and assemble at the bottom of the hill. Meanwhile, our men on the hill, seeing what had happened, gave us supporting fire which kept the NKs' heads down and prevented them from pursuing us.

When we got back to the top of hill, the battalion commander came running to me and chewed me out for starting the fire fight in the village. He wanted an explanation. After I explained what happened, he said he was going to send a company to clean out the village.

"I tell you what, colonel," I said. "Let me take some of my men back to the village and maybe I can convince them to surrender." He mulled over my suggestion quietly for a few seconds and then approved it.

I took a dozen of my KATUSAs with me and went back down to the village. When we got to perimeter of the village, I sent two point men forward into the village while the rest of us waited. In about ten minutes they came back and said that they were seen by the NKs but were not shot at. It could be a trap, I thought, but because a dozen had surrendered earlier there was a chance that the rest would, too.

When we entered the village several NKs came out from the houses with their hands raised. One appeared to be an officer, judging from his uniform. I called him over and told him if his men surrendered they would receive good treatment. One of my KATUSAs repeated the same instructions. "Give up now! We will give you tobacco. We will give you candy. We will give you food. Throw down your weapons now." The officer went back to his men and shouted some orders. Ninety-six NKs came out and surrendered without a shot being fired.

They came out from hiding, some singly but most in small groups. My men ordered them to place their weapons on the side of the road. A detail was sent down from the hill to help us carry the surrendered weapons and escort the prisoners. When we got back to the company, the battalion commander wasn't there to congratulate us on our successful mission. He later sent his intelligence officer to debrief me.

While we were resting, I noticed that several NKs had stars sewn on their uniforms. These were large red stars, larger than those our generals wore on their uniforms. I had the prisoners remove fifteen stars and had them sew five in a circle on my fatigue cap and five each on my shoulder. I then declared myself general of the army for that day, September 18, 1950.

As I was having chow that evening, my battalion commander came by and asked how many prisoners my patrol captured. I told him, "Ninety-six, sir!"

He looked at the stars on my uniform and replied, "Very goooood, general, very goooood. I see you got a promotion."

"Yes, colonel. Nobody in this chicken shit outfit promoted me, so I promoted myself."

The next morning the battalion commander told me to take two jeeps and check the valley up ahead before the main column moved out. He wanted us to go about 10 miles into the valley.

I asked my KATUSAs for volunteers and they practically fought among themselves to go with me. I picked seven men. Each jeep had a driver, a shotgun rider, and two men on the mounted light .30 caliber machine guns. I drove the lead jeep.

We raced down the valley floor out of sight of friendly forces. We had gone about 8 miles when we came upon five unarmed, wounded North Korean soldiers sitting by the side of the road. We approached cautiously and stopped about 30 yards from them. I told the medics to cover me with the machine gun while I walked to the NKs. It was no trap. They were stragglers from a retreating North Korea regiment and were left behind because they couldn't keep up with their unit. The North Koreans said they were also victims of an American air strike the day before. Figuring that our intelligence would be happy to question the prisoners, we piled them into the two jeeps and returned to our unit. We weren't gone for more than an hour and no one missed us.

That evening while I was having chow, the battalion commander again stopped by to talk to me. "Ikeda, how many prisoners you got today?"

"Five, sir," I replied. I didn't think he believed me. "They are now with S-2."

"Take off them stars," he shot back.

"Yes, sir," I said. "What a chicken shit outfit," I said under my breath but loud enough for the colonel to hear. "One day I'm a general of the army and the next day I'm a private."

SEPTEMBER 1950
PFC. SUSUMU SHINAGAWA
Able Company, 34th Infantry
Manpo, POW camp, North Korea

We had been put on a train five days before we arrived at Manpo, our new home, a little town on the Yalu River. Because it took so long to get there we guessed that our last POW camp was not too far from where the fighting was taking place.

We were put in a compound consisting of several long buildings with wooden floors. As usual, there were many guards patrolling the area. A small building served as a hospital for the sick and wounded. We were lucky this time to have an American doctor, but he couldn't do too much because he lacked the medical supplies to treat us. All he had to work with were gauze and bandages. I was his patient and his translator.

We were given quite a bit of freedom, unlike the other camps we were in. The setup was good and an American officer was in charge of us. We cooked our own meals and ate "cafeteria" style. The food was poor, but we didn't complain. With this kind of setup, why should we? The civilians were allowed to bring us rice, turnips, won bok cabbage, and green onions in an ox cart. We were pretty much on our own with little directions from the guards. The guards came to check our sleeping quarters only during the evening.

One night, Tadaki and I were sitting on a platform in the open field with a big moon shining above. We were just chatting to kill time when a NK guard came and tried to make small talk with us in Japanese. He looked at the moon, pointed to it, and asked us if we had a moon in America. Tadaki and I looked at each other and just wanted to bust out laughing. Instead, Tadaki, with a serious face said, "In America, the moon is blue."

The guard said, "Oh," and walked away. I recalled the incident of the black and blond hair when I was first captured. Same very low intelligence.

I had never seen lice before. It was a creature new to me but it was a common thing with the farmers. Lice were everywhere, and some even found their way into my cast. They fed off the skin and sucked my blood. The bites itched. They were in my groin, underarms, and eyelashes as well. I had no way to get them out. The itching was unbearable and tortuous. We would spend hours a day trying get rid of them but they always returned with a vengeance.

It was time to take the cast off my arm. The medical staff first tried using a knife but couldn't remove it. They then tried a saw and still failed. They boiled hot water, as hot as I could stand it, and put my cast and arm in it. It softened the cast and they were able to peel the cast off layer by layer. The wounds were healed except for one. Tissue was still sticking out of the skin and wouldn't heal. I had to keep a bandage on it for the rest of my stay in Korea.

SEPTEMBER 1950

CPL. JAY HIDANO
Easy Company, 8th Cavalry
Vicinity of Sabu-dong, South Korea

We were ordered to attack a North Korean stronghold that was at least several hundred feet high. Braving enemy fire was one thing, but having to crawl up the steep slopes with bullets buzzing and striking all around us was just madness. Casualties were heavy as I watched men get hit, some struggling to get up, others not moving.

I had to move up the hill or get clobbered by mortars. I would rather face hand grenades because there was a chance I could dodge them.

It took us several hours before we got to within a few yards of the crest. The NKs must have saved all their hand grenades for that moment because it rained grenades for several minutes, causing a lot of casualties. We made a final charge and gained the crest. The NKs retreated down the slope and up another hill about 200 yards away. While others fired away at the fleeing NKs, I found a hole and plopped in. I didn't want to push my luck.

As we prepared our defensive positions for the night, the NKs threw some mortar shells at us. One of the men jumped out of his foxhole and screamed, "They blown my ass off," ran a few feet, and fell to the ground. A small mortar round had landed in the two-man foxhole he was in and tore his backside open. His foxhole buddy was not so lucky. The mortar barrage lasted for only a few minutes, and we continued to work on our defenses.

Just before dark Captain McClain called a meeting of two other platoon sergeants and me to lay plans for the night. We were in a circle with the captain talking when a couple of NK mortar rounds came in. One mortar round exploded several feet behind me and I felt stabbing pains in my back. The two other platoon sergeants were also injured but not severely. Luckily for the captain the mortar round had burst on our side of the circle, the three of us shielding him from mortar fragments.

After we were tended to by a medic, the captain ordered us to report to the battalion aid station. The platoon sergeants were treated and were sent back to the company. My wound was more serious so I was sent to the division hospital in Taegu. One of the doctors took one look at my back and ordered me to the 8th Army hospital in Pusan.

The next day I was put on a train to Pusan, where a doctor told me I had two metal fragments in my back. He removed one and could not take the other out because it required a delicate operation and it would be better if he didn't remove it. However, he said that it should not bother me and I could return to my unit. Geez! I had a vision of recuperating in a hospital in Japan and being with my wife and kids.

I stayed in the hospital for about a week. I then caught a train back to Taegu and found my company in the same general area where I had left it. Captain McClain was surprised but happy to see me back. He thought that I had earned a plane ride to Japan.

A short time later we were relieved by another unit and went into reserve about a mile behind the lines along a stream. The first thing all of us did was to bathe in the stream and wash our dirty clothes. It was the first bath most of us had since we arrived in Korea but I cannot remember changing my clothes and socks during that time.

While we were in reserve, our company received approximately seventy KATUSAs as replacements. About twenty were assigned to each platoon, but this didn't work out because there was a major communication problem. Another problem arose when we found out that the KATUSAs couldn't stomach our food rations and many became ill. They wanted Korean food. In some cases they were physically abused by our men, forced to carry heavy loads of ammunition and supplies.

To solve this problem Captain McClain had an idea. Since both the KATUSA soldiers and I could speak and understand Japanese, Captain McClain put most of the KATUSAs in one platoon and put me in charge. The company now had an extra platoon made up entirely of KATUSAs and, for that matter, all Asians. The captain promoted the two brightest to second lieutenant and platoon sergeant. He then surprised me. He told me that I was now promoted to sergeant first class and papers for my promotion would be submitted immediately. However, someone changed the orders to staff sergeant, and that is how it read when the orders came down from the battalion later.

To solve the KATUSAs' food problems, I sent them out foraging for Korean food whenever the opportunity arose. They especially wanted kimch'i, a very spicy, pickled cabbage dish. But after a couple of weeks they adapted to our food rations.

Like the KATUSAs I also craved Korean food. One evening a Korean woman came to my platoon and offered us some food. It was the spiciest food I had ever eaten.

We entered Seoul in late September and pushed farther north to Kaesong just below the 38th parallel and remained there for several days until we received the go-ahead to cross the border into North Korea.

SEPTEMBER 1950

Pfc. WALTER OGASAWARA
Item Company, 5th RCT
Vicinity of Waegwan, South Korea

Our B-29s had just bombed the hell out of the city of Waegwan. The smoke and dust after the bombing drifted to where we had dug in on the side of a hill. We had a running fight with the NKs for several days. It was so thick that I had trouble breathing. I practically had to put my nose to the ground to get under the layer of smoke and dust.

I was still the gunner of the 57mm recoilless rifle. In my crew were two big haoles. One was my assistant gunner and loader and the other the ammo bearer. We had had several fire missions since I arrived in Korea but never hit a target. I came close a couple of times but no teddy bear. Our gun position was on the reverse slope just below the crest of the hill and probably looked like a silhouette to the North Koreans who were on a nearby knoll a couple hundred yards away. Since I was the smallest of the three I would put myself between the two haoles because it gave me protection on both sides. Even at night I would get between the two.

One day the ammo bearer said he wanted to be in the middle and, since he was bigger than me, I said fine. The next morning we fired a few rounds at the NK hill and received a few mortar rounds in return. Then for about twenty minutes things got quiet so all three of us got up to see what was up. Wrong decision. A machine gun opened up on us and just stitched us good. I got hit in the right shoulder and I was knocked flat on my ass. The two haoles also were knocked back into the hole.

When I recovered I looked at the ammo bearer next to me, the one who wanted to be in the middle. He was hit in the chest and was all bloody. My assistant gunner was sitting up and holding his left shoulder. I yelled for a medic continuously for ten minutes until one came. I told him to check the one who was hit in the chest. He looked him over for about a minute and turned to me without saying anything. I knew my ammo bearer was dead. In retrospect, if I hadn't changed places with him, I probably would have been the one killed.

I was able to walk off the hill with some help and was taken to the forward aid station, where a chaplain told me that I had a "million dollar" wound. I didn't know what he was talking about.

I was taken by ambulance to Pusan, where I was put on a British ship and sent to Japan. I ended up at Tokyo General Hospital, where I was operated on. I was told that the bullet had entered my right shoulder and was deflected downward near my spine. I was flown to Army Tripler General Hospital, Hawaii, where I thought the bullet would be removed. The bullet is still in my back today.

SEPTEMBER 1950

PFC. NICK NISHIMOTO
Baker Company, 35th Infantry
C-ration Hill, South Korea

While I was improving my foxhole, my platoon sergeant came up to me and said that I had been selected to go on R&R. The reasons for my being selected were that I had never missed a day on line, had not been to sick call, never was wounded, and was on line for almost three months. I was to go to Chin-hae Airfield near Pusan for my R&R.

Chin Hae, South Korea

What was weird, though, I almost cracked up on my R&R. I constantly thought about my buddies on line, especially the guys from Hawaii. Every time I took a hot bath, ate a hot meal, and slept on a nice bed it bothered me. I felt guilty as hell and worried about the Hawaii guys back at the company. The only time I felt good was when Al Jolsen came to perform.

My R&R was over and I had to report back to my unit. I hitched a ride to where I had left the company but found that it had pulled out just ten minutes before I got there. Fortunately, the company had gone on foot so I was able to catch up. I learned that UN forces in the Pusan Perimeter had gone on the offensive in coordination with the Inchon landing west of Seoul.

We often met with some stiff resistance along the way and just bar-reled our way through roadblocks. On one occasion we had to stop and dig in while enemy mortar shells were falling on our positions. I was standing looking for a better place to hide when I heard a crunching sound less than 5 yards from where I was standing. It was a mortar round, which embedded itself in the ground without exploding, its fins stick-ing out of the ground. It wasn't a small round like our 60mm but larger, probably an 82mm round. I threw myself to the ground thinking it might explode. I would have been history if it had, and graves registration would have had a hard time putting my body parts back together. After a few seconds I hauled ass out of there to another spot. When I finally settled in my hole, my whole body trembled, and I suddenly realized that it could have been the end of me.

We finally got a break. Instead of going on foot we were put on tanks. I was on the second tank as we barreled up north without encoun-tering stiff resistance. The terrain was pretty much the same. Rice pad-dies on one side and hills on the other side. Sometimes there were hills on both sides of the road. We stayed on the road and cleared the hillside of North Koreans who decided to fight it out with us.

On the second day the first tank hit a mine and was put out of action. Almost instantly we began receiving machine gun and rifle fire from the hillside about 200 yards away. Bullets struck the side of the tank, making weird sounds as they ricocheted in the air. No one had to be told to get off the tank. I jumped off the tank with the tripod in my hand and took shelter behind the tank. My assistant gunner followed me with the gun. I tried to spot a place where we could set up the gun but couldn't because of the intense enemy fire. I could see puffs of smoke on the hillside.

Our tanks now swept the hillside with their machine guns and 76mm cannons. By this time I found a spot to set up the gun and joined in the firing. With this cover fire, a platoon led by a West Point lieu-tenant stormed the hill and took it. The lieutenant was killed. We got on the tanks and continued north again.

SEPTEMBER 1950

PFC. FRED ITO
Easy Company, 5th Cavalry
Vicinity of Taegu, South Korea

We were nearing Taegu when we were told to relieve units of the 5th RCT on Hill 303. Hill 303 was also named Massacre Hill because, earlier, some GIs had been captured by the North Koreans during the fight for the hill, had their hands tied behind their backs, were shot in the back of the head, and were dumped into a gulch.

When it got dark we packed up again and took to the hills in the direction of Waegwan. Then it rained. *Monsoon season*, I thought. Those of us who had been stationed in Japan knew about the monsoon rain. The rain came so fast that no one could put a poncho on in time to stay dry. This one was a heavy downpour that lasted for about an hour. I didn't bother to put on my poncho. I welcomed the rain because it washed the dirt and grime off my clothes. I took off my steel helmet, separated the liner from the steel helmet, and caught some rain water and drank it. It sure tasted good, better then the chlorinated water we had in our canteens.

My feet hurt and I knew I was getting blisters on them. When we got to the next hill I had a medic check my feet. It was so bad that I was sent to Taegu to have my feet treated. I stayed there for two days until my feet got better. They were not completely healed, and were still tender and sore.

The company was on Hill 303 when I caught up to it. Going up the trail to where the company was dug in, I saw several North Korean corpses on the side of the trail. No one bothered to bury them. I was told that while I was gone the North Koreans had attacked the company but were driven back. The NK bodies I had seen were of those who had slipped to the rear of the company but were killed by an alert GI.

It was 100 percent alert when it got dark because it was suspected the NKs might mount another attack.

At 2200 hours, we saw a torch moving on a hill about 300 yards to our right. It drew all our attention for a few minutes and distracted us. Before I could turn my eyes back to the front of our positions, hand grenades began bursting and bullets from NKs' automatic weapons snapped in the air above me, digging dirt in front of me. While we were mesmerized by the torch, the NKs had crawled within hand grenade range and surprised us. "Mansei! Banzai!" they screamed.

I was between a machine gun team and a flame thrower. I was glad to be next to the flame thrower because every time he let out a burst of fire it would light up the area for a split second, enabling us to see the NKs. I fired as fast as I could. Our guys were firing and yelling at the NKs at the same time. I ran out of hand grenades and wished that I had carried more.

Then the operator of the flame thrower was hit, depriving me of

FIGURE 10   5th RCT soldiers from Hawaii rest after capturing Hill 268 from the North Koreans. In the foreground is a dead North Korean soldier. September 1950. Courtesy of Al Chang.

what little light he had been able to provide. Someone vaulted over my foxhole and fell behind me with a thud. I sat down, pointed my rifle straight up in the air, and emptied a clip of ammo, hoping to discourage any NK who might be in the area. I jumped out of my foxhole and lay beside it, firing at figures in the dark. I didn't want to be caught in the hole should a NK toss a grenade in it. Someone running tripped over me and fell, got up, and continued running. It couldn't have been a GI because the swearing was not American.

   Then I heard shouts of, "Cease fire. Cease fire," and it became very quiet. We had beaten back the NK attack.

OCTOBER 1950

CPL. IRWIN COCKETT
Dog Company, 5th RCT
Vicinity of Suwon, North Korea

We were in reserve and we had dug in on the reverse slope of a bare hillside. Bright signal panels were in full view so our pilots would not mistake us for the enemy.

FIGURE 11   Ragged and beaten North Korean communist soldiers surrender to Hawaii's 5th RCT men near Taegu, South Korea. September 1950. Courtesy of Al Chang.

Hugh Whitford, a high school classmate of mine who was in Able Company, came to visit me one afternoon. We were sharing our rations when a flight of our P-51 Mustangs came over and strafed and rocketed the hell out of us. Before they could come around for a second pass they were called off via radio by one of the air force ground controllers. Luckily, there were no serious injuries but we sure cussed the hell out of the air force.

After the incident, Whitford said it was more dangerous where we were so he left to return to his company. When I saw him again, he told me that when he went back to his foxhole after the "friendly" attack, there was no foxhole. Instead, there was gigantic hole where his foxhole used to be. A rocket had scored a direct hit on it.

We were on the move again, nearing Seoul. Whenever we got to a

FIGURE 12   In the battle for Sobuk-san, Sgt. Albert
Corioso and Cpl. Robert Jimenez of Hawaii blast
away at enemy positions with their mortar. August
1950. Courtesy of Al Chang.

village, local boys used their scrounging skills to get kimch'i, chili
pepper, rice, and other kinds of Korean delicacies. The haoles looked at
us with great disgust. They couldn't understand how we could eat that
stuff.

We used the chili pepper to spice our rations. When we found rice
we would stuff it in our pockets and packs. Whenever we rested
we would cook the rice in cans or even in our canteen cups. We rarely
went hungry. But as food became scarce the haoles soon came to us
for food.

During this time replacements were few and our ranks were slowly
being depleted. You might say we were desperate. As we moved through
villages we picked up able-bodied Koreans and used them as porters. At
one village, my squad drafted three young Korean boys. We called then
Tom, Dick, and Harry and outfitted them with uniforms and rifles. They
were with us all the way into North Korea. I lost track of them when the
Chinese entered the war.

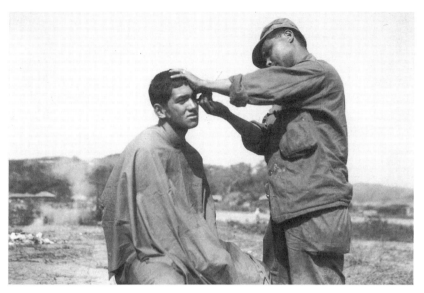

FIGURE 13   While in reserve, Cpl. Irwin Cockett gets a free haircut from a buddy. October 1950. Courtesy of Al Chang.

FIGURE 14   Sgt. Florantino Romano, a medic with the 5th RCT, receives the Silver Star for heroism from Colonel John L. Throckmorton, regimental commander of the 5th RCT. October 1950. Courtesy of Al Chang.

OCTOBER 1950

CPL. BERTRAM SEBRESOS
Fort Shafter, Territory of Hawaii

The 5th Regimental Combat Team, based at Schofield Barracks, Wahiawa, was looking for men to fill its ranks. Many of my friends volunteered but I didn't because Fort Shafter was real easy duty.

My good friend, Leo Labang, and I had joined the boxing team but after a while I quit the team because I didn't enjoy getting hit on the head. Two men from our detachment were picked to go and got killed as soon as they got there.

I now began to take a serious interest in the war since the 5th RCT was in the thick of the fighting in the months of August and September in the Pusan Perimeter. The call came again for more men to go to Korea, not necessarily for the 5th RCT but for other frontline units as well. Like the first call, I didn't volunteer but within a few days my name, along with those of other local boys, appeared on the bulletin board destined for Korea. We were given two weeks to put our personal life in order and report to Hickam Air Force Base for transportation to the Far East.

OCTOBER 1950

1ST LT. HERBERT IKEDA
Charlie Company, 5th RCT
Vicinity of Kaesong, South Korea

Our last big battle was at Waegwan and from there we really hauled ass to the 38th parallel. We knew the 1st Marine Division and the 7th Division had taken the capital city of Seoul from the NKs. We passed the cities of Taejon and Seoul and stopped just short of the 38th parallel at Kaesong, where we had to wait for orders from the big brass to cross into North Korea. I think we had taken less than three weeks from our breakout of the Pusan Perimeter to reach the 38th parallel.

Units of the 1st Cavalry Division had already entered Kaesong when we got there. Seemed like they were always ahead of us. The North Koreans were simply bugging out and we moved out again. The going was easy. We entered Pyongyang, the capital city of North Korea, and found the 1st Cavalry Division already there.

Sunchon, North Korea

When we got to the town of Sunchon, my platoon was given the task of reconnoitering the valley and ridges about 3 miles farther north. It took us the better part of the day running the ridges, climbing one hill after another, and at the same time, keeping an eye on the valley below. There was one more hill to climb and I had decided that after that hill, I was going to call the battalion and tell them it was all clear and to move the column forward. I was at the point of the patrol when I topped the hill standing up. I stopped abruptly and threw myself to the ground. I turned around and motioned my men to hit the ground and crawl to me. When they were up with me I pointed to the valley below, which was alive with enemy activity. There must have been about 1,000 NK soldiers, so I thought, with many tanks. We didn't know at the time that they were units of the CCF that had crossed the Yalu River undetected from Manchuria into North Korea.

We must have been about 400 feet above the valley floor and about a mile away. After determining the coordinates for the artillery, I told my radio operator, Ben Terukina, to request artillery fire. Let me tell you, we had the best seats in the house, watching the artillery pound the commies in the valley. The first few rounds weren't that off and with a couple of adjustments the artillery was right on target. It was like watching ants scatter after you have destroyed their ant hill. While the enemy was scattering Terukina said, "Let's go after them."

"With our thirty against their 1,000, you're crazy," I said. I radioed to the battalion what we had seen and we returned to our company.

OCTOBER 1950

Pfc. Susumu Shinagawa
Able Company, 34th Infantry
Kosan, POW camp, North Korea

We were on the move again, this time walking, moving southwest along the Yalu River to the small village of Kosan. It was during this march that I first saw Chinese soldiers as they crossed the Yalu River from Manchuria into North Korea. There were thousands of them. At first I thought they were walking on water, but it was an underwater bridge they had built, probably at night. From Kosan we were marched to the nearby village of Danakon. It was there we heard artillery fire and saw the first North Korean wounded coming home. Our hopes were lifted, for we were sure that our liberation was not far away.

Vicinity of Danakon, North Korea

Waiting to be rescued by friendly forces was just a dream for me because we moved out again. Why all this moving from one camp to another?

Why didn't they leave us at one camp and be done with it? This time they separated the sick and wounded, about a dozen of them, from the main group. I was ordered to remain with the sick and wounded because an interpreter was needed. We didn't have to walk. They put us on a cart pulled by an ox. Our progress was slow but we caught up with the main group that was camped in a cornfield. They had been there for four nights. I would like to think that they had waited for us but it was not likely.

Up until this time we were under the control of the North Korean Army, but that soon changed. We were transferred to the North Korean Security Police and soon learned of the brutality of that unit. They were a fanatical and sadistic group who would kill anyone without reason. Until then I didn't know how lucky I had been under the control of the North Korean Army.

One day at a bull session with some other POWs, someone heard a rumor and passed it on to us that General MacArthur had promised the boys that we would be home for Christmas. Our morale shot up because this meant that we were winning the war and could be liberated soon. But our hopes were soon dashed because we were told we would be moving to another camp, Chunggang-jin, northeast of Manpo, about 100 miles to the northeast. Hell, we had just come from that direction, and now we were going back the same way. It just didn't make sense.

On October 31, Halloween Day, a short, stocky North Korean officer of the North Korean Security Police was put in charge of the march. No one knew what his name was but he had a nickname, "The Tiger." We soon discovered that he had absolutely no regard for human life.

Our group now consisted of about 700 POWs and over a dozen civilians. We were divided into fourteen companies, fifty men per company, with an American officer in charge. We were told that the guards were going to enforce strict discipline and if a man should fall behind, the officer in charge must assist him or the officer in charge would be shot. To prove how serious they were, they picked out one officer and shot him, just like that, in front of us. That was the second time I witnessed an American officer shot by our captors. We were stunned. They repeated the order and the consequence. This was no idle threat. This was the beginning of a horrible nightmare—"The Tiger Death March."

The civilians who were with us were mostly French, and there was a Catholic priest who had been captured in Seoul. The priest, who spoke fluent Korean, was our interpreter during the march. There were five of us from Hawaii who were Japanese so we were also used as interpreters.

The terrain we had to negotiate was extremely rugged, nothing but high mountains and big valleys. In one instance, it took us more than a day to climb a mountain and half a day to get to the valley floor. Since I had just been released from the hospital and couldn't walk very fast, I was used as the pace setter for our company, and since I was in the lead company, I actually set the pace for the other companies as well. This was a lucky break for everyone because I was short, didn't have a long stride, and was still too weak to walk fast so my pace was very slow. Once in a while I was prodded by the guards to walk faster.

We were now two days into the march. At one time we were three-quarters of the way up a mountain when I looked back and saw the last three companies literally running to catch up with us. And here I thought I wasn't moving fast enough. We tried to help each other by encouraging one another and physically assisting those who were faltering. I told the NK officer that we should slow down some more but the guards would push us on. Every so often we would hear a rifle shot, which meant that some American would not see home again.

About the fourth day, the "Tiger" announced that no prisoner was to help another prisoner. If a prisoner could not make it on his own, he would have to drop out. No one could break ranks to relieve himself. There was a lot of shooting until the end of the march.

From then on it was a pathetic and sorrowful sight. We ate as we marched and many defecated in their pants at the same time. It was a miracle that most of us survived the nights. There were a couple of times when the GI who had leaned on me for the night was dead in the morning.

OCTOBER 1950

SGT. FUMIO HIDANO
Easy Company, 8th Cavalry
Vicinity of Kaesong, North Korea

Captain McClain had gone on R&R leave and was temporarily replaced by Lieutenant Hayden.

It was around 0800 hours on October 9 when Easy Company, the lead company of the 2d Battalion, started on foot across the 38th parallel into North Korea. It was not a dramatic crossing, no shouting or much talking and pretty much a glum disposition on the face of everyone I saw. What was very audible was the pounding of heavy boots on the ground and the clinking of the equipment we carried. Prior to moving out we had loaded ourselves with ammunition, grenades, and rations. The morning air was pretty cool.

Several miles into our march we came to a ninety degree dogleg left turn in the road that was only wide enough for one vehicle. The road was flanked by high ground on both sides. As soon as the lead platoon turned the bend of the road, the entire company came under machine gun fire from the hills on both sides of the road. My platoon was behind the lead platoon and took several casualties immediately. I dove for cover into a shallow ditch that ran the length of the road. It was only about a foot deep but offered some protection. My platoon followed me into the ditch. I tried to contact Lieutenant Hayden but got only static on the radio.

No one made an attempt to dislodge the enemy from the hills, so I motioned to my KATUSA lieutenant to take a few men and find out where the North Korean machine gun was located. Before he could move out, a KATUSA next to me tapped me on the shoulder and cried out, "Nisan, look," and pointed to the third KATUSA on my left who was slumped over his rifle. One of the soldiers turned the body over. There was bullet hole smack between his eyes with a little blood oozing out of it. That was the first time I saw anyone get shot between the eyes.

The KATUSA lieutenant finally set out but returned half an hour later to report that he had been turned back by machine gun fire. By now the company was pouring rifle and machine gun fire on the hillsides. However, the column was still receiving machine gun fire and there was still no contact with Lieutenant Hayden so I told my ROK lieutenant we were going to attack the hill to our right. I shouted to the tail end of the lead platoon that my platoon was going to attack the hill to our right and to give us covering fire.

We took off in small groups across the open space to the bottom of the hill and began climbing the hill, but not until several of my men got hit. We were halfway up the hill when the firing from the top of the hill stopped. We finished the climb uncontested. There were no North Koreans on the crest, only hundreds and hundreds, maybe thousands, of spent cartridges. But at the bottom of the hill and running to the next hill were several NKs. It gave my platoon some target practice as they dropped several fleeing North Koreans.

The NKs, now on the other hill with an elevation higher than the one we were on, looked down on us and raked us with machine gun fire. Several of my men got hit. One soldier, who couldn't have been more than sixteen years of age, was hit in the stomach and kept calling for his mother. For nearly two hours he groaned while his buddies tried to comfort him.

Later in the afternoon two forward observers, a lieutenant and a sergeant, joined us on the hill and told me that they were going to call in an air strike on the hill. I told them we were pretty close to the NKs so to be sure that the air strikes were on target.

Not more than five minutes later several F-80s roared in and strafed, rocketed, and dropped napalm on the hill. Napalm is something to see but very scary close up. Thick, black smoke billowed when it hit the ground and then turned into a fiery red and orange color. The KATUSAs got out of their holes, waved their fists, and cheered.

But after the F-80s departed the NKs came out of their holes and harassed us with mortar and machine gun fire. The lead platoon reinforced us before dark and we set up our defenses for the night.

The next morning Lieutenant Hayden called and said that my platoon was to seize the hill that was holding up the advance. I asked him if he had any plans for me but he said to just take the hill and there would be no supporting mortar fire. I wanted to leave half of my platoon on the hill to give me supporting rifle fire but I had already lost one-third of my platoon. I needed everyone in my platoon to take the hill. I asked Lieutenant Hayden if I could have a couple of machine guns for covering fire and he reluctantly approved. We waited almost an hour before two light machine guns were brought up the hill.

With two skirmish lines about 30 yards apart, we descended the hill running, crossed a 70-yard open space, and began the tough climb up the hill in the face of NK rifle and machine gun fire. Several of my men were down, but I had to move about to keep the rest of the platoon moving. There were three bunkers in our way, which we neutralized with hand grenades. I was really proud of my KATUSAs.

When we neared the crest we were showered with hand grenades, which slowed us down momentarily, but with a second effort we gained the crest, forcing the NKs off the hill.

When it was over Lieutenant Hayden joined us on the hill and said, "Hidano, you will get the Silver Star for this." He never followed through with his promise.

Pyongyang, North Korea

We entered the North Korean capital of Pyongyang on October 19, and took a short rest. The city had been bombed flat by our B-29 bombers and most of its population had fled. My platoon occupied one of the few homes spared from the bombings.

One night one of my KATUSAs warned me that I had to be careful because he had heard talk that I might get shot in the back in the next battle. Admittedly, I was hard on my KATUSA platoon but only because they were an undisciplined bunch when they first joined us, having been conscripted off the streets and farms with very little military training. Military discipline was sorely missing and I had to develop them into a fighting, disciplined unit. I never gave them a task that I wouldn't do myself and, for that, I gained the respect from most of my KATUSAs. But there were always a few disgruntled men in every outfit.

That problem became moot because on the very next day, all the KATUSAs were transferred to a ROK division. Those I had come to know well wished me luck before they left. A few didn't want to leave.

OCTOBER 1950

CPL. PEDRO BEHASA
Item Company, 5th RCT
Vicinity of Pakchon, North Korea

Since the breakout from the Pusan Perimeter and the Inchon landing, we had moved pretty fast, deep into North Korea, and met little enemy resistance. Sometimes we would be on foot doing the dirty work while other units rode. Sometimes we would be in trucks while other units did the fighting ahead of us.

At one point the battalion commander decided to send out a motorized patrol to check out what lay ahead since we were about 50 or so miles from the Yalu River, the boundary between Manchuria and North Korea. The patrol consisted of six men in two jeeps. I was picked to drive one of the jeeps. Two battalion S-2 officers and a couple of captains made up the patrol.

The route was by way of a narrow, winding road that led into a long but slender valley. When we had gone about 3 miles into the valley, all of us smelled horse manure. The officer in charge stopped the patrol to discuss the situation with the other officers. "I don't like it one bit," one of the officers commented. "Let's get out of here." We turned around and raced back to the main column. The battalion officers huddled and came up with the decision to move forward despite what the patrol had reported. Their orders were to drive to the Yalu River.

Item Company was to lead the way, with one platoon combing the left ridge and another the right ridge. The platoon I was in was to take the road. Behind Item Company came the rest of the battalion with its trucks and artillery. I drove down the road with two squads of infantrymen walking ahead of me. When we got to the valley floor we stopped to let the men on the ridges catch up because it was rough going in the hills. While waiting I picked up a pair of field glasses and looked at the ridge line to the right of the valley where one of our platoons was advancing. With the powerful field glasses, I could see many men in green uniforms ahead of our advancing platoon on the right ridge, and couldn't tell whether they were the enemy or friendly forces. I gave the glasses to my platoon leader and pointed in the direction of what I had seen. He saw the same thing but also couldn't identify them. He said there were hundreds moving on the ridge toward our platoon. He then looked at the ridge to left of the valley and saw the same thing. My platoon leader radioed our company commander and informed him of what we had seen. "Stand by," was the reply.

The narrow, winding road would make it difficult for our vehicles if we had to turn around. Behind us the vehicles of the battalion were lined up bumper to bumper and there was the fear that one wrecked vehicle on the road would simply stall the column. While we waited for orders firing broke out on the ridges on both sides of the valley. Our platoons had made contact with the unidentified units. They were not North Koreans. They were Chinese troops. The column now came under enemy mortar fire.

The word came for the column to withdraw. The vehicles already on the valley floor had room to turn around but those still on the narrow, winding road could not, so the drivers began backing up the road. It was slow going, waiting for the entire column to move. In half an hour I don't think I moved 50 yards and it was apparent that we were on the verge of panicking.

There was now a fierce fire fight going on both ridges, and our column was under heavy mortar attack, causing damage to a few vehicles, which blocked the road. These were pushed over the side of the road quickly so the column could move. About this time our air support arrived and rocketed and napalmed the ridges where the enemy were concentrated.

"Leave the jeeps!" barked my platoon sergeant.

"What?" I replied in shock.

"Leave the damn jeeps! We'll walk!"

I joined many who were already walking or trying to hitch rides on vehicles that were able to be turned around. I came to a tank that was stopped so I jumped on it along with others, assuming the driver would reverse his way back up. Not so! The tank commander ordered us off the tank and told us that he could not turn the tank around with us on the tank. I didn't think he had room to turn the tank around. With some choice four-letter words directed at him, we jumped off the tank.

The column was spared only because of the air support and the hard fighting of the platoons on the ridge line.

NOVEMBER 1950

CPL. LARRY ACOSTA
Item Company, 5th RCT
Vicinity of Taechon, North Korea

It was getting pretty cold and we were on our way to the Yalu River with little opposition from the North Koreans. We stopped at a village for some rest and some of the men from Hawaii went scrounging for food. Hawaii guys were always scrounging for Korean food. They came back with a pig they said they bought from a farmer, but I seriously doubted that. They had probably stolen it.

The mess sergeant and the kitchen had not caught up with the company yet so we had to cook the pig ourselves. One of our guys butchered the animal and the others made a fire and built a crude spit over it. The cold and light falling snow hampered the roasting process. Almost five hours into the roasting the pig was not yet done. But the outside part of the pig was cooked, so we sliced off pieces and ate. There was no salt and it sure didn't taste like the roast pig the Filipinos made in Hawaii. But it was meat.

The dreaded words came again: "Pack up, we're moving out." I cut off a huge chunk of half-cooked pork, which must have weighed about 5 pounds, and wrapped it in one of my spare undershirts and put it my pack. We left the rest of the meat, still on the spit, to the villagers.

We stopped near a village the next day and I asked one of the Korean porters in the platoon to accompany me into the village to get some rice. At this time of the year, rice was very hard to come by in the villages. We went from house to house without any luck until we came to the last house. An elderly man, wearing a tall, black hat, came out. Judging from the hat and his appearance, he must have been a person of high standing in the village. The porter pleaded his case and, to my surprise, the elderly gentleman went back into the house and returned with a small package of rice. I took out some money, but he refused to accept it. The porter thanked him, and we ran back to my platoon.

I took the half-cooked pork out of my pack while the Korean porter prepared the rice. We were laughed at by our friends but I knew they were laughing with envy. "You mean you carried that thing from yesterday?" Leonard Kaae remarked. "It's spoiled." But it wasn't spoiled. I cut the meat up into one-inch pieces and put them on sticks like shish kabob and roasted them over the fire. Now the men were getting interested in what I was doing and began to gather around the fire. They weren't laughing now. The 5 pounds of pork were plenty enough for the squad.

[Although over 300,000 Chinese communist troops had crossed the Yalu River in mid-October, their attacks against the advancing UN forces in the war had been limited, and, after each attack, they had disappeared into the mountainous terrain. In November the Chinese launched their counteroffensive and drove the UN troops back to the 38th parallel and beyond. Humiliating defeats were suffered at the Changjin Reservoir on the eastern front and at Unsan and Kunuri on the western front. It was the worst defeat suffered by American forces in the annals of American military history.]

NOVEMBER 1950

Honolulu, Territory of Hawaii

The *Honolulu Star-Bulletin* reported the following story:

FAMILY PAYS HEAVY PRICE IN KOREAN WAR
The price which the Teiki Miyashiro family of Kukuila, Koloa, Kauai, is paying in the fight of United Nations forces to stem the tide of communism, is high. One son, Corporal Tomoyshi Miyashiro, once listed as wounded, is now listed as killed. His brother, Private 1st Class Daniel T. Miyashiro, is missing. The third son of the family, Yaichi, is fighting with U.S. forces in Korea.

Cpl. Miyashiro, recently reported killed, was a member of the 5th Regimental Combat Team. Daniel, who is missing, was stationed with the Itajima command before going to the Korea War front. He attended Lahainaluna and Waimea high schools before enlisting in 1948.

The father of the three soldiers, Teiki Miyashiro, has worked for McBryde Sugar Co., for 30 years.

There are two daughters in the family, Mrs. Betty Konishi of Kiele and Mrs. Amy Sarmento of Kalaheo, Kauai.

NOVEMBER 1950

SGT. JAY HIDANO
Easy Company, 8th Calvary
Unsan, North Korea

From Pyongyang, we were ordered to relieve two ROK battalions in the vicinity of Unsan. The ROKs were happy to see us and warned us of Chinese units in the area. This was discounted by the higher brass as only Chinese volunteers in token numbers. The 1st Battalion dug in about a mile north of Unsan and the 2d Battalion was positioned also a mile west of Unsan. The 3d Battalion was southwest of Unsan and east of the Nammyon River near a bridge. There was a large gap between the 1st and 2d Battalions.

On the night of November 1, the enemy struck without any prepatory fire. Directly in front of Easy Company's position, I heard the chilling bugles and whistles which gave the enemy the order to attack. Immediately our mortars lit the area above our hill with illuminating flares, revealing movement at the bottom of the hill. Now I could clearly see bunches of men walking up the hill toward us, firing their weapons. Gunfire and exploding grenades were deafening as the enemy attack took in the entire company front. Despite our concentrated fire and, who knows how many hand grenades we had thrown, the enemy kept coming.

It didn't take long for the enemy to overrun our positions, as well as the entire battalion sector. Most of us fought out of our foxholes because no one wanted to get bayoneted while in the holes and the enemy was flipping hand grenades in them too. I remember getting out of the company's CP and firing down the reverse slope. Men were yelling, "The chinks are all over the place! The chinks are all over the place!"

I moved to where Captain McClain was standing, trying to rally his men. He yelled, "Let's get out of here!" It was difficult to tell whether everyone heard the order over the noise. We started back to our secondary defensive position to a hill about 200 yards back. Men were moving back, firing, covering front and rear. I could hear the voices of the enemy, unmistakably Chinese.

Our secondary defensive position was a small knoll covered with thick vegetation. Captain McClain vainly tried to organize our defenses to get ready for another attack, but in less than fifteen minutes the Chinese attacked again, this time from the right flank of the company.

The darkness and tall shrubs made it difficult to see the enemy until they were almost on top of us. It was now hand-to-hand fighting, and the distinct sound of the Chinese burp gun clearly indicated that the enemy had the upper hand. Some of our men retreated down the hill as Captain McClain yelled to them, "You sons-of-bitches!"

About this time a call from regiment came through for all battalions to withdraw to a road fork south of Unsan. The order of withdrawal was 2d, 1st, and 3d Battalions. Heck, we were already bugging out.

I stayed close to Captain McClain and helped to rally the men, but like on the previous hill, we were going to be overrun. The captain gave the order to follow him and we took off south over a series of small hills, all the while being pursued by the Chinese in the dark. We reached a road that ran east to Unsan and followed it until we came to a couple of tanks. The tankers told us that there was an enemy roadblock between Unsan and us and that is why they were headed west.

Another radio message came through, instructing us to head for the 3d Battalion defensive positions, which had not yet been engaged by the enemy. It was about 2300 hours when we started out in search of the 3d Battalion. When we reached its vicinity, we were stopped by one of its listening posts, which refused to let us enter the defensive perimeter. After some heated words back and forth, the listening post finally agreed to let us through.

But Captain McClain told the rest of the company to wait and set up a defensive perimeter back of the listening post. He then picked William Hue, also from Hawaii, and me to accompany him into the perimeter in search of the 3d Battalion's command post. Hue, a recent replacement, and I had been classmates in high school and lived in the same neighborhood.

We reached the 3d Battalion command post sometime around 0200 hours on November 2. The command post was in an open area next to a road and near a bridge that spanned the Nammyon River. It was still quiet in the perimeter. Before we entered the command post, Captain McClain sent Hue back to the company with a message. What it was, the captain didn't tell me. But more than likely, it was for what was left of Easy Company to join him in the perimeter.

The command post was heavily sandbagged and camouflaged with brush. A three-man machine gun crew guarded the entrance to the command post, which was really a dugout. The entrance was covered with a shelter half and steps led down into the dugout. The dugout was about 10 by 12 feet and 7 feet deep and was lit by candles. Several officers greeted Captain McClain, and he gave a quick report as to what had happened to the 2d Battalion and where his company was located.

We were in the command post for less than five minutes when we heard the faint sound of rifle fire. It sounded like it was some distance away so no one bothered to go outside and investigate. Then we heard sounds of footsteps on top of the dugout and the chattering of Chinese voices. The candles were snuffed out and we stood still in the darkness, no one giving any kind of orders or even saying one word.

I remembered the machine gun crew outside. What had happened to them? We would have been given a warning or the firing of the gun would have alerted us that Chinese were in the area. The machine gun crew must have been taken by surprise.

I had to get out of the dugout because if the Chinese were to throw a satchel charge of dynamite or even several hand grenades, we all would have it. I nudged Captain McClain and told him we would have a better chance outside and that is where I was going. Without hearing a reply from him, I flipped open the shelter half at the entrance and ran up the few steps. The captain was right behind me. The machine gun crew was lying on the ground, dead.

There was now clattering of small arms fire in the perimeter. I looked around and saw about a dozen Chinese milling around at the other end of the command post. They were more concerned about the men in the command post and didn't see me emerge from the dugout. There was also another group of Chinese between the road and the command post. Even closer, not more than 10 feet away, four Chinese were prodding one of our men with their bayonets. The soldier was minus his helmet and weapon.

I leaped to within 4 feet of this group and shot the Chinese whose back was toward me and yelled at the soldier to get the hell out of there. When the other three surprised Chinese turned to me, I shot and killed all three.

When I turned around to look for Captain McClain, he was nowhere to be seen. That was the last time I saw him until forty years later.

There was now bedlam in the perimeter as the intensity of the fighting increased. It seemed that the fighting was centered in the vicinity of the command post. The officers in the command post had decided to come out and were now engaged in the fighting, which was hand-to-hand. Other men had come to the rescue of the command post. The Chinese were everywhere, running and dumping satchel charges of dynamite into vehicles. A truck nearby erupted into flames, lighting up the area, and I could plainly see the faces of the Chinese.

On the road I saw about twenty Chinese sitting or in prone positions firing at our men. When they saw me I ducked behind some sandbags and fired at them as fast as I could. Then I left my cover to try to outflank them, which was not the smartest thing to do at the time. As I ran I could see the flashes as they fired at me. Bullets zipped and snapped around me.

My left knee buckled and I fell to the ground, grabbing my left leg below the knee. Damn, one or two bullets had cut me down. Pain came in a hurry and when I felt my leg, I knew that I was badly injured. I felt blood and shattered bones with my hand so I knew I wouldn't be able to stand. I dragged myself to a small depression near the command post. There was no sense in calling for a medic because there were too many Chinese around.

I had to stop the bleeding so I took off my belt and, with my bayonet, fashioned a tourniquet and applied it above my left knee. Fighting still continued around me but I lay as still as I could and the Chinese never bothered me. I was hoping they wouldn't use me as a dummy for bayonet practice to make sure I was dead. For nearly two hours I loosened and tightened the tourniquet to stop the bleeding and, finally, it did. I think the cold helped the blood coagulate.

I was lying on my left side and happened to glance over my right shoulder when I saw a Chinese, probably an officer because of his uniform, with a pistol in his hand, walking toward me. When he came to me he stopped, walked to the back of me, and instantly I heard the roar of his pistol twice. I felt like my back was hit with a baseball bat and went sprawling on my stomach. I thought, *This is it, my time to die is now.* I just lay there, waiting for my last breath to leave my body, and I silently said my goodbyes to my family.

It was very cold. The air was hazy and the ground frozen on the morning of November 2, 1950. The smell of gun powder still lingered in the air. I could barely move but I could see out of the shallow depression. It was quiet, no gunfire of any kind. The Chinese had withdrawn to the hills before our air support arrived.

I heard someone call out, "Is anybody around?" The voice came from some distance away, probably 100 yards or so. I yelled back that I couldn't walk and needed help. But they told me I had to make it by myself, not knowing how badly injured I was.

I dragged myself out of the hole and holding my left leg with my arm I started to crawl to where the voice came from. The pain was excruciating. Dragging myself on my right side, I made it to the nearest foxhole in about two hours. There were two men in the foxhole. "Come on in," one of the men invited. With one yell I went head first into the foxhole on top of the two men.

To say it was crowded was an understatement. One of the men was a big guy who introduced himself as M. Sgt. Lloyd Quinsy of the 3d Battalion. With some difficulty, because of my injured leg, the two men managed to make room for me in their foxhole.

During the day our planes came over and kept the Chinese away, which gave the 3d Battalion a chance to pull in the perimeter around the command post. Since we were close to the command post we didn't have to move. Some men in the perimeter, braving sniper fire, were salvaging weapons, ammunition, and food. There were a lot of dead bodies, ours and theirs.

During the night, word came down to us that what was left of Easy Company, whom we had left at the listening post, had slipped through the enemy lines from the hills. Their arrival was just in time because they helped beat back several Chinese attacks that night. I couldn't do much with my leg and back injury except to give them all my ammunition and stay out their way. They fought like mad men and kept the Chinese away from our foxhole.

The next day one of our small planes flew low over the perimeter and left just as suddenly as it arrived. I wondered what was up. Then word was passed down to us that the plane had delivered a message saying that a battalion from the 5th Cavalry was on its way from the west to rescue us. That was great news and it renewed our hopes.

I was hungry and thirsty. I had eaten some food two days before and had not eaten since. Master Sergeant Quinsy shared with me what little food and water he had. I owe him a lot.

Then we got the bad news on November 3. The relief battalion from the 5th Cavalry ran into a Chinese roadblock only a couple of miles to the west and couldn't bust through. No further rescue attempt was going to be made. We were on our own. The 1st Cavalry Division had given up on us. We all knew now that our position was hopeless and another large attack was going to overrun us. There was no air support. We were short of ammunition and food and there was no talk of resupplying us by air. The Chinese in the hills were like vultures waiting for the opportune time to come sweeping down on us. They wouldn't have long to wait. At that moment I believed that we were all going to die. What I couldn't understand was that with all the firepower the UN forces had, why had we been abandoned?

On the morning of November 4, there were more wounded than able-bodied men. Much later I learned that there were about 250 wounded and 200 who could still fight. A decision was made by the officers to let the nonwounded attempt an escape through the Chinese lines. The wounded were to be left behind to take their chances with the Chinese. Master Sergeant Quinsy and I were seriously wounded, so we would be left behind.

At about 1400 hours, the Chinese bombarded the perimeter with white phosphorous shells, creating a layer of smoke over most of the area. Taking advantage of the poor visibility, the nonwounded assembled and slipped through the east side of the perimeter where the smoke was the thickest. Many years later I learned that Captain McClain was in that group. The evening of November 4 was the most chilling, if not the most memorable, night of my life. It was a clear night and I think there was a moon. It was cold and we had not been issued winter clothing. The cold numbed the pain in my leg and back.

Captain Anderson, a medical officer, called out to the Chinese several times. "We surrender. We surrender." I have never forgotten those words.

Thirty minutes after Captain Anderson's words, Chinese with torches appeared near my foxhole. Some were on horseback. They motioned Master Sergeant Quinsy and me out of the foxhole. Master Sergeant Quinsy, with some difficulty, scrambled out, and when I tried to get out I fell back on my ass. Two Chinese took me by both arms and pulled me out of the hole. I howled and grabbed my leg. Without any pause they dragged me across the frozen ground to the road and dumped me into a wooden cart. I muffled my cry of pain.

It took several hours for the Chinese to gather and sort out the wounded. Only the more seriously wounded were put on carts. The others had to walk. Captain Yantis, who had five bullet holes in him, had to walk.

It must have been close to midnight when we began moving. The ride was bumpy and with every bounce I gritted my teeth and tried not to yell in pain. The other wounded men in the cart expressed their pain with four-letter words.

I don't know how far we traveled but when morning came, we stopped to rest in a village and were put in small huts. I was now able to see how large our group was. There must have been at least 150 wounded.

A detail of North Korean Security Police was added to the Chinese guard force. The NKs continually harassed us and on one occasion threatened to throw hand grenades in our midst. They stripped some of the wounded of their personal possessions, like watches, rings, and pictures. Most of the victims were too severely wounded to offer any kind of resistance. If they had, they probably would have been shot.

We finally were given food on our third day at the village, if you could call it food. It resembled food we fed to pigs back home. But no one complained. We were so hungry we ate every bit of it.

I was again put on a cart when we moved out the next evening. We always traveled at night and hid during the day because the Chinese feared our planes. Sometimes we rested in villages or huddled tightly under trees to keep warm.

One of the wounded who walked behind my cart fed us garlic he took from the huts we passed on the road. He even found a container and brought us water. That saved me because my injuries made me terribly thirsty. When we stopped the next morning, the wounded soldier next to me in the cart was dead. He didn't utter one sound during the night. Every day a few would die either from their wounds or from the cold. The North Korean Security Police stripped the bodies of their clothing and boots and unceremoniously dumped the bodies on the side of the road.

I had seen men die in so many different ways—by bullets, mortar and artillery rounds, mines, bayonet, and napalm—but seeing naked dead men just thrown to the side of the road was the worst I had ever seen. It strengthened my resolve to live, and I told myself that I would never give in to my injuries or to the cold despite the fact that we had never been treated for our injuries and were not given any warm clothing or blankets.

Our ride on the carts ended about a week after our capture because we were now entering the foothills to begin our journey into the mountains. We were put on litters carried by Chinese soldiers. They were strong and you might call them somewhat gentle because at no time during our march did they stumble or drop a litter.

At the next stop, I decided to get rid of my left boot because my injured leg couldn't support it. I couldn't just pull it off because it meant tugging at my leg so I decided to cut off the boot with my pocket knife that I always carried with me.

I started cutting from the top of the boot and slowly worked down. At every stop, without any help, I cut off the boot piece by piece and finally, after three days of cutting, I got the boot off. I now had only one boot.

The blood had frozen in my socks. The bandage that I had applied to my leg was crusted with blood and needed to be changed. Others were in the same predicament, but no one had a spare bandage, much less a clean one. Our captors still ignored our injuries.

The untreated injuries attracted flies that fed on our wounds. One morning I felt something crawling on my injured leg and when I looked I saw maggots in my wound. It scared the hell out of me because I didn't know then that maggots ate the dead flesh and actually cleaned the wounds. The guards just laughed when I called their attention to it.

I had no idea how serious my back wound was and apparently it couldn't have been bad because it hardly bothered me on the march except on one occasion. I don't know why but I never asked anyone to take a look at it. There was no exit wound and I concluded that if I had been shot in the back the bullet was still in there. Anyway, I was more concerned with my leg injury.

At the time, being on the march for about a week with no relief in sight or hope of being rescued, I was in total despair. For three nights I kept my shirt and fatigue jacket open in hopes of freezing to death. One night I tore up the photos of my family. Each night I would say a silent prayer and bid my family goodbye. But I was breathing every morning.

No one knew where we were being taken. We kept moving from village to village and it didn't make sense because I thought by this time, if they had intended to put us in a prison camp, we would have reached one.

About two weeks after my capture, I was taken to a house, where a Chinese doctor looked at my leg and told me that he had to remove the shattered bones. There was a hole about 2 inches in diameter and I could see little pieces of bone. I watched while he probed and took out bone fragments. I could hear the clinking sounds the pieces of bone made when the doctor threw them into a tin can. I was given a shot and a splint was put on my leg. I had lost a lot of blood, which weakened me considerably, but the Chinese had no blood to give me.

One evening just before the march started again, the Chinese took all of us who couldn't walk and put us in a shack by the side of the road. They just laid us on the floor, which was very, very cold. I thought the Chinese were humanitarians after all and instead of shooting us, they left us in the shack to die. A few lucky ones had field jackets, but that wasn't enough protection from the freezing cold. My left foot was still bare.

It was very quiet the next morning. The chattering of the Chinese was absent and there was no gunfire. Someone crawled to the door and looked out. He turned to us and excitedly said that there was no one outside. The Chinese were gone!

About 1000 hours the roar of tank engines was heard in the distance and, as they got closer, we became very excited, although we weren't sure whether they were ours or the Chinese's. When the tanks ground to a halt we took a chance and yelled, "We're in here. We're in here," hoping they were friendly troops. Moments later a couple of American soldiers burst through the doorway. There was no other feeling that could be compared with how we felt at the time. We were rescued and it was a miracle. Most of us cried unashamedly. Our rescuers were part of Task Force Dolvin from the 25th Infantry Division. There were twenty-nine of us when we were rescued on November 24, 1950.

The only thing I can remember after we were found was that Maj. Gen. Hobart Gay, commander of the 1st Cavalry Division, visited us and told his staff officers to notify our families immediately. I am not sure if he explained to us why the 3d Battalion of the 8th Cavalry was left to die.

Osaka, Japan

I was in a hospital in Osaka, Japan, when I came to my senses. I must have been heavily drugged right after our rescue because I can't remember any part of the trip from Korea to Japan. I can only guess that we were evacuated by ambulances to the nearest airfield and flown directly to a hospital in Osaka, Japan. It must have taken less than a day to get to Japan.

After I was cleaned up and dressed in a hospital gown, the orderly brought my dirty uniform to me and asked me about the holes in my field jacket, fatigue shirt, and undershirt. He looked at my back to see if there was a wound, and sure enough, there was a partially closed bullet hole. I put on the three pieces of clothing. The holes in the clothing lined up perfectly with the hole in my back.

An X ray showed a bullet lodged in my back about a quarter of inch from my spine. I remember hearing several shots after the Chinese walked up behind me. The Chinese officer must have aimed at the back of my head but hit me with only one shot, even at that close range. Talk about being lucky. No attempt was made to remove the bullet because the surgeon felt that the operation was too difficult to perform and could leave me paralyzed. He asked how I felt and I told him I agreed with him.

I was transferred to Tokyo General Hospital, where doctors looked at my leg and quickly decided that it was a job for the doctors at Tripler Army General Hospital in Hawaii.

NOVEMBER 1950

CPL. IRWIN COCKETT
Dog Company, 5th RCT
Vicinity of Chongju, North Korea

The North Korean army was practically destroyed, and talk of going home before Christmas put us in a festive mood. A hot Thanksgiving dinner complete with turkey, cranberry sauce, minced pie, and other goodies on the front lines convinced us that the war was almost over.

But before sunup the next morning, we were told to break contact with the enemy and head south. Here we were, about 40 or 50 miles from the Yalu River with victory practically in our grasp, and now we were being ordered to turn around? What the hell was going on? But south we went until we were told that the Chinese had entered the war and we were in danger of being cut off.

We rode, walked, and fought our way south. Most of the time the 5th RCT was used as the delaying force or blocking unit while the other units passed through us on their way south. That didn't sit too well with us. We were called "The Bastard Outfit."

We learned of the disasters of the 8th Cavalry regiment at Unsan, the 2d Division at Kunuri, and the trapped 1st Marine Division at the Changjin (Chosin) Reservoir. The entire 8th Army was in full retreat.

Vicinity of Seoul

When we got to the Han River we saw several train cars parked to the front of our positions. Our engineers were ordered to blow up the train cars. What we didn't know at the time was that the train cars were loaded with cold weather supplies and equipment. If we had known that, we would have been all over the train cars. I doubt that the engineers would have carried out their orders with us on the train cars.

NOVEMBER 1950

CPL. SUSUMU SHINAGAWA
Able Company, 34th Infantry
Somewhere in North Korea

We wore the same clothes we were captured in and they were pretty much in rags. Huddling in groups was our only way to keep warm during the night.

The following day we were finally issued some warm clothing—a quilted cap and either a quilted jacket or pants, but not both. I got a quilted jacket. The only food given to us was whole dry corn grain, which was boiled until it became fluffy. We stopped long enough to fill our caps with it and ate while walking. This diet made many of us want to crap along the way. One of the guys did just that and broke rank to do it. One of the guards shot him as he was squatting. The Catholic priest went up and down the column to warn everyone not to break ranks and, if they had to crap, to do it while walking. Better dirty than dead, we said.

Words could not describe the pitiful condition we were in. Looking at the others I thought, *Do I really look like the rest of the prisoners?* It was a miracle that most of us survived the near-freezing temperatures.

There were a couple of times when the GI who slept next to me froze to death.

There was an incident which all of us were not proud of. We were all American prisoners and the feeling that all or most of us had was to try and help each other as best as we could. For the most part, we did. There was an airman who had a severe leg injury but walked with crutches for two days. He kept up with us and did not complain at all. One morning this airman could not find one of his crutches. We had to assemble quickly to resume our march so there was no time to investigate the disappearance of his crutch. For a while he was able to keep up with the group with only one crutch but later had to fall back. A guard came by and shoved him out of the column. An American officer begged the guard to let the airman continue but the guard pushed the officer back into the ranks. A few minutes later, we heard a shot and assumed that the airman was killed. Later we found out why the airman had lost his crutch. One of the soldiers had stolen it while the airman was asleep and burned it to keep warm. Only the strong and cowardly survive.

Chunggang-jin, North Korea

"The Lord is my shepherd, I shall not want. He maketh me to lie down in green pastures. He leadeth me in the path of righteousness for His name's sake. Yea, though I walk through the valley of the shadow of death, I will fear no evil, for thou art with me, thy rod and staff they comfort me." This was the recollection of the prayer which was given by the Catholic priest.

After eight days of hard marching we arrived at Chunggan-jin. Much to our dismay the "Tiger" remained with us for another three months.

I can account for about 100 Americans, either shot or frozen to death during the march. Most were shot for not being able to keep up. It's not that we didn't help each other because we tried our very best, but the guards would push us along and force us to leave the weak behind. During the march, many were frostbitten, or had dysentery, pneumonia, and other kinds of illnesses. One of the victims was my friend from the 34th Regiment who died from frostbite. I can't remember his name. Another soldier from Kona, Hawaii, who was in the same regiment as Tamaye and Tadaki, contracted some kind of disease and died after the march. Both these men were on the boxing teams for their respective regiments. There were about 700 Americans when we started out on the death march. About half survived.

I was in a group of 400 who were billeted in a large building that looked as though it had once been used as a school. The rest of the men were put in village huts that had been taken from the villagers. When the guard found out that I spoke Japanese, he assigned me the duty of interpreter in the kitchen detail. I told the guard that I spoke very little Japanese. He asked me if I was Japanese. When I said yes, he lost his temper and slapped me on the face and kicked me. "Bakayaro, Nihonjin de Nihongo ga wakaran no ka?" he screamed at me. Translation: "You fool. A Japanese and not knowing the Japanese language. What do you mean?" The other Hawaii men who were used as interpreters were also beaten by the guards.

Following that incident, I was more careful how I answered their questions. If my answers to any of their questions showed a lack of understanding of the Japanese language, another beating was in store for me. But my Japanese was really poor and I regretted that I had not learned more of the Japanese language from my parents. The beatings made it necessary for me to try to recall some Japanese I had learned from my parents if I were to avoid those vicious slaps and kicks.

Our first meal at our new home was won bok cabbage soup and millet. The kitchen detail was given twelve heads of won bok cabbage to make soup for 400 men. It was winter and the twelve heads of cabbage were frozen solid. We used an ax to chop up the cabbage because we had no knife. There was no salt or anything to add some taste to the soup. I broke the news to the men, telling them what they were going to eat. There was nothing they could do or say. The untasty, boiled millet we washed down our throats with thin cabbage broth. If you got one small piece of cabbage, you were fortunate. At least the broth was very hot on the cold November night and warmed us a bit, if only for a few minutes. It had been about five months since I was captured and I was used to eating very little. My small body frame didn't require much to keep it going. This was one time when my small body had an advantage over those of the big haoles from the mainland.

Food was difficult to come by during the winter and our food staples consisted mainly of millet, sorghum grain, and dried corn. When I first saw the millet, it reminded me of what I saw at home. It was what we fed pigs.

After a couple of days in the building, we were put in huts that were on the perimeter of the village. Each hut was about 12 feet wide and 40 feet long and was divided into four sections. The roof was made of straw and the floor of straw and mud covered with mats. One section at one end of the hut was the kitchen. The other three sections were our sleeping quarters.

The kitchen was about 3 feet lower than the floors. From the kitchen, there was a trench about a foot wide and 6 inches deep which ran under the floor and branched out to the sleeping quarters. In the center of the kitchen there was a cooking platform about 3 feet high made of mud and on it was a big wok. It was designed in such a way that the heat from the stove was channeled down to the trench, heating the mud floors and keeping the hut warm in the winter. If you were in the section next to the kitchen, the floor would really be hot, so hot sometimes you would have to leave the area. It was really comfortable in the second section, where I was. It took a long time for the heat to get to the third section because most of the heat would dissipate before it got there.

We were moved again to smaller one-room huts. Thirty men were assigned to each hut, which measured 9 by 12 feet. We were not able to lie down, so we sat with our legs folded in front of us. To keep from getting cramps we took turns stretching our legs whenever we could. When night came we simply put our arms on our knees and rested our heads on our arms. Sometimes, to keep warm, some would sit with their knees spread apart so a buddy could squeeze and sit backward between his knees. I wouldn't say we had pleasant nights, and there was a lot of grumbling going on. Then, too, there were men who complained more than others. It's a wonder we didn't have fist fights, for that would have made the guards really happy to see Americans fighting one another. I suppose everyone was too weak to raise a hand.

We were issued cotton padded jackets and pants, which were full of lice. No one wanted to put on the lice-infested clothing, but we had no choice because it was so cold. Either tolerate the lice or freeze to death. We tried to delouse ourselves every day by taking off our clothes and hunting down the lice in the seams of the jackets and pants. I could feel the lice crawling over my body, which made me itchy. Like everything else, I got used to it. On a nice day we would go outside to stretch our legs, but couldn't stay out too long for it was very cold.

In every room, there would be at least one or two GIs who would get so frustrated that after a while they would refuse to delouse themselves or even go outside to exercise. They would just about give up and would lie down and not do anything to help themselves. Whenever I could I would try to force them to move. Sometimes, some of us would get together and physically throw them out in the cold to get their blood circulating, but they would just crawl back to their places in the hut wishing to die. Most got their wish.

Day in and day out we saw so many men die that we became experts in predicting when a particular person was going to die. It may sound cruel, but most of that person's possessions, even before he died, would be reserved for someone who needed a particular item. The dead were stripped of all possessions and clothing.

Many of the prisoners who died were not very sick at all. They simply lost the will to live and gave up. The North Korean medics came by every day and shouted, "Anybody sick? Anybody sick?" When someone died, the procedure was to place the dead body outside of the hut by the door. As the death rate increased the North Korean medics now yelled, "Anybody dead? Anybody dead?" I don't really know how many men died the winter of 1950, but there must have been hundreds.

Dysentery was something everyone dreaded. It could hit you any time. You could be healthy one day and catch it the next. There was no medication to treat it. Yet, if we were home, a simple medication could stop it. If you had a toothache or an earache, you just had to bear it until it went away. I saw many cases of severe dysentery. The men who had to go to the latrine frequently didn't keep their pants on because it was too hard to keep taking them off and putting them on. I also saw guys running to the latrine with cotton stuffed in their rectums. One of the happiest moments after having dysentery for days was when only a healthy fart came out. You should have seen the smile on guys' faces.

Before I left Japan for Korea, I was warned not to eat raw vegetables or drink water from Korean wells for they could make you sick. I ignored this warning. I did not get sick eating vegetables but got worms. Yes, worms, like earthworms you see when you work in the garden. The only difference is the worms in my stomach were white. Whenever I defecated a ball of worms would come out. When it hit the ground the worms, some as long as seven inches, would splatter in every direction. The experience was terrible at first but I got used to it. I had to.

NOVEMBER 1950

PFC. PETE BEHASA
Item Company, 5th RCT
Vicinity of Anju, North Korea

We had our asses kicked by the Chinese, who had now entered the war, and the entire 8th Army was retreating south. At one of our rest stops, Sgt. Herbert Ohia of Hawaii provided us with a rare treat. He was in charge of a group of Koreans called the Korean Service Corps, made up mostly of elderly Korean men who were too old to fight yet able to pack considerable amounts of weight on their A-frames (backpacks made of wood).

Ohia had a knack for scrounging things up for our company. Sometimes he would go into a village with his Koreans and bring back rice. One night he came to us with a hindquarter of something. I think it was beef. He didn't explain how he got it or whether it was a steer, mule, or horse. We didn't question him either. He hung it over a fire and cooked it and we all took turns slicing a piece out of it when we were not on watch. It was the first fresh meat we had eaten in two months.

Vicinity of Taechon, North Korea

There was humor even under the harshest conditions in combat. It was cold in North Korea. One of my mainland buddies fell asleep with his rifle cradled in his arms with the muzzle cupped in his left hand. When he awoke he found the muzzle of his rifle frozen to the palm of his hand. He couldn't remove his hand from the muzzle without tearing the skin off his hand. One of the guys, identity unknown, volunteered to urinate on the GI's hand to thaw out the ice. Now we had layers of clothing on at the time and the volunteer had a great deal of difficulty retrieving his organ, much less urinating in the cold. But he did manage a few squirts and freed the GI from his rifle. We all laughed while this was going on.

[The landing of the 1st Marine Division, 3d and 7th Infantry Divisions, and ROK units on the east coast and the rapid advance of the 8th Army in the west had everyone talking about being home for Christmas. Supply ships on the way to Korea were diverted or were turned back, giving the impression the Korean War was just about over.]

NOVEMBER 1950

CPL. BERTRAM SEBRESOS
Baker Company, 7th Infantry
Wonsan, North Korea

Late in the afternoon on November 26 we landed in Wonsan Harbor on the east coast of North Korea, which was already in friendly hands. I had joined the 3d Division in Japan and was assigned to Company B, 7th Infantry.

We bivouacked on the outskirts of Wonsan, where we were briefed. The 1st Marine and 7th Divisions were farther north in the Changjin Reservoir area. Our main objective was to maintain the supply routes between those divisions and the port of Hungnam. Our battalion's assignment was to keep a secondary MSR open west of Hungnam. I thought this was an easy assignment, not knowing that in a few days we were going to be up to our ears in chinks.

The next morning after a C-ration breakfast our battalion boarded a train north to Hungnam and then switched to trucks for our journey west into the mountains. The terrain was rugged. High peaks, narrow valleys, sharp slopes, and steep heights boggled my mind. I could see patches of snow at the upper elevations. The air turned very chilly as we climbed the narrow mountain road. We were not supplied with full winter clothing.

In the truck I couldn't help but notice the very young baby faces, whose ages I guessed were between seventeen and nineteen. I was an old man compared to them. They were very talkative when the ride began but now their faces were silent and showing signs of worry and fear although we all knew that the NKs had been on the run since the middle of September. There was a chance that the war might be over even before we got to see our first North Korean soldier.

After several human nature stops and hours of bouncing in the truck, we finally arrived at the village of Sach'ang-ni, our destination. It sat astride a road junction in a very long, narrow valley with steep sides. The road was a secondary MSR that ran north to Hagaru near the Changjin Reservoir. Then from Sachang-ni it went east to Hungnam, the route we took getting there.

Looking north I couldn't see the end of the valley. It just disappeared into the distance. The spurs leading down from mountain ridges on both sides of the valley were steep and sharp. No way the Chinese could climb those ridges to get to us. They would have to come through the valley. A river ran alongside the road.

Sach'ang-ni, North Korea

Our defense was set up with Charlie Company on the north and northeast part of the town and Baker Company on the right flank of Charlie Company at the base of the ridge. Able Company was on the flats. Dog Company's heavy weapons were scattered throughout the defense line. The 1st Battalion CP and the ammunition dump were behind Baker Company.

Just about dusk the Chinese gave Charlie Company to our left a taste of 120mm mortar shells. Then just before midnight the Chinese came down from the ridge and attacked Charlie Company. From our position to the right of Charlie Company, we could hear the action and see the flashes of gunfire. The Chinese shot a green flare and there was a hell of a noise in front of Charlie Company's perimeter.

Sergeant Savage, my squad leader, came running and told us to get ready to give support to Charlie Company. An enemy force had infiltrated from the hills and attacked Charlie Company's CP and was trying to get to the ammo dump and 60mm mortar positions. While he was talking to us, another fire fight broke out in the Able Company area at the roadblock. A ROK soldier, who was my foxhole partner and whom we called 48 because we couldn't pronounce his name, jumped up, pointed to the roadblock, and yelled, "Chinese! Chinese!" Chinese! I had thought we were fighting North Koreans. Charlie Company took the brunt of the attacks. The fighting continued until just before dawn, when the Chinese broke off the attack.

Sergeant Savage had gone back to battalion to find out what had happened the previous night and came back with the information. The Chinese had somehow managed to climb down the almost vertical cliffs and caught one of the platoons by surprise. Another force hit the roadblock dead on, penetrated it, and attacked Charlie's command post. They also got back to the 60mm mortar pits and killed a number of mortar men. If they had gotten any farther they would have run into Baker Company's CP, the ammo dump, and the battalion's CP. Charlie Company took a lot of casualties. So did the Chinese, who left their dead behind. Number 48 was right. We were fighting the Chinese.

I was returning to my foxhole from a hot breakfast at the battalion rear when Platoon Sergeant Mays came running up shouting, "Pack up, we're leaving."

"Forward or backward?" I replied, just getting smart.

"Back where we came from," he yelled.

Something is up, I thought to myself, but I didn't ask why. Others were shouting the same orders. What gave an indication as to the seriousness of the withdrawal was that equipment and supplies that couldn't be loaded or carried were being burned in a hurry.

I hurriedly put my gear together and went looking for my squad leader, Sergeant Savage, who was getting the squad together at the roadside. Since we rode in, my guess was that we were going to ride out. The only problem was that there weren't enough vehicles so half the platoon had to walk, including my squad. We threw our gear except our weapons into the trucks and started walking. It turned out that walking was better because it kept us warm. The men in the trucks sat and froze.

It took a while before the column moved east toward the sea. Along the way we got the word why we had to pack and get out of Sach'ang-ni. The marines and army units at the Changjin Reservoir north of us were being clobbered by the Chinese and at this very moment were retreating south. Also, elements of a Chinese division were observed moving south in the valley toward Sach'ang-ni. I asked an officer if we were retreating and he said, "Hell no, Americans don't retreat. It's a strategic withdrawal."

It was in the afternoon after we had only traveled a couple of miles when the column began receiving long-range machine gun and light mortar fire from the hills on both sides of the valley. The Chinese were catching up to us. I could see the plunging fire of the Chinese machine gun tracer bullets from the ridges, which were mostly ineffective. But the mortars caused casualties. One of the trucks that our platoon was riding on was hit. Lieutenant Evans, our platoon leader, and Sergeant Savage, my squad leader, were seriously wounded. Platoon Sergeant Mays was slightly wounded. He became the platoon leader and I was made squad leader. Private First Class Chevalier became my assistant.

Those of us who were walking fired our M-1 rifles blindly into the hills. Men in the trucks threw us ammunition. I swore at them and said, "Why don't you cowards get off the truck and fight!" But the heavy weapons company did stop to fire their big guns into the hills. The 81mm mortar and 75mm recoilless rifle teams would stop, set up their weapons, fire several rounds into the hills, mount up, and catch up. They would repeat this tactic all the way into Hungnam.

The machine gun and mortar fire from the Chinese was now becoming more accurate, which indicated that the Chinese were even closer. And we started to panic. Those of us walking began to beg for rides, climbing into trucks that were already overloaded. Others were hanging on to the sides of the trucks. I finally realized that I was the only one in my squad walking and I had lost sight of my squad. What a squad leader!

Finally, a truck stopped and I jumped on the running board on the driver's side. The driver told me he couldn't give me a ride. "You sure as hell can," I told him.

"Oh, you speak English," he replied.

"You're damn right. I'm a GI just like you."

"Get in the back."

I rode in the truck for about an hour but it seemed that the guys walking were making better time. I jumped off the truck and started running and passed several trucks along the way, hoping to catch up with my squad. I came to a jeep stopped in the middle of the road, which had slowed the column down. A body was slumped over the steering wheel, apparently dead. Vehicles were slowly driving around it but nobody was trying to move the jeep off the road because of harassing machine gun and mortar fire. To the side of the road were several officers, probably passengers of the jeep, seeking shelter from mortar fire. Someone yelled, "Move the damn jeep."

"If the jeep belonged to the officers, they should move it," I said to myself. "On the other hand, if I moved it and drove it, I've got transportation." Those few moments of indecision cost me. Another GI ran to the jeep and dumped the dead body on the side of the road. At the same instant the officers dashed to the jeep from their hiding places and jumped into the jeep, and the driver drove off.

NOVEMBER 1950

PFC. NICK NISHIMOTO
Baker Company, 35th Infantry
Vicinity of Unsan, North Korea

Winter was coming and we still were not issued winter clothing except for pile caps, long johns, and mittens. We were issued field jackets in October, but they couldn't keep us warm enough.

After weeks of driving north we finally were told to hold up and dig in on a hill that had been vacated by the enemy. There was some talk about the Chinese entering the war. In improving the foxholes we found that the enemy had dug short tunnels on the sides of the trenches large enough to accommodate one person. At night you would overlook that feature if you took only a quick glance into the trench. Just before being overrun, they would scoot into these tunnels and stay there until our guys passed them. Then they would come out of the tunnels and shoot our guys in the back. We found out later that this feature was developed by the Chinese.

The last few days were tough. We were engaged by the enemy several days running and suffered heavy casualties. Then early in the morning we found that our company was completely surrounded by the Chinese. They tried several times to take the hill but we managed to drive them off with hand grenades.

At 0300 hours the next morning, word came down to everyone that no help was coming from other units because they were also fighting to save themselves. When the Chinese pulled back to regroup, our company decided to try and break out. We started to work down the side of the hill we thought was not heavily defended by the Chinese. The Chinese knew what we were up to and began blowing bugles and yelling and talking up a storm just to let us know that there was no way out. They never fired a shot, just made a lot of noise. They were all around us and they knew they had us and we knew it, too. It was decided that we should return to the top of hill and discuss what to do. To continue the fight was senseless and, besides, we were just about out of ammo. But no one wanted to surrender.

When I got back to my position, my machine gun was still there but there was no ammo. I took the gun apart and scattered the parts down the hillside so the Chinese couldn't use the gun against us. I had brought the gun with me from Japan and sure hated to part with it.

Our platoon sergeant told us that anyone would be free to try to escape but to do it in pairs. Any group larger than that would be easily detected by the Chinese. Henry Higa and I decided to give it a shot. Instead of heading south to friendly lines, which was the most obvious to the Chinese, we decided to head north for a while and later turn south. The only weapon we had between us was a Browning Automatic Rifle I had picked up when someone had dropped it. When I checked the magazine it had only one round. When fully loaded, it would have twenty rounds. But I kept the BAR because I felt that later I would stumble upon a few loose rounds of .30 caliber ammo and reload the magazine.

It was still dark when we slowly worked our way down the hill, often coming within a few yards of the Chinese. But we were never challenged. In the dark, being short of stature and being Orientals, we must have looked like them. We got off the hill without being discovered. We crossed some open ground and headed for a ridge. The dark morning was not yet graying and we did not want to be caught in the open at first light. We started running to the ridge and got to the top just as it was getting light. We found a foxhole but a black guy was sitting in it. It was hard to tell if he was wounded but he said, "I got this hole, man!" So we moved farther up the ridge.

We were just about to round a turn on the ridge when a Chinese appeared no more than 30 yards away. I pointed the BAR at the Chinese but before I could get off a shot, more Chinese appeared, about fifteen of them. Common sense prevailed over valor and immediately I threw my weapon to the ground and Higa and I both threw our hands up in the air. The day was November 27, 1950, sometime around 0900 hours in the morning.

The Chinese didn't tie us up, but we had to keep our hands in the air as they led us into a ravine. Our captors cut some small branches off a tree and gave them to us. We carried them above our heads. This was for camouflage in case our planes came by. The Chinese didn't speak English and communicated with us using hand and arm gestures.

We came to a small village and were put into a room that contained other captured GIs from our company. Higa and I were relieved that we were not the only ones from our company who were captured. But we had a feeling that our company, Baker Company, was wiped out.

NOVEMBER 1950

SGT. LUCIO SANICO
Baker Company, 35th Infantry
Vicinity of Unsan, North Korea

Baker Company was part of a task force called Task Force Dolvin of the 25th Infantry Division whose job was to locate and determine the strength of the Chinese in the Unsan area where the 8th Cavalry had been literally smashed by the Chinese about two weeks before. But after that battle the Chinese had withdrawn into the hills.

The task force had stopped a couple miles east of Unsan to wait for further orders before continuing its advance. One of its advance units found a group of badly wounded Americans who had been captured at Unsan. The men had been held as prisoners by the Chinese for about two weeks and left in a village, presumably to be found by us. There were about two dozen of them. They would have probably frozen to death in another day or two if they had not been found.

The task force deployed in a perimeter with the infantry dug in on several hills. Baker Company was dug in on the right of the perimeter on a small hill. The kitchen and company command post was set up about 400 yards south of the hill in a small draw between two tanks. Captain Dillard, our company commander, told all the drivers to turn the vehicles around just in case we had to bug out. We were told to be especially on the alert and to post security even though we were hundreds of yards behind the lines. There were light snow flurries and it got pretty cold.

For several days there were probing night attacks by the Chinese but our infantry was able to beat them back. During the day our air strikes kept the Chinese in their holes.

One night the commanding officer told us to prepare doughnuts and hot coffee for the troops. If there was no action on the hill we were to take them to the troops. It was about 2000 hours and it was still quiet.

At about midnight Sergeant First Class McConnell, our mess sergeant, told me to get the doughnuts and coffee loaded on two jeeps since it appeared that tonight might be a quiet night. I told one of the drivers to back up a jeep to the kitchen tent when I heard scattered rifle fire coming from the hills. It didn't bother anyone because that had been pretty much routine the past several nights. It would die down.

The sound of distant bugles pierced the quiet night. Sergeant First Class McConnell said, "Hold it, don't load the coffee and doughnuts." Flares lit the night and the sound of heavy gunfire came from the hills. We all ran to the command post to see what was happening. The captain was on the radio listening to incoming reports. When he was through he told us that all the companies on the hills were under heavy attack. He said he was going to join the company on the hill.

While he was getting ready, mortar rounds bracketed our area and hit one of our tanks. We all went flying for cover. The captain's radio operator said something to the captain. He took the phone for not more than a minute and handed it back to the radio operator. Then amid the bursting mortar rounds Captain Dillard yelled, "Let's get out of here."

Everyone tumbled into a vehicle. I was near the captain's jeep and he told me to hop on and we barreled out of there. We reached a collecting point several miles south and waited. We lost one jeep on our way out. The captain finally told us why we had to leave in such a hurry. The message the captain got was that Baker Company was being overrun and the other companies were also in trouble. He was told to get the hell out of there.

When morning came Captain Dillard counted heads and found that less than twenty men, mostly from headquarters, had survived the night. A few more came straggling in during the day but of the 150 men in Baker Company most were captured or killed. Later reports said that Baker Company was surrounded but fought on until the next day until killed or captured. I think I was the only one from Hawaii who was not either killed or captured, and I wondered about Nishimoto and the other Hawaii guys.

NOVEMBER 1950

PFC. MOSES PAKAKI
4.2 *Inch Mortar Company, 35th Infantry*
Vicinity of Yongsan-dong, North Korea

It was early in the morning—it must have been about 0300 hours—and it was cold. We were told to pack up our equipment and to get the hell out of there. Someone said that we were moving south. South? We were gaining ground moving north and now we were moving south? It sure was a funny kind of a war.

We loaded up and got on about ten trucks. A jeep led the way and a single tank brought up the rear. My truck was the fourth in the convoy. As soon as we got into the truck, many of the men quickly got into their sleeping bags to keep warm. We had no idea how serious the situation was at the time. The convoy was under way for only about half an hour when it stopped. I got out of the truck and walked to one of the trucks ahead of us and asked the driver why we had stopped. "Another column ahead of us ran into an enemy roadblock and we are waiting until the roadblock is removed," said the driver. I walked back to my truck and relayed the information to the vehicles I passed.

While walking back I was able to take a look at the terrain. We were in a small, narrow valley with a ridge line to our right and rice paddies on the left. The road was so narrow that vehicles would not be able to maneuver around a stalled or wrecked vehicle. All vehicles were now stopped, bumper to bumper.

Before I could get back into my truck and into my warm sleeping bag, rifle and automatic fire erupted from the hillside to our right. I looked up the hill and saw figures firing and moving down the hillside toward our column. Although daylight was about an hour away, I could clearly see the enemy and yellow and orange flashes as they fired into the column.

I yelled to the men in my truck, "Get out of the truck! Get out the truck!" The men piled out of the truck, some trying to get out of their sleeping bags, and took cover on the left side of the road, their backs to the rice paddies. I couldn't tell right away if any of our guys were returning the fire. Now firing was coming from the head of the column as well as from the hillside. We were just a few feet away from the vehicles, and I had a feeling that being close to the vehicles was not safe. I yelled for the men to move farther back into the rice paddies behind a dike, which offered some cover. Fortunately, the rice paddies had only ankle-deep water. As I ran, small geysers of water erupted around me. I made it to the dike and so did the rest of my men. We were about 50 yards from the road. When I looked back at the column, it appeared that most of the men had also followed us into the rice paddies.

Enemy machine gun fire swept the column and I could hear the sound of bullets striking the vehicles. Then there were several explosions. Some of the trucks blew up, including mine. The trucks on fire lit up the column and the lower part of the hillside, and we could see the enemy only a few yards from the roadside firing into the trucks. At this time the men who were able to hang on to their weapons fired into the hillside.

It was cold and although there was little water in the rice paddies we still had to slosh through icy paddy water and mud. I only had a .45 pistol with me so it was easier to run with both hands pumping. I had left my carbine in the truck when I walked to the head of the column. Those with the M-1s and carbines had a more difficult time running, having to hold on to their weapons with both hands. I could hear the soft plunk of bullets hitting the water and mud as we ran.

I remembered a tank that brought up the rear and I figured being close to the tank would give us some protection. But I couldn't see the tank from where we were because there was a bend in the road. I told my men to run for the tank.

We needed to get to the tank before the others did and we kept on running. I shot a glance at the road and saw some men lying on the road next to some of the burning vehicles. Theirs or ours, I couldn't tell. We made it to the tank after slipping, falling, and swearing at no one in particular. Six of us, out of ten that left the truck, made it to the tank.

When we got to the tank, I saw that the tank turret hatch cover was not closed and the tank's gun was silent. The tank commander's head was barely visible in the open turret. I yelled at him and pointed to figures not more than 100 yards up the hill. "Fire up the hill! That's the enemy!" What the tank commander did next almost put me into shock. He dropped into the tank and pulled the hatch cover shut. I think he panicked when he saw what I had pointed to. Then I realized that the tank was disabled and was a prize target for the enemy.

I yelled for my men to get back into the rice paddies. "Get away from the tank! They want the tank!" We took cover behind a dike about 100 yards into the rice paddies and began firing at the enemy, now only a few yards from the tank. Although we saw several figures fall, there were just too many of them to make a difference. The enemy was now all over the tank, trying to find a way to get to the crew inside.

By now it was just getting light and I could see that the entire column was under attack from the hillside. Many of the vehicles either were burning or were completely destroyed. There was no question that the enemy had the upper hand and it was time to see if we could get away. There was a ridge about 200 yards away that ran in a southerly direction. I made a run for it, with the other men following close behind. I thought I would get a bullet in the back, but there was no fire coming in our direction even though I could hear the distinct sounds of the enemy's burp gun.

We got to the base of the ridge out of breath, dropped down, and looked back toward the column. We were not being pursued. I could see smoke coming out of the tank's engine compartment, and suddenly the tank erupted in flames. The enemy probably used a satchel charge of dynamite to blow it up. I don't think the tank crew ever got out. I could see men with white winter clothing milling around on the road. We were never issued white winter clothing.

I stood up to climb the hill when I felt something hit my foot. It felt like a branch had whipped around and struck me there. When I got to the top of the hill I examined my left foot. The heel of my left foot was gone. It had been shot off. One of the men told me that we had lost a couple of men in the rice paddies to enemy fire.

On the other side of the ridge I was surprised to see friendly troops crouching and waiting. I asked one of them what was happening. He pointed to a distant hill and said there were snipers on that hill taking pot shots at them when they tried to go over the crest of the hill. They had to move one at a time to avoid giving the snipers better shots. He said friendly troops were on the other side of the hill. I was so damn tired that I didn't care anymore. About a dozen men took their turns dashing over the crest of the hill. I could hear the pinging of bullets as the snipers searched the area around us with their fire. My turn came, and keeping as low as I could, I ran over the crest of the hill and down the other side.

What I saw at the bottom of the hill was a column of friendly trucks, jeeps, and tanks moving south. Apparently, while our column was being clobbered by the enemy, units ahead of us had cleared the enemy roadblock. I didn't know whether to laugh or cry when I saw them. I kept on running until I came to the column. My momentum carried me straight to a moving tank already loaded with men. A couple of the men on the rear of tank offered their hands and, with one leap, I got on the tank. I found a place to sit and just sat there, too tired to say or do anything else. I never thought about where the rest of my squad was. Next thing I knew, someone had grabbed me and said, "What are you doing? You wanna get killed?" I had fallen asleep and if he had not grabbed me, I would have fallen off the tank and been run over by the one following us. This guy saved my ass.

We traveled all morning until we passed one of our roadblocks and made it safely to an assembly area to regroup. Then by trucks, we moved farther south, where we dug in again.

NOVEMBER 1950

CPL. HARRISON LEE
Love Company, 19th Infantry
Vicinity of Anju, North Korea

Because I spoke fluent Chinese (Cantonese) I was often called by Battalion S-2 (Intelligence Section) to interrogate Chinese prisoners. While moving north two Chinese prisoners were brought into battalion headquarters. Major Powell of S-2, in charge of intelligence, knew that I was a linguist and sent a runner to get me. I was happy to go because it meant getting into a tent that was warm. He said for me to ask them for their names and the unit they belonged to. So I squatted with the prisoners and put on the ground a piece of paper on which to record the interrogation. I took one aside and began questioning him. When I asked him for his name he spat on the paper I had placed on the ground. Hard-core Chinese! Hell, when he did that it pissed me off. I took my M-1 rifle and, with the butt end, flattened him with a blow to the side of his head. I picked him up and made him sit up again. I told him that I was not going to fool around with him so he had better answer my questions. I got his attention. He never gave me any trouble after that and he answered all my questions. I found that he was a railroad engineer. The other prisoner was a schoolteacher and just blabbed his head off.

When the interrogation was over, the major thanked me for my help and said, "Gosh, I didn't think you would treat your own countryman like that," referring to the butt stroke I gave the Chinese.

I said, "Hey, major, he is Chinese. I am not his countryman. I am an American. He would shoot me if he had the chance."

DECEMBER 1950

PVT. GARY HASHIMOTO
Ford Ord, California

After completing Wheel Vehicle Maintenance and Repair School, I received orders to report to a camp in Seattle, Washington. I had enlisted in the army on February 17, 1950, with my buddy, Jack Hiwatashi, who hailed from Camp 3, Spreckelsville, Maui. I was from Lower Paia, Maui. Both of us were 1949 graduates of Maui High School.

Jack and I were fortunate in that we were together all the time we were in the army—through basic training, army schools, and shipping out to Korea, where we were assigned to the same unit. Being single and young, we were eager to do our share.

We knew our parents were worried about us because we never called or wrote to let them know how we were. We felt guilty. The same thing happened when we enlisted together. We only told our parents the night before leaving for Fort Ord that we had joined the army and the papers were all signed. They would have objected if we had told them our plans before enlisting. Both of us realized we had broken their hearts.

Jack and I took a two-week furlough in Chicago before reporting to

Seattle, where our orders told us to go. We had no idea what to expect in Chicago as this was our first time there. As it turned out, we arrived at the time of Chicago's worst snowstorm in twenty years. It was cold and miserable. Aside from staying in the room, our only trip outside was to go to the Salvation Army for hot coffee and doughnuts. After four days we cut our leave short and caught the train to Seattle for assignment to Korea.

DECEMBER 1950

CPL. BERTRAM SEBRESOS
Baker Company, 7th Infantry
Huksu-ri, North Korea

Thinking that we had outrun the Chinese, the battalion stopped for the night at Huksu-ri, a small village, to regroup. We were reinforced by the 2d Battalion, which came from Hamhung.

My platoon was on a small hill overlooking the village. Callahan, our machine gunner, was 10 yards to my right. The barrel of his gun was sticking way out and overly exposed so I told him to pull the gun back in a bit. He said he was a World War II veteran and told me to mind my own business. He was right. If he wanted to get killed, that was his business.

We were on 50 percent alert so I had a chance to get into my sleeping bag, hoping that the night would pass without any interruptions. It was not to be. Using green and red flares as signals, the Chinese penetrated our defenses at several points but were hurled back. Talk about confusion. The fighting continued throughout the night and when morning came we had to retreat to the surrounding ridges and reorganize. From the ridges we could see the Chinese moving around our flanks to surround us and cut us off. But after air strikes from our planes the Chinese attacks slowed down and we were able to continue our march to Hamhung.

Vicinity of Hamhung, North Korea

It took us almost two days to get to the defense perimeter outside Hamhung, where the 3d Division had established a semicircle defense 5 miles from the city. The area was flat with only a few low, rolling hills.

Attached to our battalion were five tanks and two half-tracks. The tanks had the high-velocity 76mm cannons and the half-tracks each had four .50 caliber machine guns mounted to fire simultaneously. We called them quad fifties; they could fire at a rate of 2,000 rounds per minute. They were to play a significant role in the next Chinese attack.

My squad was on a small knoll overlooking the flat terrain so we had a good view of the approaches to our perimeter. There were some apple trees on the knoll. Chevalier and I paired off and dug our hole. We covered it with scraps of wood, logs, and steel pickets and about 3 feet of dirt. We finished our little fort in less than five hours, just before dark. We found some rice straws, laid them on the ground outside of the hole, and put our sleeping bags on them. Private First Class Gilbert from my squad joined us to chew the fat while we laid back and looked at the sky.

At about 2300 hours I got up and happened to glance to my right when I saw a figure hiding behind an apple tree about 50 feet away. Both my rifle and Chevalier's were in the hole but Gilbert had his. I motioned to Gilbert and pointed in the direction of the figure. Gilbert fired several rounds but missed. The figure, whom we guessed was Chinese, ran into the rice paddy and hid behind a dike. At that hour no one went after him, but his presence indicated that something was up and the alert went out for everyone to get into his hole and to expect an attack. Chevalier and I emptied our cartridge belts and bandoleers and placed all the ammo clips in front of us. We did the same with our hand grenades, about ten of them.

Shortly before midnight there was a wailing bugle call, a sad kind of a call, followed by a similar call as if in answer to the first. There was a third call. It was real eerie and sounded like a death call. It gave me goose bumps. Then there were six quick, snappy blasts of the bugle that set off green rocket flares into the night.

Knowing that this was a signal for the Chinese to attack, our mortars threw up illuminating flares, exposing hundreds of Chinese in the flats about 400 yards away. I never saw anything like it before. "Here they come," several of our guys shouted. Our mortars and tanks got the range but the human mass continued forward. At about 300 yards our quad fifties opened up. It was sheer joy to see the .50 caliber tracer rounds disappear into the bunched-up Chinese. Then our entire line erupted in a firing frenzy.

Just the gun flashes alone lit the night. The air was thick with smoke and gun powder and the cold air kept them close to the ground, making it tough to breathe. At less than 200 yards I fired my M-1 rifle, not aiming but just pointing it to the still charging Chinese. I must have fired about ten clips of ammo, which made the stock of my M-1 rifle pretty hot.

The Chinese charge was stopped, with only a few Chinese penetrating the perimeter. They were killed or captured. Our illuminating flares continued to light the battlefield, revealing Chinese bodies all over the place. There were walking wounded, some crawling, others dragging their bodies back. We watched as the Chinese tended to their casualties.

Some of our guys wanted to go out and get souvenirs but were told to stand fast. And lucky they did because the quick bugle blast sounded again. Shit! Two attacks in an hour. It reminded me of the cowboy and Indian movies I saw as a kid when the Indians attacked the wagon train again and again.

This time they added a cavalry charge to their attack using small ponies followed by infantry. They kept coming with absolutely no regard for their lives. It was like committing suicide. I emptied clip after clip and so did Chevalier. The quad fifties tracer rounds were spiraling into the sky because their barrels got so hot, but they halted the charge again. Many of the ponies were gunned down and a few ended up in our perimeter. This was the longest and strongest attack made on the perimeter during our withdrawal.

The next day, anticipating another mass night attack, we withdrew closer to Hamhung, shrinking the perimeter by a few miles. Then on December 19 the perimeter was shifted to the port of Hungnam, which made the 3d Division the only large unit on line while the other units boarded ships in the harbor.

While the evacuation took place the navy saturated the area in front of us with thousands of shells, which discouraged the Chinese from making an attack. All day and night shells whistled overhead without any letup. During the day our aircraft ranged overhead to spot anything that moved and call navy guns on them. Those with binoculars could see large groups of Chinese in the distant hills watching the evacuation take place. For three days, December 21–23, there was no enemy activity to our front. We were told later that four Chinese divisions surrounded the perimeter.

On December 23, we made our final withdrawal to the immediate outskirts of Hungnam with still no enemy activity. I think the Chinese just wanted us out of there.

On the morning of December 24, at about 0900 hours, our battalion got on landing crafts and headed for the large ships in the harbor. One of the hardest things I had to do was climb up the rope ladder from the landing craft to the deck of the ship. After all personnel, including thousands of Korean refugees, were safely on board, the navy pumped several shells into the hills as a parting gesture.

Then without warning the entire harbor of Hungnam exploded. The engineers didn't want to leave anything to the Chinese. The explosions were so powerful that we could feel the blast on board ship.

On Christmas Eve, December 24, 1950, we left Hungnam for the port of Pusan on the south coast of South Korea.

PART II

1951 | Chinese Firecrackers in Korea

On New Year's Day, the Chinese launched their first offensive of the year with a vengeance, committing nearly 500,000 communist troops into battle in an attempt to keep the UN off balance and to capture the South Korean capital. UN forces, still smarting from their defeat in North Korea, particularly at the Changjin Reservoir, Unsan, and Kunuri, were driven farther southward, as far as 50 miles below the 38th parallel, allowing communist forces to take Seoul for the second time.

Pvt. Gary Hashimoto
Pusan, South Korea

We didn't stay long in Seattle and shipped out on a Liberty troop ship, which was packed with soldiers. About the third day out at sea we hit a violent storm and everybody got sick. The way the ship was rocking and rolling, I thought it would capsize.

After a couple of weeks in Japan, we caught the ferry to Pusan, Korea, and waited for our assignments. It seemed like Korea was colder than Japan.

The tents we stayed in while waiting for orders did not have heaters. We were joined by Norman Ahakuelo of Honolulu. The three of us were the only local boys from Hawaii there at the time.

Jack and I were disappointed when we finally got our orders. Instead of being assigned to a frontline unit, we were assigned to guard trains that took troops and supplies to the front. Guards were needed because the trains were frequently ambushed by North Korean guerrillas. When our troops broke out of the Pusan Perimeter in mid-September 1950, thousands of North Koreans were trapped and bypassed by UN forces. Republic of Korea army units were supposed to have cleaned out these pockets of resistance but apparently missed quite a few. They fled into the mountains and conducted guerrilla warfare.

Pvt. Hisashi Morita
Item Company, 23d Infantry
Vicinity of Chunchon, South Korea

I joined my unit in December when it was on line below the 38th parallel. I was assigned to a rifle squad. A couple of old-timers told me that the entire division took a severe beating in November and December in North Korea south of the town of Kunuri. The division suffered thousands of casualties.

Vicinity of Hoengsong, South Korea

The January offensive by the Chinese sent us reeling back for miles. A buddy of mine, whom I knew since basic training, was shell-shocked, and would have been killed or captured if I hadn't helped him.

For two and half weeks I literally dragged him along, carrying his pack and weapon. The fact that I was still in good physical condition helped. Oftentimes we were left behind by the main body but managed to catch up when it took a break.

When we had outdistanced the Chinese, I left him in the care of a medic. That was the last I saw of him until fifty years later. I learned through some friends that he made it back to Hawaii and was all right.

JANUARY 1951

PFC. MOSES PAKAKI
4.2 Inch Mortar Company, 35th Infantry
Vicinity of Suwon, South Korea

We got our asses kicked by the Chinese in November 1950. Not only us, but also all of the UN and Republic of Korea forces as well. The capital city of South Korea, Seoul, was again taken by communist forces. But somehow the North Koreans and Chinese had run out gas and the front lines stabilized south of Seoul.

We got word that there was going to be an all-out push along the front to regain the ground that had been lost. I guess the brass had had enough bug-outs and decided to take the offensive.

The attack began on January 23 at about 1500 hours. We moved out behind the infantry and it appeared that we had things pretty much in control the first couple of days. We were not moving as fast as the time we broke out of the Pusan Perimeter in September 1950.

On the fourth day, the infantry units ahead of us found the going rough and called for mortar support. Our mortar company pulled into a draw to set up the mortars. The area had patches of potatoes, corn, and other vegetables and a small, dry rice paddy. We had no time to dig pits for the guns because the cry for support fire was urgent. While my mortar crew was putting the mortar in position, several shots rang out. One of the perimeter guards yelled, "The gooks in our positions! The gooks in our positions!" He had seen a North Korean trying to slip into an open irrigation ditch that ran through the length and middle of our position and took a shot at him. Fortunately for the North Korean, the guard was a poor shot and he surrendered. We all looked around but saw no other North Koreans. The one who surrendered had a couple of potato masher grenades but no weapon.

An officer quickly gave the order to search the area. About twelve of us lined up in a staggered skirmish line about 20 yards apart and began sweeping the area toward the roadside. A local boy from Hawaii, and I cannot remember his name, yelled for us to stop. He held up a grenade, motioned for us to hit the ground, and then threw a hand grenade into a thick patch of brush about 30 yards to our front. After the grenade burst five North Koreans jumped out of the patch with their hands in the air. Two of our men escorted them to the company's command post.

The rest of us continued to sweep the area down to the road. A shot rang out directly behind me and I turned just in time to see a North Korean about 20 yards away slump to the ground, a rifle falling from his hand. He was shot by one of our men who was bringing up the rear. The North Korean had been well camouflaged in a 3-foot-deep hole and I had walked right past him. Apparently, the North Korean didn't see the rear guard as the skirmish line moved past him. He couldn't get off a round because of the alert rear guard. Man, that was close! As we continued with the sweep, three North Koreans emerged from a thicket 50 yards ahead of us with their hands up to surrender. Before I could react, someone started firing at them. Others picked up the fire and, I don't know why, I joined in on the firing with the BAR I was carrying. They were all killed. If no one had fired I wouldn't have fired, too. But, like all the others, I reacted at the first shot and fired. When we got to them they were riddled with bullets.

We finished the sweep to the road without running into any more North Koreans. I immediately sought out the GI who saved my ass and couldn't thank him enough.

After the five North Koreans had been interrogated we learned that they had been in the area for several days and were waiting to ambush us during the night.

FEBRUARY 1951

SGT. CLARENCE YOUNG
George Company, 5th RCT
Somewhere in South Korea

I cannot count the number of hills we had taken in our drive north, but we were always on the go, moving from hill to hill. After a while, all the hills looked alike. But that wasn't so bad. It was moving through the rice paddies in the valley that was bad because of the stench of human fertilizer. Anyway, I got wounded on one of those hills.

We had moved up to take this particular hill, with the artillery laying down a tremendous moving barrage ahead of us. Several rounds fell short behind us, causing some casualties. Some of the men turned to the rear, raised their fists, and cussed like hell but for nothing because the guns were a couple of miles behind us. The barrage kept the Chinese in

FIGURE 15   While in reserve, Sfc. Clarence Young of Honolulu rides a calf.
December 1950. Courtesy of Al Chang.

their holes. When the artillery fire was lifted, we were about 100 yards
from the enemy positions.

As I got closer, a camouflaged cover about 30 yards to my right
popped open and a hand grenade came sailing in my direction. All I saw
was the arm tossing the bottle-shaped hand grenade. I leaped to the side
and the hand grenade exploded several yards downhill from me. I got up
and rushed to the spot where the grenade came from. The hole was so
well camouflaged that I almost ran past it. Standing a yard from the edge
of the hole, I aimed my rifle at the cover and pulled the trigger of my
M-1 rifle. My goddamn rifle jammed. I worked the bolt back and a round
ejected. I pulled the trigger again but the rifle still didn't fire. I was getting angry and excited. One of the guys yelled, "Hey, Young, don't get
crazy, take it easy." When he came to my side I grabbed his M-1 rifle and
emptied the entire clip, all eight rounds, into the hole. I never opened
the foxhole cover to see what I had done. I gave the M-1 rifle back to the
soldier, picked up my own, and got it working again.

As I continued my climb, I heard a crunching blast and the next
thing I knew I found myself on my belly on the ground. A single mortar round had exploded several yards in back of me.

I sat up, dazed. My neck hurt. I felt the back of my neck with my

FIGURE 16   Hawaii's decorated men chat between battles. *Left to right,* Sgt. Douglas McQuillan of Honolulu, Silver Star; Sgt. James Kawamura of Kauai, Distinguished Service Cross; and Cpl. Carl Higa of Honolulu, Silver Star. January 1951. Courtesy of Al Chang.

hand and it was wet. It sure wasn't sweat. When I looked at my hand there was blood on it. Someone cried, "Medic!" and a few minutes later the platoon medic came to my side. He looked at my neck and head and told me that a piece of shrapnel had struck me on the back of my neck and it was still there. He said he would have to send me to the aid station. He put a bandage on the wound and got one of the men to escort me to the battalion aid station, where a group of wounded men were waiting to be treated. Six hours later, a doctor said, "Okay, yobo, you're next."

"Wait a minute," I told the doctor. "I'm no yobo. I'm a GI." The poor doctor had to apologize to me. He said that he thought I was a ROK soldier. I knew then why I had waited so long to be treated. The medics and doctors were treating GIs first and ROK soldiers last. And I remembered that there were many haole GIs who were not as seriously wounded as I was, who were treated ahead of me. Another reason was that I didn't complain or show I was in pain, which indicated that I wasn't seriously wounded.

The doctor told me that the shrapnel was too deep for him to remove

FIGURE 17   Sfc. Mamoru Ikemura of Hawaii fires at the enemy while Cpl. Sitgreaves of California reloads. January 1951. Courtesy of Al Chang.

FIGURE 18   Taking time out to sing their favorite Hawaiian songs are (*left to right*), M. Sgt. Alfred Alfonso, Pfc. Tony Buan, Cpl. Vic Barbadillo, Cpl. Edward Kaulauli, Lt. Leonard Warner, and Cpl. Miyahira. Standing, *left to right*, Pfc. Cappy Panagacian, Cpl. Walter Chong, Cpl. William Silver, and Pfc. Felix Tormis. January 1951. Courtesy of Al Chang.

FIGURE 19   5th RCT soldiers root out a Chinese survivor after a battle. February 1951. Courtesy of Al Chang.

and that I needed to be sent to Japan to have the shrapnel taken out. With other wounded men I was put in an ambulance and taken to Kimpo Airfield, from where we were flown to a hospital in Kyoto, Japan.

In Kyoto, doctors removed the shrapnel from my neck and hands. I was hospitalized for thirty days. I thought that I was going to be sent home to Hawaii, but that's not how the army works. But it was better than being on the front lines. Food was good. I had a bed to sleep in and I had clean clothes every day. Thirty days was too short and I soon found myself on a ship headed for Pusan, Korea. A long train ride north took me back to my unit.

FEBRUARY 1951

PFC. GARY HASHIMOTO
Baker Company, 32d Infantry
Vicinity of Wonju, South Korea

After a month of riding shotgun on trains, Jack and I finally got our wish and were assigned to Baker Company, 1st Battalion, 32d Infantry Regiment, 7th Infantry Division.

Baker Company was in reserve, waiting for replacements to fill its depleted ranks when we arrived. Finally, after two weeks, even though still under strength, we were told we were going on the offensive—an operation called Operation Killer. This was going to be the first combat action for most of us in Baker Company.

February 21 was the date that Operation Killer was to start. I couldn't sleep a wink on the eve of the battle because thinking about it made my stomach turn. We were all scared and none of the old-timers gave us any words of encouragement. I guess they were just as scared as we were.

I can't remember how long Operation Killer took, but I remember how cold it was. I think the temperature range was from zero at night to 50 degrees during the day. In a steady, cold rain we fixed bayonets and moved out. There was ice in the stream we crossed, and when we got to the other side, I thought my feet would freeze. We had to keep moving and didn't stop to change our socks.

FIGURE 20   Sfc. Arthur McColgan, eating canned *poi* during a lull in the fighting. Courtesy of Al Chang.

FIGURE 21   Sfc. Robert Cho of Honolulu. Courtesy of Al Chang.

FIGURE 22   Sfc. Tokuzo Tamashiro of Waimanalo. Courtesy of Al Chang.

FIGURE 23   M. Sgt. Fernando Batungbacal of Honolulu. Courtesy of Al Chang.

FIGURE 24   Sfc. Clarence Choy of Honolulu. Courtesy of Al Chang.

FIGURE 25 Cpl. George Kealakai of Pearl City. Courtesy of Al Chang.

FIGURE 26   Sfc. Manuel Cabos of Honolulu. Courtesy of Al Chang.

MARCH 1951

SFC. JAY HIDANO
Easy Company, 8th Cavalry
Army Tripler General Hospital, Territory of Hawaii

My leg wasn't responding to treatment in spite of all the efforts by surgeons to save it. One surgeon told me of the consequences if the leg was not amputated. He asked how I felt about it and without hesitation I told him to go ahead with the amputation.

FIGURE 27   Cpl. Bertram Sebresos of Hawaii taking a break in reserve. March 1951. Courtesy of Bertram Sebresos.

It was amputated below the knee and as soon as I was able to walk with crutches I was retired from the army with a permanent disability. The war was still on but I returned to civilian life.

I was later fitted with a prosthesis. To this day I still carry the bullet and the mortar fragment in me.

MARCH 1951

SGT. CLARENCE YOUNG
George Company, 5th RCT
Somewhere in South Korea

On a train heading north to join my unit, I saw a Korean mother with a baby in her arms a couple of rows in front of me. It was cold and both had no warm clothing whatsoever. All she could do was hold the baby tightly in her arms. It was a sad sight so I got my duffel bag and dug out two GI blankets. I got up from my seat and walked over and gave her the two blankets. I gestured to her to wrap themselves up in the blankets. This she did and then tried to thank me in Korean.

I went back to my seat and got a piece of paper and wrote a note

FIGURE 28   Hawaii's soldiers dig into a watermelon after fierce fighting along the 38th parallel. March 1951. Courtesy of Al Chang.

FIGURE 29   The "J. Aku Head Pupule" tank, named after a Honolulu disc jockey. Second from left is William Kapaku of Nanakuli. March 1951. Courtesy of Al Chang.

FIGURE 30   Inductees from Kauai prepare to leave for Oahu for basic training. Standing, sixth from the left, is John Iwamoto. March 1951. Courtesy of John Iwamoto.

explaining how she got the blankets in case she was questioned by military authorities. On the note I put my name, rank, and unit I belonged to. I went back to her and tried to explain what the note was for. I also gave her about $50 in American money and told her to buy food for themselves. What made me do that? I don't know. I did it without even thinking. Maybe subconsciously, I was thinking about my own family.

Vicinity of the 38th parallel, North Korea

I finally got back to my unit, which was in blocking position a few miles north of the 38th parallel in central North Korea. It was half a mile behind the front lines. The company commander informed me that I was now the leader of the 2d Squad. Most of the guys I knew before I left were still there and were happy to see me back. But there were a lot of new faces, which indicated that many old-timers were gone.

   In the chow line one morning, I had on a nice warm parka jacket that can be worn inside out. It was given to me by my air force friend while I was waiting to catch the train in Pusan. Behind me were two haoles who had recently joined the company while I was hospitalized in Japan and who didn't know who I was. One called out to me and said,

FIGURE 31 Sgt. Leroy A. Mendonca, Company B, Seventh Infantry Regiment, 3d Infantry Division, was awarded the Medal of Honor posthumously for conspicuous gallantry in action at the risk of his life above and beyond the call of duty against the enemy mear Chich-on, Korea, on July 4, 1951. Courtesy of the U.S. Army War Museum.

FIGURE 32   Pfc. Herbert K. Piliaau, Company C, 23d Infantry Regiment, 2d Infantry Division, was awarded the Medal of Honor posthumously for conspicuous gallantry in action at the risk of his life above and beyond the call of duty against the enemy near Pia-ri, Korea, on September 17, 1951. Courtesy of the U.S. Army War Museum.

"Hey, yobo, that jacket you have on is worn only by Americans." I didn't say anything. The next thing I knew I was grabbed from behind and spun around. "Take off that jacket, it's mine," said one of them. Without answering I took my M-1 rifle off my shoulder. I suppose the move made it appear that I had taken the rifle off my shoulder to take the jacket off, and I could see the smiles on their faces. What they didn't know was that my rifle was loaded. I flicked the safety off my M-1 rifle, took about three steps backward out of the mess line, and fired two rounds into the ground in front of them. They jumped back, shocked. Others near the two scattered.

I aimed the rifle at the head of one of them and said, "If you touch me one more time, I'll blow your fucking head off." Our company commander heard the two shots and came running up to me from his tent and demanded to know what had happened. I was shaking and still had the rifle in my hands. I pointed to the two GIs and explained to the captain that they tried to take my jacket and I wasn't about to let them do it.

The captain was livid. He charged the two men and gave them hell. He went nose to nose with one of them and shouted, "This is Sergeant Young and he is an American soldier from Hawaii, not a KATUSA. He is one of my squad leaders and has just returned from the hospital. I have a good mind to put the two of you in his squad." The two were visibly shaken. He also made it clear to all the other replacements who I was. He tried to calm me down and asked if I was all right. I nodded, and he said for me to take it easy and left. As soon as the company commander left, the two stunned GIs immediately came to apologize. Hell, I was still pissed off. The other guys who knew me told me to cool off, which I did, eventually. Later, though, I became good friends with the two.

MARCH 1951

PFC. SUSUMU SHINAGAWA
Able Company, 34th Infantry
Camp 7, North Korea

I spent the winter at Chunggang-jin and Hanjang-ni prison camps. From Hanjang-ni we were moved to Andong. The "Tiger" was relieved of his duties and the North Korean army personnel took over. We were moved again to another village a few miles west and put in an old Japanese barracks. This was Camp 7. There was only one frame building with very large rooms. Each room had a stove. During this time the civilians who were in our group were moved across the Yalu River into Manchuria. We never saw them again. Of the 700 Americans who began the "Tiger March," less than 300 had survived.

MARCH 1951

SGT. IRWIN COCKETT
Dog Company, 5th RCT
Vicinity of Yangpyong, South Korea

Between January and March the fighting took place between the 38th and 37th parallels. It was at this time that I was called to report to the company's command post. When I got there, Captain Hisaka, our company commander, told me that Dog Company had received its first R&R allocation. My name was drawn from a bunch of names to go to Japan on R&R. I thought that it was just great, but I had one problem. I was broke.

Before I could explain what my financial status was, Captain Hisaka presented me with a steel helmet full of money. He had anticipated the problem and had collected money before I reported to him. I asked him what I could bring back and he said to bring back a case of C&C. Hell, I didn't know what C&C stood for although I knew it was some kind of liquor.

I flew out of Kimpo Airfield in a C-47 with other soldiers also on R&R and was taken to an army camp in Beppu, Japan. The first thing I did was to go to a store and ask a lady clerk if she had any C&C. She said she did and it was a popular item with soldiers on R&R in Japan. I said I wanted a case, still not knowing what kind of liquor it was. When she brought the case, the label read Canadian Club Whiskey. I took the case to the barracks, secured it, and went on to enjoy my R&R in Japan.

MARCH 1951

1ST LT. HERBERT IKEDA
I&R Platoon, 5th RCT
Vicinity of Hongchon, South Korea

For some reason, I received orders to transfer to regiment, which shocked the hell out of me. Even my company commander was shocked. The only reason that I could think of was the dislike my battalion commander had for me. I wasn't given a chance to pick up all my personal belongings. I got on a jeep and was driven to regimental headquarters, where I was put in charge of the Intelligence and Reconnaissance Platoon.

One of battalion's advances was stopped while attacking a hill mass near Hongchon, so the regimental commander told me to take my platoon and support it in whatever way I could. A tank would accompany us to give fire support if we needed it. He also attached a 57mm recoilless rifle team to my platoon.

Under enemy small arms fire, we moved out to within 100 yards to the base of the hill. The tank drew mortar fire and sought cover behind a mound. I spotted a machine gun bunker halfway up the slope and told my platoon sergeant to bring up the 57mm recoilless rifle team so we could take the machine gun position under fire. When the team arrived I took the recoilless from the gunner and told him to load it. I set the sights at 200 yards. From the kneeling position, I fired. Lucky shot! I got a direct hit on the bunker. With smoke pouring out of the destroyed bunker, enemy soldiers came running out of it.

I told my men to hold their positions while I sprinted to where the tank was parked. I told the tank commander that my squad would be making a charge up the hill and I needed his tank to support us. I would be carrying a signal panel on my back to keep his fire well above and ahead of me.

With a .45 caliber pistol in my hand and the signal panel draped over my back, I led the attack up the hill in a skirmish line. I turned around and pumped my fist to my men to signal double time. I yelled encouragement as I made my way up the hill. We were now drawing heavy automatic and rifle fire from the hill. I moved to the left side of the hill and almost stumbled into a Chinese machine gun pit no more than 20 yards away, firing down into my attacking platoon. They caught sight of me at almost the same time that I saw them. They scrambled and tried to turn the machine gun in my direction but before they could I was already about 10 feet from them. The first round from my .45 killed the gunner and the second, the assistant gunner. When I got to them I raised my pistol to fire to make sure they were both dead. The pistol jammed. I pulled back the pistol's slide and pulled the trigger again. I emptied the pistol into them.

Then I saw another enemy machine gun to the right of the one I had just destroyed. Apparently, the North Korean gun crew was not aware I had taken out the gun to their left. I made a mad dash to a small shell crater a few yards below the enemy machine gun. I threw two hand grenades, which exploded in or near the gun pit. When I looked up I saw the gun crew scrambling out of the pit and running up the hill. They were too far away for my pistol. With my back to the hill, I sat down and waited for the rest of the platoon to catch up.

Before I could muster my men for a final assault, my radio man received a message from battalion to hold up where I was so the other platoons from the company could catch up with us. While I was waiting for this to take place, I received another message to report to the battalion commander, Colonel Kane, at the command post. I put Sgt. Gabriel Simoneta in charge of the platoon and made my way down the hill and up another hill to see Colonel Kane. The battalion CP was on the reserve slope of that hill. When I got to battalion headquarters, one of the staff officers told me Colonel Kane was busy but that I should wait. While waiting, a heavy enemy artillery barrage fell on the hill where my platoon was holed up. Reports coming in by radio told of heavy casualties. I was told to get my butt back to my platoon as quickly as I could. I never got see Colonel Kane and never found out why he wanted to see me.

When I got back to my platoon on the hill, I was shocked to see the number of casualties we had taken. My platoon was down to less than two squads. We were ordered off the hill because of the heavy casualties we had taken.

Colonel Kane was replaced by Col. Sherman Pratt. Colonel Pratt personally commended me for my action in destroying the two enemy machine gun positions and for leading the charge up the hill. He was going to recommend me for one of the highest decorations. It was even mentioned I was going to be recommended for the Medal of Honor. Apparently, someone from the battalion staff had heard about what I had done and I was flabbergasted when he mentioned the Medal of Honor. However, Colonel Pratt needed witnesses to confirm my actions. Heck! In the heat of combat no one has the time to follow the actions of another man and to record his deeds. I didn't know of anyone who saw what I did and I sure wasn't going to ask my men to make me a hero. I never pursued the matter and it was not brought up again, which I regretted many years later.

MARCH 1951

CPL. BERTRAM SEBRESOS
Baker Company, 7th Infantry
Vicinity of Kumwha, North Korea

I was relieved as squad leader and demoted to bazooka gunner in the weapons squad. We were assigned a pretty good sector, where the terrain was pretty steep and was supposedly quite defensible.

My foxhole buddy was Barnett, an ex-navy man from World War

II. On my left about 50 yards away was a heavy machine gun manned by Sergeant Davis and the same distance away on my right was another machine gun manned by Sergeant Rosada from Hawaii. A narrow footpath joined our positions.

Between Davis and me were two foxholes. The occupants of one were an Englishman we nicknamed Limey and a KATUSA we called #48, because we couldn't pronounce his name. A BAR team was in the other foxhole.

It got dark pretty fast but at about 2200 hours the bright moon rose and lit the landscape. Then we heard bird calls. Heck, we hadn't seen or heard birds for weeks so we knew they were Chinese signals. Immediately, our illuminating flares popped above us.

To my left I heard two loud explosions and Chinese voices. Someone came running on the path toward me, so I raised my rifle to fire when the running figure shouted, "Number 48! Number 48!" and dove into my position. It was the KATUSA.

Footsteps again on the path. Chinese only 30 feet away. I picked off two of them with my M-1 and the rest leaped to the side of the path to avoid my fire. But I could see their heads so I emptied a clip in their direction.

I saw this dark object in the air that froze me for a split second. It exploded among the three of us. It must have knocked me unconscious for a few seconds. I found myself in a sitting position. Then I heard the voice of Barnett yelling, "Don't shoot! Don't shoot!"

I looked up and saw a Chinese on the opposite side of the hole fire at Barnett and just as he swung his gun around toward me, I fell to one side. He fired but missed. I stayed still and held my breath, trying not to move. The Chinese never checked me out, thinking I was dead.

After about a minute I peeked and saw several Chinese jump into the already crowded position. One grabbed me by the collar and pulled my head up. I thought he was going to slit my throat. Then he slammed my face into the ground, thinking I was dead. I didn't know it at the time but my bloody face saved my life.

The Chinese took my wrist watch, my crucifix, and a *Reader's Digest* that I carried in my shirt pocket.

For the next seven hours or so they stepped and sat on me. I laid on my stomach with my head turned to the middle of the hole but with my face in the shadows so I could take short peeks from the time to time. I counted five Chinese in my hole.

Barnett was not dead because I could hear him calling my name. I wondered why the Chinese didn't finish him off. The Chinese now were having a duel with Rosada's machine gun and the hot, empty shells fell on me but I kept quiet. I couldn't hear the BAR team on my right so I assumed the Chinese got them too.

This went on for hours until finally I sensed that the Chinese were leaving. I peeked and found them leaping out of the hole one by one. Then I realized that it was almost daylight. The last Chinese didn't have a weapon and took his time so I jumped up and grabbed him before he could get out. I had his shirt with one hand and tried to punch him out with my right hand but I just didn't have the strength so I just hung on to him until Sergeant Bowman from the second squad came to my rescue. I had captured a Chinese prisoner.

Barnett was still alive but not for long. Number 48, the KATUSA, was dead. The BAR team was also killed. Sergeant Davis was dead, his skull half blown off.

On my own power, I went down the hill looking for a medic.

APRIL 1951

SGT. STANLEY KAU
Service Company, 5th RCT
Vicinity of Pukhan Dam
Letter home

Dear Folks,

Sure hope that this letter finds you all in the best of health. I am okay but tired as the dickens. Am now on the switchboard shift from 2 to 4 in the morning and my eyes can hardly stay open but figured I'd write a letter or else I may fall asleep.

Well, folks, the unfortunate has happened as those damn chink commies have launched their spring offensive in a big way and have hit us pretty hard. In two days, our company moved back about thirty road miles. Yes, the same old grind as before, moving back again. This damn war is surely getting sickening as we go back and forth, just like a game of checkers. Really burns one up! Sure hope that the withdrawal this time won't be too serious as the last one. We have had a tremendous amount of casualties but understand thru the radio news that the commies have suffered over 15,000 casualties in the first 24 hours of this new offensive of theirs. We are just above the dam where we once were a month ago.

Sure hope we can have many more replacements over here or it will hurt our chances of an early rotation home. More good Hawaii boys have given their lives in this latest encounter with the enemy. It is sickening and sad to hear this from friends coming back from the lines. The commies came in hordes they say and just overran our positions with great disregard for their lives. Commies are a group of fanatics, most likely under the influence of dope.

We moved twice in two days and it is a lot of hard work and with the few hours of sleep I did manage to get, I am all pooped out. We were but five miles from the front when we moved out two mornings ago. Had a brief stay of two days across the 38th parallel this time. Sure hope we can hold at the 38th and not get shoved back too far. The artillery batteries have been really putting rounds out steadily day and nite.

Well, folks, guess this letter hasn't been too cheerful but hope to have good news in my next letter. Will close now and my God bless you all.

Love,
Stanley

APRIL 1951

CPL. GARY HASHIMOTO
Baker Company, 32nd Infantry
Vicinity of Wonju, South Korea

After being on the front lines a couple of months, I received field promotions to private first class and corporal and eventually became first scout or point man for Baker Company. Point man was the most dangerous position in the company, platoon, or squad. In retrospect, I could have been the first one to get killed or captured. But that was my job and I was counted on to do just that.

On one occasion an anxious camouflaged Chinese machine gunner opened up on me too soon. Although I was pinned down, it warned the company of the ambush up ahead. Our tanks took the point and plastered the hillside with cannon fire and forced the Chinese to withdraw.

Jack Hiwatashi was promoted to staff sergeant and he and Norman Ahakuelo were made squad leaders. Jack and I had been on line for only three months and he was already a sergeant and me a corporal.

Jack and I had a couple of close calls but were lucky to get out alive so he and I talked about separating. Being in the same squad together could mean getting killed at the same time. We talked to our platoon sergeant about splitting us up and the reason for it. He agreed and pulled me out of Jack's squad and put me with another squad but still in the same platoon. I felt much better.

Vicinity of Hwachon Reservoir, North Korea

We fought all the way to the Hwachon Reservoir, which was several miles above the 38th parallel, and then ran into a Chinese counteroffensive, which drove us back well below the 38th parallel. We marched south for five days and were joined by other UN forces moving south. I recall seeing Turks, Ethiopians, Canadians, Australians, Filipinos, and English troops coming down from the hills retreating from the Chinese. It was a sad but awesome sight to see thousands of our men in full retreat from the Chinese. I couldn't believe that I was part of what was called a huge retrograde movement.

APRIL 1951

Cpl. Arsanio Vendiola
George Company, 5th RCT
Vicinity of Chongpyong, South Korea

The 2d Battalion, along with the 1st Battalion, was given the assignment of holding a rear guard to screen the withdrawal of the 24th Infantry Division. The 3d Battalion was to lead the column. With us were 105mm howitzers and a tank battalion. Just when we were given the orders to withdraw, we were told to hold things up because a company of rangers was surrounded by a Chinese regiment just to the north of us. We were to hold our positions while five Patton tanks were sent to rescue them. Several hours later, the tanks returned with sixty-five survivors, most of them wounded.

When we started moving south again, word was passed back to us from the head of the column that the Chinese had established a roadblock ahead and had stalled the column. We were at the tail end of the column trailing the 1st Battalion. As if on signal, Chinese began to appear on the ridge lines to the east and in the rice paddies to our right.

Then I heard the sound of enemy mortars popping. The Chinese must have positioned their guns close to the road. A few seconds later their rounds burst along the length of the column. The Chinese mortar men were good because very few rounds missed the road.

Enemy automatic fire from both sides of the road swept the column, causing heavy casualties in the crossfire. Ahead of me a truck burst into flames and flipped over on the road, blocking the way. By this time our guys were jumping off the trucks and taking positions facing either the hillside or the rice paddies. The Chinese came right down from the hillside to only a few yards from the road, exchanging grenades and small arms fire with us. I yelled for my recoilless rifle team to set up the gun in the rice paddy facing the hillside where most of the enemy fire was coming from. I told the gunner to fire all the rounds as quickly as he could because I thought we would sure as hell would not make it out of there.

After several rounds were fired, I told the men to fix their bayonets. The way things were going we were going to get killed on the road anyway so we might as well get killed charging up the hillside. Besides, I thought that was the only way we could get out of the trap.

Looking at the hillside I saw scores of Chinese moving down on us. But before I could give the order to charge, a sergeant came running toward us. I stopped him and asked what we were going to do. Since he outranked me, I thought it would be better to follow his orders than to make that bayonet charge. He said he was going to the back of the column to see what was happening.

After he left us, three of our tanks tried to make their way to the head of the column. I hailed the first tank and it slowed down. My squad jumped on it and I asked the tank commander what he was going to do. He said he was going to try to break through the roadblock. I told my men to get off the tank and get on the second tank, which I thought was safer going through the roadblock. I was now lugging the recoilless rifle because the gunner had a leg wound. The gun was already loaded.

The tanks were at 30-yard intervals. The first tank stopped, causing our tank and the tank behind us to stop too. Scanning the hillside, my eyes almost popped out of their sockets. I saw several Chinese with a bazooka on a rock outcropping in full view about 50 yards away. Shit! The Chinese gunner was aiming at our tank. I saw the back blast of the shot fired and saw the bazooka round heading in our direction. It seemed like it was in slow motion. I thought I had it. He missed. The bazooka round cleared the barrel of the tank's gun by several inches and exploded beyond the tank and among our troops who were in the rice paddy. Before the Chinese could reload, I fired one round at the Chinese and missed, the round bursting far beyond my target. I jumped off the tank with my squad following me and took a position on the other side of the tank. I told the assistant gunner to load me up again. I fired a second round in the direction where I had seen the chink bazooka and then dove for cover in the rice paddy. We were about 40 yards from the first tank when it exploded in a roar. Then was a second explosion, probably from the tank's ammunition. Nobody got out. The second tank took a hit, probably from the same chink bazooka that missed us. But this time the crew got out. The blast from the round that got the second tank knocked me backwards and momentarily stunned me. My shoulder was bleeding and I wasn't sure from what. Probably pieces of metal from the tank.

My squad was scattered so I called out for them to meet me behind the third tank. Two of my men were missing. When I got there, Sergeant Nattad from the 4.2 Mortar Section was already there. I asked him where he had come from and he pulled me over to the side where I could see the back of the column. He said, "Look down the road." I turned my head to where he pointed and saw vehicles burning, all belonging to the 4.2 Mortar Section.

The third tank had stalled and the crew had abandoned it. I sprinted to the tank, climbed in, and tried working the radio. I began flipping switches but all I got was a humming sound. I started to talk into the mike, "This is George Company and we need help." There was no answer. I could hear bullets bouncing off the tank. I looked around and saw the stack of 90mm rounds for the tank's gun. Was I wide-eyed! I thought, *If a mortar round hits this tank, it's aloha for me.* I quickly scrambled out of the tank and went to the rear underside of the tank. I looked back down the road and saw a half-track with someone firing the mounted .30 caliber machine gun. It was Sgt. Clarence Young, firing at the Chinese who were swarming down the hillside. He saw me and yelled, but I couldn't hear him. I yelled back, "I gotta look for my men," but I don't think he heard me. Besides, all armored vehicles were now prime targets for the Chinese gunners and I was not going to commit suicide that way. I turned to go into the rice paddy and I still could hear Sergeant Young firing away. He was doing an Audie Murphy.

About 100 yards away I heard several explosions in quick succession. I turned to look and saw Young's half-track on its side. I didn't think Young could have lived through that so I didn't bother going back to see if he had been killed. I learned later that Sergeant Welch, who was taking cover behind a damaged tank in the rice paddy, also saw what happened to Sergeant Young.

The roadside looked like hell. Incoming rounds bracketed the road, setting more vehicles on fire. GIs were scurrying around looking for cover behind vehicles and rice paddy dikes. I turned around and saw other friendly troops in the rice paddies heading for a ridge line. I decided to follow them.

I was armed only with my .45 pistol. I had left the recoilless rifle by the roadside after being knocked almost unconscious. With only the pistol I was able to make good time through the rice paddies and to the bottom of the ridge line. The dust and haze from the smoke of the burning vehicles and brush fires created some sort of smoke screen. However, I wondered when I was going to get a bullet in the back because there were Chinese in the rice paddies when the battle began.

Halfway up the ridge line, I got tired and sat down to rest. I looked back at the column. Less than a mile away I could see burning vehicles extending almost the entire length of the column. I finally got to the top of the ridge and joined about a dozen of our men. I was the only one from Hawaii. With us were a truck driver and a cook. It was late afternoon.

I was so tired. I sat down and put my head in my arms. I never heard the incoming mortar round because of the noise our attacking jets were making. Wham! It struck several yards to the right from where I was sitting, injuring half of us, including me. We had made a mistake bunching up. I caught shrapnel in my head and legs, but the wounds were not serious. It was my second injury in two hours. Another person was more seriously injured than I was. One of his legs was cut open, exposing the bone. Others had only minor wounds. Knowing we were seen, we moved south, each of us taking turns assisting the soldier with the injured leg.

It was now getting dark and there was no trail so we stumbled along, depending on whoever was at the point to lead us to safety. We were still on the ridge but now walking downhill. As we neared the valley floor a burst of burp gun fire sent everyone to the ground. I braced myself for the barrage of Chinese hand grenades and more burp gun fire but nothing happened. Probably a trigger-happy Chinese. About half an hour later we saw a figure about 30 yards away, shouting to us in Chinese. I wondered if the Chinese was the one who had fired at us earlier. He could be alone. Those with rifles fired a volley at the Chinese, expecting return fire but got none. About a minute later we got up and cautiously approached the area where the Chinese had been. I was right. He was alone, dead, a bloody mess. We continued walking.

We walked all night, climbing and crossing several ridges and, to our best judgment, headed south. I still had my .45 caliber pistol. I noticed several of the men threw away their weapons and their canteens. No one stopped them because there was no leader. No one wanted to assume command of the group and, as a result, we were always arguing as to what direction we would take.

We finally came to a small gully that had a rice paddy with water. My canteen had been empty for a long time and those who still had their canteens joined me in refilling theirs. We shared the water with the others. Sure tasted muddy. No one had purification tablets but we were thirsty as hell! Now I was the only one with a weapon.

We were climbing a ridge at about 0630 hours when we were greeted by several bursts of automatic fire, which drove all of us to the ground. I felt a tug on the left side of my field jacket. I later found a bullet hole there. A bullet must have passed between my left arm and left side, making a hole in my field jacket.

The firing continued for a few more seconds. Then I noticed that the firing was not that of a Chinese burp gun. Its rate of fire was too slow. It sounded more like our slow-firing BAR. I said to the others, "Hey, they must be friendlies! It must be one of our listening posts, who don't know who we are."

"But nobody asked for the password," someone spoke up.

"Hell, I don't think there is any password, the way things are going," I said. And if there was one, we sure didn't know what it was. By this time the firing had stopped and we debated for a few seconds as to what we should do.

"Let's go in," one guy said.

"You go first," another one replied.

Finally we decided to identify ourselves. "We're GIs, don't fire," someone shouted. No response.

I shouted, "We're GIs, don't fire."

Silence. Then a voice in English shouted, "Come ahead with your hands up."

Talk about a happy bunch of GIs! We hurried to where the voice came from, not caring if there were land mines in our path. When we got to the outpost we saw the BAR man who fired at us. He was shaking all over, shaking more than us. The first thing we did was ask him for cigarettes.

APRIL 1951

SGT. MARCELLO VENDIOLA
Item Company, 5th RCT
Vicinity of Chongpyong, South Korea

It had been a month since I had seen my younger brother, Arsanio, who was in George Company in the 2d Battalion. We never got to see much of each other, even when the entire regiment was in reserve, because we were in different battalions.

In one of our retrogrades, my company was fortunate to be riding on trucks. I rode in the cab of the truck. Other units had to walk. It was almost dark and the truck and infantry column were crawling south. As we slowly passed tired, plodding men of the 5th RCT, I looked at every face. Some were familiar faces and we waved at each other. One of the faces was too familiar. It was my kid brother Arsanio, whom I hadn't seen in a couple of months.

I jumped out of the cab and went to him. We hugged while walking and had a quick hello and "take care" conversation. My truck was moving ahead so I had to run after it, giving my brother a wave as I leaped on the running board of the vehicle. I worried about him.

Our company followed the heavy weapons company in the march order south. On one of our breaks, an 81mm mortar crew from heavy weapons was given a fire mission. The gun crew set up their mortar in a dry rice paddy about 100 yards away from the road. While we waited, I watched the gun crew fire several rounds. Then there was a blinding flash and smoke above the gun. One of the rounds had exploded prematurely only a few feet above the gun, killing the entire crew. We all ran down to the gun but there was nothing anyone could do. The gun crew was just cut to pieces. This was the most tragic incident I witnessed in the war.

APRIL 1951

SGT. CLARENCE YOUNG
George Company, 5th RCT
Vicinity of Chongpyong, South Korea

I was promoted to sergeant first class and became the platoon sergeant of the 2d Platoon. I also was the acting platoon leader, a position normally held by a lieutenant, because our company was short of officers.

My platoon was given the mission of providing flank security for our battalion when UN forces were pushed back to the 38th parallel. My platoon occupied a small knoll above the road on the left side of a valley while the 5th RCT column made its way just south of the 38th parallel. The knoll was almost at the valley floor at the end of a ridge. A few men tried to dig foxholes, but most of us tried to position ourselves behind boulders or bushes or holes dug previously since we would have to move out quickly once the tail end of the battalion passed by.

In the afternoon I thought I would check on my men. I found everyone pretty much settled in their defensive positions. While doing this, I happened to look up the ridge and saw a large number of men moving down the ridge line toward us about 300 yards away. I glanced at the other ridges and saw the same thing: masses of men moving down the ridges toward the valley floor. Now I could hear small arms and machine gun fire coming from the head of the column. I called my radio operator over and told him to get hold of the company commander. I told him that enemy forces were attacking the column from the ridges to our left. He said, "No, that can't be. Those men must be ROK units pulling back."

"It can't be because they are shooting at us and we are shooting back," I answered.

"Hold that position at any cost," he shouted over the radio.

At that instant, the entire column was engulfed in small arms, automatic, and mortar fire. Some of the vehicles burst into flames and I saw men piling out of them.

My platoon fired up the ridge and slowed down the attacking Chinese. Just ahead of us six Patton tanks tried to back up and support us but were unable to because of the bumper-to-bumper traffic and the narrow road. All they could do was fire blindly over our heads into the hills above us. At the same time they were sitting ducks for the enemy's bazooka teams.

The enemy now had gotten to less than 100 yards from my platoon's position, causing several casualties. There was a half-track below us on the road so I told my men to get the wounded into the half-track and to pull back across the road into the rice paddies. The roadside bank next to the paddies offered some protection. The half-track mounted a .30 caliber machine gun but the gunner was wounded and couldn't fire the weapon.

While my men were putting the wounded on the half-track, I jumped on it and manned the machine gun, firing into the hillside. The gun's red tracer ammo slammed into groups of Chinese attempting to reach the column. I emptied the ammo can in less than a minute. I was loading up another can of ammo when out of the corner of my eye, I saw a GI running toward me. It was Arsanio Vendiola from Hawaii. I yelled, "Vendy, Vendy, give me a hand. I need help to fire this gun!"

He screamed back with words I couldn't understand or hear because of exploding mortar rounds and small arms fire. I kept on firing with one hand and feeding the gun with the other. At this point I was so busy concentrating on firing that I didn't know what was happening to the rest of the column. Then there was this bright, yellow flash in front of me. The vehicle tipped over on its side and spilled everyone out, the wounded and me included. I must have been knocked unconscious for a few seconds from the explosion. I came to my senses when my radio operator shook me and asked if I was okay. My nose and ears were bleeding. I was able to stand but was still wobbly from the concussion. I asked, "What happened?"

"A mortar round burst just a few feet from the half-track," the radio operator replied.

"What about the others?"

"They had it," someone replied.

There was much confusion on the road—men milling around, vehicles on fire, occasional bursts of mortar rounds, and men in the paddies trying to get as far away from the road as possible. I gathered several men, about a dozen from the platoon, and started jogging in a southerly direction across the rice paddies to a distant ridge. What we didn't know was that the commies had set up a roadblock ahead of the column and had it stalled. They also had infiltrated several miles south of the roadblock.

We found a deserted village and took refuge in a large house. We hid in every nook and cranny we could find in the house and stayed there for the night. The next morning I heard voices but I told the guys to stay put just to make sure. Before I could take a look North Korean soldiers burst through the door and pointed their burp guns at us. We couldn't do anything but throw our weapons down and raise our hands above our heads. We were pulled out of the house and herded into an open area. The badly wounded were set apart from the rest of us.

What happened next was something I will never forget. All the badly wounded GIs, about five of them, were shot as they lay before us. I thought the rest of us were next and I was just shaking. What saved us was a group of Chinese soldiers who had ventured into the village and saw what happened to the wounded GIs. They ordered the North Koreans to stop the killing and took us into their custody. They searched us and took some personal items from the other men but never took anything from me. After a few questions we were then led from the village and marched north.

Somewhere in North Korea

We had nothing to eat the first two days of our march but were given frequent rest stops. The water we were allowed to drink came from the rice paddies and smelled terrible. It didn't matter because we were thirsty. During our breaks the Chinese never stopped their interrogation. Questions about our units were asked but we only gave them our name, rank, and serial number. They repeated the same questions over and over and got the same answer.

Before we started out again, each prisoner was given a 50 pound bag of rice to carry, which was most difficult because we were weak from lack of food and water. At the next village, the group was divided into ten groups of six each. The radio operator, the driver, and I were still together. When we started out again, our armed escorts now numbered only six, one per group of prisoners.

A break was called at this village and we all sprawled on the ground in exhaustion. We had been marching for a couple of weeks now and had no idea where we were. All of us had lost some weight, and as I looked at the men around me, I wondered if I looked like them—thin, ragged, and eyes seemingly not caring. Then I noticed there was another group of prisoners in huts across from where we were.

Fortunately for us, this village had a well with nice, clear water, and we were allowed to drink as much as we wanted. When my turn came, I drank as much as I could until I felt my stomach get bloated. When I was done and turned to go back to my group, I saw this tall, white, skinny, bearded, white-haired old man come out of a hut, making his way to the well. He seemed like he wanted to talk to me, so I waited until he came to me. The universal question that prisoners of war asked each other is what unit they were from, so I asked, "Hey, Pop, what outfit you belong to?"

"Twenty-fourth Division," he said very quietly, almost in a whisper.

"What company?" I asked again.

"I was the commander of the 24th Division," he answered softly, "but you can call me Pop."

I laughed and said, "Yeah, if you are the commander of the 24th Division, then I'm a jet pilot." He burst out laughing and I laughed along with him. He asked what outfit I was from and how I got captured. When I told him that I was from the 5th RCT, his eyes lit up. He said he knew that the 5th RCT was in Hawaii but didn't know that it had arrived in Korea. He was anxious to know what had happened to the 24th Division so I gave him a quick briefing. He was surprised to learn that the 5th RCT had replaced the 34th Infantry in the division. After a few minutes of chatting, he said he had to go and perhaps we would meet again. He said good luck and I wished him the same.

When I rejoined my group I was asked what all the laughing was about. I told them that the guy was nuts because he believed that he was the commander of the 24th Division. When my group gathered to continue our journey, I had a chance to talk to him again before we left. I told him, "Take it easy, Pop."

"You, too, son," he replied.
Much later, our paths would cross again.

MAY 1951

PFC. HISASHI MORITA
Item Company, 23d Infantry
Vicinity of Naepyong-ni, South Korea

Another Chinese offensive almost surrounded our division and had us fighting for our lives. Our company took defensive position on one of the hills while other friendly units withdrew through our position.

During this time I had become good friends with a lieutenant. We had just finished talking and he got up to check on his platoon. I was sitting on the back edge of my foxhole when enemy artillery rounds began falling on our positions. He was about 50 yards away when a shell landed at his feet and blew him away. Before I could drop in my foxhole, an object came hurtling toward me and struck me on the chest. It was a helmet—the lieutenant's helmet. I dropped in the hole, devastated. I knew he had been killed instantly.

We withdrew to another hill farther back that did not have any foxholes. Before we could dig a decent hole, the Chinese unleashed a murderous artillery barrage. I dove behind an uprooted tree trunk for cover. As soon as the enemy artillery lifted, I peeked over the tree trunk down the hill and saw many Chinese advancing up the hill about 100 yards away. We poured rifle and machine gun fire on them but the Chinese wouldn't be stopped.

I started throwing hand grenades when they were 40 yards from my position. Other GIs nearby tossed me their grenades. I felt like a baseball pitcher with several catchers tossing me baseballs. Why they didn't throw the grenades themselves, I never had the opportunity to ask. Anyway, I threw the hand grenades as fast as they were handed to me.

The Chinese kept coming. Several enemy hand grenades burst near me and I felt pain in my right arm and hand. They were bloody when I looked at them. I grabbed a hand grenade with my left hand and tried to pull the pin with my right hand but couldn't do it. I looked up and there was a Chinese soldier with a burp gun pointed straight at me. I still had the grenade in my left hand, which he saw, and it was a wonder he didn't blow my head off. I showed him the grenade with the pin still in. He motioned with his burp gun for me to drop the hand grenade. I looked around and saw only Chinese, no GIs. The Chinese had overrun our positions. I wondered what the hell happened to the rest of my squad.

The date of my capture was May 18, 1951. After surviving several Chinese offensives and UN counteroffensives, my luck finally ran out.

JUNE 1951

SFC. CLARENCE YOUNG
George Company, 5th RCT
Mining Camp, North Korea

It had been a couple months since my capture, and I was sure we were deep in North Korea. We did a lot of walking, losing men along the way, either dying from their wounds or sickness or just left behind because they were unable to walk and were shot by the guards.

While on the trail I met another local boy from Hawaii who was a veteran of World War II who had served with the 442d RCT in Europe. At the time he was very sick with dysentery. We talked a lot and I remember him telling me about his favorite cakes. One day, the guards took him away and that was the last time I saw him. This was standard procedure for the Chinese. If you were sick, badly wounded, and a burden to the rest of the group, you would be taken away. When I got home I visited his family and spoke to his mother and described him to her. "Yes," she said, "that is my son." I told her not to have her hopes up because of the condition he was in.

We finally came to a large camp located in a deep ravine boxed in by high ridges. There were several rows of long, barrack-type buildings. Each contained a number of rooms about 12 feet square. At one end of the barracks there was a small kitchen. In the back of the camp there was a large "L"-shaped building with many rooms. It looked like a school building. We found out later that it was once a school and a mining camp. The entire camp was called "The Mining Camp."

Our meal came once a day made up of soupy rice or millet. The boys from Hawaii were able to stomach this diet, but the haoles could not and refused to eat. Many starved to death.

One of the problems that faced many of the prisoners were thoughts about their families back home and feeling sorry for themselves. Once in that frame of mind, the chances of survival were pretty slim. I was determined not to be caught in that kind of a predicament. I thought the best chance for me to survive was to try to erase my family from my mind. To do that, I had to do out of the ordinary things, crazy things, even at the risk of being killed. But I had one thing going for me. My captors were Chinese, and being Chinese myself, I believed that some leniency might be accorded me.

One day I had my hair cut very short, much like the Chinese guards. That night I snuck to the clothesline where the Chinese guards hung their clothes to dry and stole a pair of pants. The next morning I put on the pants, and barefooted with no shirt, walked past the Chinese guard at the compound gate and went to a village down the road. I was surprised I wasn't stopped by the guard. He must have thought I was one of them or a Korean laborer who worked in the camp.

The Koreans in the village thought that I was one of the Chinese guards. Whenever I ran into a Korean I muttered some Chinese mixed with pidgin, which left them shaking their heads at me. But no one questioned me.

I had some American money. When the Chinese took us away from our Korean captors, I was allowed to keep my money, wrist watch, and rosary. After quite a bit of haggling with the Koreans, I was able to buy some Korean taffy candy, which I later gave to some of the men who were very ill.

Almost every day for two weeks I pulled the same stunt. I bought food until my money ran out. When it did, I began raiding the vegetable garden and fruit orchards in the village during the evening hours for turnips, cabbages, peppers, and apples. I gave whatever I could scrounge to the men who needed it the most. Some of the men gave me money to get food for them.

Finally, the guards wised up. One day I was stopped when I was on my way back from the village and was hauled off to the camp commander. There was no need to explain myself, for I was guilty of every act I was accused of. They took away my Chinese pants and put me in solitary confinement for a week.

When I was released from confinement I was more determined than ever to harass my captors. One day I asked Defontes to distract the guard so I could get into the shack and get some matches. Defontes tried to talk me out of this crazy idea, but I wouldn't listen to him.

The guard was several yards from the guard shack. Defontes went over to the guard and talked to him. When the guard turned his back to talk to Defontes, I quickly and quietly ran into the shack and took a book of matches. I wanted to make things a bit exciting, even to the point of gambling with my life.

There was another village down the road from the prison compound and I wanted to go there and see what it had. From my earlier observations, there didn't seem to be much security between the village and the compound so I decided to visit the village. I asked Defontes to go with me, but he refused. A cook named Shoeberry said that he would go with me. That night, we slipped under the wire and walked to the village.

I knew that many Chinese soldiers slept in the village, so we had to be careful. We came across a hut where Chinese soldiers slept, their shoes left outside the door. We collected about a dozen pairs of shoes and took them to the village well and threw them in. Then I went to another hut, and with the matches I had stolen from the guard shack, lit the straw roof.

Before anyone could see us, Shoeberry and I ran back to the fence, went under the wire, and were back in the prison compound. Briefly, from inside the fence we watched the hut burn while the Chinese soldiers ran around shouting at each other. Then we quickly ran back to our quarters, where I buried the book of matches. It was a good night's work for us. There was an unsuccessful shakedown for matches the next day.

We were told by the guards that a Chinese general was going to visit the camp so we needed to clean up the camp and be on our best behavior. We were all taking a break when the Chinese general arrived. When he approached our group, everyone stood up except me. The other prisoners urged me to stand, but I refused and started to laugh. The general looked down at me and asked the interpreter why I was laughing. The interpreter asked me why I was laughing. "I am proud of my grandmother," I replied.

"Why?" the general asked through his interpreter.

"Because my grandmother was smart enough to leave China when she did," I shot back.

"You know, you act sassy and smart, but if I have the power I will see to it that if and when prisoners are released, you will be the last one to go, or maybe never," he said, with a menacing look.

He ordered the interpreter to lock me up. I was put in a small cell containing only a small stool in the middle of the room and was ordered to sit with my back straight twelve hours a day. I couldn't move the stool to the wall to lean on it because a guard stood in front of me to see that I did as I was told. When I tried to ease my aching back, I would get cuffed across the face by the guard.

What kept me going were the words of encouragement from the other prisoners as they passed my cell on their way to some work detail.

They would say, "How zit going, Young?" When I was let out after two weeks in the cell, I was as white as a sheet. My back hurt like hell. There were prisoners from other UN forces, including Park and Anarita from Hawaii. I estimate there were over a thousand of us in the camp, most of whom were Canadians, British, Australians, and Americans. There were no South Koreans. This was my first permanent POW camp. The camps before this were called "collection camps," where small groups of POWs were sent until there was a sizable number to be sent to a permanent camp.

The commies broke us up into groups of sixty and herded us into a room that measured 20 feet by 20 feet. No one could lie down or sit. We all had to stand, packed like sardines. Later that day we were moved to another building, where we were able to lie down and rest.

Quickly we knew what was going to be in store for us because of the condition of the POWs who had arrived there before us. Many were sick and just skin and bones. As many as forty died a day. A good day was when less than ten died. The diet and the lack of medical supplies contributed to the death rate. Most died from dysentery, an illness all of us dreaded, because once you got it, more than likely death would come after a week. I saw men cough blood and pus, unable to take any food down, lose considerable weight, and die.

We all took turns burying the dead. I must have been on at least 100 burial details. First, we removed the two dog tags. One was given to someone who kept all the dog tag records and the other was jammed between the dead man's teeth. The body was taken outside of the camp to a small valley where large pits were already dug. There was no ceremony. The body was placed in the pit and covered with dirt.

After several weeks at the Mining Camp, we were again divided into many large groups and led northward. Park and Anarita were still with me. We had stopped at a river bank to rest and drink water when this big, haole guy, a sergeant, came down to where we were and gave Park, who was lying next to me, a kick and said, "Move, yobo, move." Park looked up at the haole and was kicked again. So Park slid over and the haole guy slid into the spot where Park had been lying down. So I asked Park why he let the haole guy do that to him. Park murmured something and turned away. I got so angry that I stood up and stepped on the guy's jacket so he couldn't get up and proceeded to kick and punch him, at the same time yelling at him that he couldn't do what he did to Park. He tried to get up, but I kept hitting him until the Chinese guards came running and pulled me off the haole guy. Later, Anarita told me I was one crazy sergeant to take on a big guy like that since I stood only 5 feet 4 inches. I told him that we had to stand up for our rights and not let the haoles push us around.

Several days later, the group was split up again, each taking a different path. We came to a second camp, which already had prisoners. The officers were separated from the enlisted men and we were led to our quarters, which was next to the officers' barracks. In our group were Turks, Britishers, and Americans. This is where I met Richard Makua, another local boy from Hawaii.

Later, one of the officers told me he heard rumors that someone was going to turn me in to the Chinese because I was a Chinese spy for Chiang Kai-shek. He said for me to watch my ass when I was among the Americans. I laughed it off.

It wasn't so funny after I was called by the Chinese interpreter and interrogated for being a spy for the Chinese Nationalist government. I told him I was an American soldier and showed him my dog tags. "No! No!" he said, "How come you fight against your motherland?"

"What do you mean, my motherland? China is not my motherland. America is my motherland. I am an American," I answered.

No matter what I said, he wouldn't believe me. I was kept in isolation in a very small room for over a week and a half without any sleep, and was grilled and beaten constantly. I was so tired that at one point I didn't give a damn what they did to me. Finally, they gave up on me, or so I thought, and returned me to my quarters.

The next day the entire camp was called out for formation, officers and enlisted men alike. I was called to the front and center by the interpreter. I guess he wanted to make an example of me. With everyone watching and listening, I was asked by the interpreter, "You are Chinese. Why are you fighting against your motherland?"

"Red China is not my motherland. Uncle Sam is my motherland!" I answered in a loud voice.

"Get back in the ranks," ordered the interpreter. He thought he had broken me.

Those prisoners who heard me cheered and clapped.

It was in this camp that the Chinese stepped up their propaganda program by enticing prisoners with wine and cigarettes to pose for their cameraman. Some accepted the invitation. They would lie in their beds with Chinese guards feeding them or pretending to receive medical treatment with Red Cross banners in the background. They were warned by other prisoners not to cooperate with the Chinese.

JUNE 1951

CPL. GARY HASHIMOTO
Baker Company, 32d Infantry
Vicinity of Hwachon Reservoir, North Korea

We went on the offensive again to regain the ground we had lost in April. We fought past the Hwachon Reservoir and took several hills west of Kumhwa. A lot of the fighting took place at night. We would dig in, set up booby traps, and wait for the enemy to attack in the early morning hours. I recall a replacement who arrived at dusk. He had dug in and was found dead in the morning from knife wounds. I never even got to know his name. He couldn't stay awake and it cost him his life.

We stayed in the same vicinity until June 23, when we were relieved by the 24th Division and went into corps reserve for a rest at Aegi-kogae.

JUNE 1951

SGT. IRWIN COCKETT
Dog Company, 5th RCT
Pukhan Valley, South Korea

I received my orders with others to rotate home but the army grudgingly let us go. We were offered promotions if we would extend our tour of duty for a couple of months because the 5th RCT was very short of men.

A few took the offer, like Sgt. Reginald Nash, who later came home a master sergeant. I thought the rank of staff sergeant was pretty high, so I declined the offer.

I remember reading somewhere that for the first time since World War II men were being drafted in the United States. It would be a while before they got to Korea.

Camp Drake, Japan

We got to Sasebo, Japan, by ship, then by train to Camp Drake, where we were processed. Transportation home was not readily available so we took advantage of that and raised hell in Tokyo for a few days. When we ran out of money we sold our spare GI clothes and went back

152 A FOXHOLE VIEW

to Tokyo. Now we had no money and no clothes. We went to the quartermaster and gave the clerk a cock and bull story why we didn't have our clothes. He gave us another set of clothing only because we were Korean War veterans and he felt sorry for us.

Our good times ended in Japan when we were put on a train to Sasebo for a boat ride home. It seemed strange that the port of Yokohama was only a few miles from Camp Drake, yet we had to travel nearly 400 miles by train for our transportation home. But, at least, we were finally on our way home.

There were a couple of hundred local boys on the ship plus several crates of caskets of KIAs in the hold below. Two days out of Honolulu, one of the boys fiddled with the radio dial of his shortwave radio and happened to tune in to a Hawaii radio station playing Hawaiian music. It was "Hawaii Calls," a popular radio program in Hawaii. You should have seen us, veterans of many battles in Korea, break down emotionally. It was something.

When we pulled into Honolulu Harbor there was a crowd waiting at the pier. A band played and our families were waiting for us under the large, posted letters of our last names. My family wasn't hard to find and it was a joyous reunion. I went home to Kauai on a thirty-day leave.

My grandfather lived on a large piece of property, and on this land there was a very steep hill. Whenever I thought about home when I was in Korea, I told myself that should I ever get home in one piece, I was going to climb that hill. I made the climb, and when I stood at the top of the hill and looked down, I couldn't believe that I was really home.

The next morning the entire family met for breakfast at my grandfather's. Nearby, there was a road that huge trucks used to transport harvested sugarcane to the mill for processing. While we were having breakfast, a truck went past and backfired with a tremendous bang. Instinctively, I dove under the table. After a few seconds, I sheepishly got up, trembling a little. When I looked around I saw several members of the family quietly sobbing. It took a little while to explain my action.

JUNE 1951

Cpl. Bertram Sebresos
Baker Company, 7th Infantry
Vicinity of Kumwha, North Korea

When the company commander heard that I hadn't gone on R&R, he was surprised and told me I would be on the next rotation list home.

When the time came to leave, Pfc. Leroy Mendonca from Honolulu, who was in another platoon, also boarded the truck. He was on his way to Japan on R&R. He had grown a beard. On the way to Kimpo Airfield I told Mendonca to be very careful and he would make it home like me. That was the last time I saw Mendonca.

JULY 1951

PVT. JOHN IWAMOTO
Love Company, 23d Infantry
Vicinity of Punchbowl, North Korea

I was twenty-one years old, working as a carpenter on Kauai, when I was drafted and sent to Schofield Barracks, Hawaii, for my sixteen weeks of army basic training. We were given two weeks of furlough before shipping out to the Far East. We heard that a Hawaii unit, the 5th RCT, was already in combat in Korea and we requested that we be assigned to that unit. The request was denied.

There were sixty of us from Hawaii who flew to Japan and spent a couple of days at Camp Drake, where we were issued rifles and given a quick orientation and unit assignments. The 23d Infantry, 2d Infantry Division got all the Hawaii boys. Thirty were assigned to the 1st Battalion and the other thirty to the 3d Battalion. My specific unit was Love Company of the 3d Battalion.

From Sasebo, Japan, we sailed to Pusan, South Korea, and by train and truck we joined Love Company somewhere in the Punchbowl area near the east coast of North Korea just above the 38th parallel. I was happy to see that there were other Hawaii guys in the company like Platoon Sergeant Herbert Sun, Glennwood Medeiros, Kalama, and Ito. I was assigned the BAR in a rifle squad in Sergeant Sun's platoon. The BAR was almost as tall as me and weighed over 20 pounds when fully loaded.

JULY 1951

CPL. BERTRAM SEBRESOS
Camp Drake, Japan

I was surprised to get a letter from one of my buddies, Pancho, who was still with the company in Korea. Rarely does one get a letter while in transit. When I read the letter, I wished that I had received it at home, instead of at Camp Drake.

Leroy Mendonca was killed in action on July 4 while covering the withdrawal of his platoon.

PFC. HISASHI MORITA
Item Company, 23d Infantry
Somewhere in North Korea

The maggots got to my wound before the Chinese doctors did. They told me maggots cleansed the wound.

A couple of months after my capture, another group of POWs joined us. Among them were two Hawaii men, Clarence Young and Joseph Park.

We were never put in a permanent POW camp but, instead, were marched to every point of the compass and, from what we were able to determine, even in circles.

Before Young and Park joined us, I had attempted three solo escapes, each unsuccessful. I was beaten every time I was brought back to camp. But that didn't dampen my desire to escape.

We had stopped at a village for the night to rest and had taken shelter in one of the houses where a farmer and his daughter lived. Young, Park, and I were able to convince the daughter to hide us in the attic until morning, which she did. We had hoped that the guards wouldn't miss us when the prisoners were formed in the morning for the march.

The next morning, however, the guards yelled at us to come down from the attic or be shot on the spot. We came down from the attic, expecting to be shot in front of the others as an example. Instead, we were clubbed and beaten.

It was passed down to us later that the girl's father had turned us in because he had feared for his daughter's life if the guards had found out that she had tried to help us escape. Who could blame him?

PFC. SUSUMU SHINAGAWA
Able Company, 34th Infantry
Andong, North Korea

An English-speaking North Korean security police officer told us that truce talks were going to take place. I thought that it was just a ploy to raise our hopes and later squash them to break us psychologically. There were rumors that our group was going to be turned over to the Chinese and taken across the Yalu River and be released. This information perked us up again and rumors began to circulate throughout the camp. The rumors were half true. We were transferred to the Chinese but no one was released.

AUGUST 1951

PFC. JOHN IWAMOTO
Love Company, 23d Infantry
Vicinity of Bloody Ridge, North Korea

I had not tasted combat yet. Our activities were limited to patrolling the valley between our hilltop position and Bloody Ridge, which the enemy occupied. One day I finally caught a glimpse of the enemy on Bloody Ridge several hundred yards away. At that distance I could only make out figures moving about in the trench line.

Our battalion then moved a few miles west to lend support to the 9th Infantry in their efforts to secure the Bloody Ridge hill complex. A ROK division had taken the hill earlier but lost it after the North Koreans counterattacked. The 9th Infantry now had the job of retaking the hill from the North Koreans.

I thought that our regiment was going to counterattack since the 9th got its nose bloodied, but it was ordered to regroup and retake the hill it had just lost. Fighter bombers appeared and they napalmed, rocketed, and strafed the hillside of Bloody Ridge while we watched. When the fighter bombers had done their job, our artillery took over and pounded whatever the planes missed. I thought no one could live through that pounding. When the artillery lifted its fire, the entire hill mass was covered with a thick layer of dust and smoke, some of which drifted over to our position. We could smell the powder and thick dust. When it cleared, the hill was even more scarred and dusty. I could make out tree stumps and felled trees and shell and bomb craters.

While the hill was being bombed and shelled, the 9th Infantry had worked its way down to the valley and the bottom of hill to wait for the support fire to end. Finally, the 9th moved out and began scaling the hill to take the three knobs it had lost the day before.

We had a grandstand seat and we watched with amazement from less than 400 yards away on a ridge line as the men of the 9th Infantry charged up the hill. I saw dust kicked up by small arms fire and when a few men reached the enemy bunkers they were greeted with grenades and the rapid fire of the North Koreans' automatic burp guns. They never made it to the top, and when dusk came, the men of 9th Infantry backed halfway down the hill and dug in. For several days and nights pitch battles were fought on the hill until it was finally taken from the North Koreans.

Under enemy artillery fire, our regiment relieved the battered 9th Infantry on Bloody Ridge. The survivors were damn happy to get off the hill, and I couldn't blame them at all because they had taken such a terrible beating. It was on this hill that I first experienced the smell of death. Rosa, a buddy of mine from Hawaii, jumped into the first foxhole he saw when we got to the top of the hill. He barely missed jumping on a dead GI in the hole. I jumped into another foxhole and when I hit the bottom of the hole there was a squishy sound. I scraped the dirt with my boot and found a dead North Korean buried in the hole.

There were many dead North Koreans and a few dead Americans, some out in the open and some partly buried. Our graves registration personnel had a tremendous task taking care of our dead. When we could, we simply threw dead North Koreans into holes, sprinkled them with lye, and covered them with a thin layer of dirt. Because the battle for the hill took several days, the North Koreans killed in the first day of battle had turned color and had begun to smell.

We had to endure the stench of the dead for many days on Bloody Ridge. I came across a dead North Korean laying on a potato masher grenade. I didn't want to pull the grenade from under his back for fear that it might be a booby trap. I threw some lye on him and that was a mistake. All the maggots started to come out the wounds and cavities. I covered him up with rocks as best as I could. I also came across a bunker that was caved in, probably from a bomb or artillery shell, with some bodies in it. I couldn't tell whether they were the enemy's or ours. We told the graves registration people to check them out. They found two bodies of Americans. We wrapped them up in ponchos and carried them to the bottom of the hill.

AUGUST 1951

PVT. ELGEN FUJIMOTO
20th Training Battalion, HITC
Schofield Barracks, Territory of Hawaii

I was inducted into the army on August 29, 1951, and took basic training at the Hawaiian Infantry Training Center at Schofield Barracks with the

20th Training Battalion, which was made up of local and mainland recruits. The battalion before us, the 10th, was made up of only local boys. When we saw them in the field, they were always walking or running. Our battalion took advantage of the transportation made available.

The training officers in our company were First Lieutenant Fujii, the commanding officer, Second Lieutenant Watanabe, and Second Lieutenant Suzuki. The latter two were freshly commissioned officers out of the University of Hawaii ROTC program. Most of the NCOs were Korean War veterans who saw combat in the early stages of the war.

AUGUST 1951

Cpl. Gary Hashimoto
Baker Company, 32d Infantry
Vicinity of Tari-dong, North Korea

The days in late August were hot and humid. Our company was ordered to take Hill 567, a piece of high ground or ridge that was to be used as a patrol base. At 0600 hours we moved out and made contact with the enemy halfway up the ridge. We had underestimated their strength. They must have had at least a dozen machine guns on the ridge and l iterally swept the slopes with a wall of bullets. I was lucky to be near a shell crater and dove for it. I must have been 100 yards from the crest of the ridge.

I tried to fire but couldn't even raise my head because of the intense enemy fire. Barrages of enemy hand grenades now came flying down from the top but burst well short of me. It must have been like this for almost half an hour; I was curled up and tried to make my body as small as possible. Then someone flopped into the crater and shouted that we were going to withdraw to the bottom of hill. He said to take off when I could. He crawled out of the crater to pass the word on to the other men. He was one brave son of a gun.

When enemy fire subsided a bit I leaped out from the crater and ran like crazy to the bottom of the ridge and took cover behind a rice paddy dike where other men were assembled. We dug in for the night.

The next morning we continued the attack after artillery and air strikes pounded the ridge for about half an hour. Again, it was a repeat of the first day, but this time we were able to gain a foothold on the ridge.

The enemy were still in well-fortified bunkers, despite the heavy concentration of artillery, air strikes, and rockets before the attack. The enemy refused to give ground.

It was a ping pong battle for ten days for the ridge, sharing it with the enemy. The bunkers had to be taken one by one. The BARs would put down a heavy cover fire to keep enemy heads down while one of us would get close enough to flip grenades into the bunker openings. We flushed them out of bunkers and they would come right back and take them away from us. It was the most bitter fighting I had ever been through.

AUGUST 1951

SFC. CLARENCE YOUNG
George Company, 5th RCT
Somewhere in North Korea

It was time for another trip, this time, to the northeast to a place called Pyoktong or Camp 5 in an inlet just off the Yalu River, the boundary between North Korea and Manchuria.

We stopped to rest one day and met six officers who were also being marched to Camp 5. As we talked for a while, Major Scott, an air force pilot, asked if we were planning an escape and if we could include them in it. I had been thinking of an escape for that very night. I told him that tonight I was going to make an attempt and he and the other officers were welcome to join me.

That night, the guards, who were just as tired as we were, were not very alert so the seven of us managed to sneak away into the hills. It was dark and we stumbled around. We came to a village and managed to sneak in and steal some food and went back into the hills. For four days we wandered in the hills, not knowing which way to go because once in the high North Korean mountains we lost all sense of direction.

It was late summer so it wasn't cold, but at night it got a little chilly without warm clothing. One clear night I looked up at the sky to see if I could locate the Big Dipper, but there were so many stars I couldn't see it. The air force major tried to read the stars to give us direction but was unsuccessful.

After some discussion we all agreed where south was and headed in that direction. We came upon a single Korean house in a small draw and stopped to decide what to do. It was still dark. While we were discussing our plans, a man came out of the house and saw us. I immediately pretended I was a Chinese guard, gave orders to the officers in my best Chinese, and marched them past the man down the trail.

But farther down the trail, we suddenly came upon a single Chinese soldier armed with a rifle slung over his soldier. Apparently, the Chinese thought I was a Korean in charge of American prisoners and stopped us to talk. Without saying one word, we jumped the Chinese soldier and one of the officers strangled him with his bare hands. We put his body in the underbrush and covered him with branches. One of the officers suggested that I put on the Chinese uniform and, like a damn fool, I did.

Armed with a weapon, we went back into the hills for the night. The next morning we saw a house in the valley below us. We needed food and water and decided to take a chance and see if there was anyone friendly living there. A Korean greeted us and I was able to convince him that I had prisoners that had to be taken south, but first we needed food and water and some rest. I told him that I needed some sleep. I asked if he could guard my prisoners while I rested and, if anyone tried to escape, to shoot him. I told the officers of my plan and for them to get some sleep and not do anything which might provoke the Korean. The plan worked and we slept until mid-morning.

I thanked the Korean for his hospitality and marched the officers down the trail. That afternoon we came upon a large town. There was no way to go around it. We decided to march through the town continuing our charade. The plan was for the officers to walk with their hands above their heads and I would be chewing them out as we went along. Some of the townspeople came out and did what I didn't expect. They threw rocks at the officers. A Korean soldier came to us and began speaking to me. I told the officers to continue walking while I answered the Korean in gibberish language. After several yards the Korean became frustrated, stopped, and watched us march by. There were no further incidents and eventually we came to the edge of town and followed a dirt road. About a mile from town we stopped to see if any of the men had been badly injured in the rock-throwing incident. Fortunately, there were only minor bruises.

Late that night we came to a small village. We still were not sure if we were heading in the right direction. For all we knew, we might be heading north again. We decided to take a chance and entered the village. Wrong move! Before we could act, we were surrounded by Chinese troops and had to surrender. I think the Korean soldier at the village was suspicious of us and alerted the Chinese. I was separated from the officers. That was the last time I saw the officers and never found out what became of them. I don't know how many miles we had traveled or in what direction we were heading.

I was not sent to Camp 5 but to another camp near the Yalu River where only enlisted men were held prisoners. I was put in solitary confinement for two weeks with little food and water. I think my stub-bornness kept me alive. After I was released I met other Hawaii guys like Sgt. Alberto Verano, Sfc. Joseph Tupa, and Hirano. I was the only Chinese American in the camp.

We were kept busy. The detail I was on was a back-breaking job. We carried huge logs from the Yalu River bank to a lumber mill. These logs were freshly cut and it took four of us to carry one. There was also the wood detail sent into the forests with hatchets to cut wood to store for the winter months. This hard work kept us in shape and forced us to eat all the meager rations and terrible food.

Along the Yalu River, North Korea

It wasn't so bad for me because I was a happy-go-lucky person and avoided thinking of my family as much as possible. To get them off my mind I did crazy things to raise the morale of the men. For instance, I would lie and tell several guys that it was the birthday of one of the men and they would get straw brooms and chase and beat the backside of the "birthday boy." One day they got even with me and told everybody that it was my birthday and had me running for my life all day long.

Other prisoners talked of escaping and I thought of breaking out for the second time, but this time it was going to be better planned than my first try.

There were eight of us in the escape group, I being the lone GI from Hawaii. The plan was to get on work details to the river as often as we could so that we would be familiar with the route at night. Once we got out of the prison compound, we would head north, swim the Yalu River into Manchuria, and try to get to the Yellow Sea to the west. On the coast we would steal a fishing boat and sail out to sea and down the west coast of Korea. For food we would take turnips, the only food item that was plentiful, although we hated it. Getting past the guards was another problem because there were two security fences manned twenty-four hours a day and, beyond that, minefields. Although it was a sketchy plan, we were desperate enough to try it.

We chose a moonless night and, with our meager food supply, left our quarters and slipped under the wires of the two fences without being detected. We sprinted across the minefield, somehow avoiding the mines. So far so good. No alarm was given at the camp.

The Yalu was quite calm when we reached it. The river flowed east to west into the Yellow Sea. From our infrequent visits to the banks of the Yalu to do our laundry or gather wood, we had guessed that the river was approximately 200 to 300 yards wide. The problem was we hardly swam to condition ourselves for the swim across the Yalu. Also, we didn't know the speed of the current and how far we were from the coast. We were hoping that the current would take us across to the north bank.

We got into the water and started to swim to the other side of the river. The first 100 yards or so were pretty easy but as we approached the middle of the river, the current was really swift, preventing us from making any headway toward the north bank. The current just carried us downriver. I looked around and saw only two or three still with me. I lost the others in the dark. I realized that we weren't going to make it across and now had to save our asses from drowning.

I don't know if the others heard me or not but I yelled to them to get back to the south bank or let the current take its course and hope that it would deposit us safely somewhere downriver. I turned around and started stroking to the south bank. Once I got out of the middle of the river I was all right. I was so damn tired I rolled on my back and tried floating downriver. I yelled for the others and I remember only one other person answered my call. I wondered if the others had drowned.

I needed a reference on land so I would have some kind of direction but it was too dark. There were no lights for me to focus on.

I don't know how far the river took me but it must have been miles. I finally stumbled into shallow water and practically crawled to the river bank, where I flopped and passed out from exhaustion.

Someone kicked me in the ribs. A stream of profanity came from my mouth but when I looked up, I was staring at the muzzle of a burp gun. I shut my mouth. The Chinese motioned with the gun for me to get up. I looked up at the sky and saw the sun high up. It must have been noon.

I finally was able to see clearly. A Chinese four-man patrol had my buddies tied up with their hands behind their backs. There were six of them. One was missing. Seven of us survived the escape attempt.

It was nearly dark when we got to camp, which indicated that we had gone pretty far down the river. We were all put in solitary confinement for a week.

SEPTEMBER 1951

PFC. HISASHI MORITA
Item Company, 23d Infantry
Somewhere in North Korea

We were being led north when another GI and I decided to escape. The nights were dark and we thought we'd seize this great opportunity to escape. We agreed that if one of us was successful in getting away and got back to the States, he would contact the parents and tell them one of us was still alive. At the time I believed we were still listed as Missing in Action.

There was nothing complicated about our escape plan. When the opportunity presented itself, we were taking it. It came a few nights later when we were walking on a narrow dike in a rice paddy and had to single-file our way across. Because of my previous attempted escapes, I was watched very carefully. At one point one of the guards had me by the back of my collar with his hand.

The quiet night was broken by screaming artillery shells in the valley, which drew the attention of the guards. I shoved my buddy, who was in front of me, into the rice paddy. The noise and the confusion created by the artillery prevented the guards from seeing or hearing my buddy splash into the rice paddy. There were no shots fired by the guards so I assumed the GI had gotten away. However, I lost my chance to get away, as the guards recovered from the confusion.

SEPTEMBER 1951

PVT. JOHN IWAMOTO
Love Company, 23d Infantry
Bloody Ridge, North Korea

We moved out to take a connecting ridge that ran between Hills 983 and 778. Although friendly forces occupied both hills, the North Koreans refused to give up the ridge.

I was standing next to a bunker when bullets struck the bunker and the slope around us. The platoon radio man, who was about 10 feet from me, fell. A .50 caliber slug got him and he died on the spot. Shimomura, from Hawaii, took the radio off him, put it on his back, and became the radio man for the platoon.

We continued up the hill until we came to a shallow shell crater and took cover in it. It was about 40 yards below an enemy bunker and the trenches. Our platoon leader, Lieutenant Woods, who preferred to be called Woody, was in another shell hole about 5 yards away. Above the noise of small arms fire, he yelled to me to tell the men to straighten out the pins of their grenades before we made the dash for the trench. This would make it easy for us to pull the pins and arm the grenades because sometimes the end of the pins were bent too sharply, making it harder to pull them out. That was dangerous because if the ring of the pin got snagged, I would have had it. "Tough shit," someone answered.

Lieutenant Woods yelled, "Go!" so we leaped out of the shell crater and made a zigzag dash for the trench line. By this time Lieutenant Woods and I had converged just below the trench line. I threw a hand grenade as hard as I could up the hill into the trench. Woody and the others did the same and there was a series of explosions. When I got to the edge of the trench, a North Korean came crawling out of a bunker. I fired a short burst from my BAR that caught him in the head. All I saw were smoke and brains. I turned and saw Woody on the top side of the trench. A concussion grenade bounced off his helmet and fell in the trench and exploded. Another landed at his feet but he kicked it off to one side and it exploded harmlessly a few yards from him. "Are you all right?" I yelled at him. He nodded and asked if my side of the hill was secure.

"Shit, no!" I shouted. At that moment from one of the bunkers came a North Korean who threw two hand grenades at me and ducked back into the bunker. Lucky for me they were the small concussion type and his aim was bad because only one came close and exploded. It just threw up a lot of dust. "You fucking son-of-a-bitch," I screamed. One of the grenades I carried was a white phosphorous grenade, which we often used as markers for our tanks and recoilless rifle crews. We called them Willie Peter grenades.

We decided to mark this particular bunker for the guys with flame throwers so I asked my assistant BAR man to cover me while I made my way to the bunker's entrance. I pulled the pin and held onto the spoon. Near the door I released the spoon, held the grenade for about two seconds, tossed it into the bunker, and took off. The Willie Peter went off with a muffled pop, and soon white-gray smoke came out from every opening of the bunker. Woody yelled for us to put some distance between the bunker and us because he suddenly remembered that the Willie Peters were also markers for our tanks and recoilless rifle crews.

We continued moving up the hill until I saw Shimomura, our radio man, standing ahead of us, watching us coming up. I yelled to him, "What are you doing, standing on the hill like a big ass bird? You want to get your head blown off?"

"No, battalion's calling. They want us to pull back."

"Don't tell me, tell Woody," I shot back. Pulling back or not, we had to be careful because there were still North Koreans on the hill and on another dominating knoll nearby. I told Yoshio Nakamura from Kaneohe, Hawaii, to get into in a hole that faced the other knoll, which was about 300 yards away. Many North Koreans came running from this knoll in our direction. I told Naka (short for Nakamura) to make sure that they didn't reach us. Meanwhile, Sekigawa from Hawaii and a haole

GI got into another hole next to Nakamura. The next instant, I heard a tremendous explosion and I was showered with dirt. When the dust and smoke cleared, I saw that a round of some kind had burst between Sekigawa's and Naka's holes. I rushed to Sekigawa and saw him and the haole crumpled in the hole. I called for a medic. I then rushed to Naka's hole and found him bleeding from his nose and mouth. He was hit pretty badly. "You're hit, Naka! You don't have a leg," I cried out.

"I know, Angel," he answered weakly. Angel was my nickname.

I got into the hole with him. I made a tourniquet from an empty bandoleer and tied it above his knee. While this was happening, we were still under enemy small arms and mortar fire. A medic came over and gave Naka a shot of morphine. He then went to Sekigawa's hole and found him badly wounded and the haole dead.

A haole by the name of Red, who was not badly injured, ordered the medic to take him off the hill. When I heard that, I told Red, "You get off the hill yourself. He's taking care of my buddy, Naka!" After the medic had tended to Naka, I told Naka that we had to get him off the hill as fast as we could because he was losing a lot of blood. Somehow, I was going to have to carry him myself but to do that, I had to have the use of both hands because I couldn't carry him and hang on to the rifle at the same time. To free my hands, I took off the trigger housing group from both our weapons and threw them as far as I could, making our weapons useless to the enemy, and left them in the hole.

One thing about Naka—he never cried out in pain. With his two arms around my neck and using his one good leg, we struggled down the hill. He muttered, "Leave me."

"If I leave you, I'll have to stay behind with you anyway, and we both might get killed," I said. Fortunately, at the time, the other men had received the orders to pull back and we were overtaken by them. I got three other guys to help me and we just picked him up by his shoulders and one good leg and carried him off the hill. We found a stretcher at the bottom and put him and a couple of others on a tank. The tank commander told us to jump on the tank since there was no need for us to remain there.

Vicinity of Bloody Ridge, North Korea

After Bloody Ridge, our unit was sent to an assembly area a mile behind the MLR for a couple of days to regroup and pick up replacements. Even after replacements our company was still not up to strength.

There were men who didn't belong on line. They were sent to the rear and assigned less hazardous jobs. We couldn't rely on them even if we wanted to. We needed men we could depend on, knowing that when it was their turn to pull watch at night, we could sleep without worrying. But I don't recall a single local boy from Hawaii who had to be removed from the line because he couldn't hack it. We had too much pride and also, we had to carry on the tradition of Hawaii's famed 442d RCT and 100th Battalion of World War II.

While in reserve I was surprised to see Yamane from Kauai in our company area. I was surprised because he was with a rear echelon unit when I last saw him. Naturally, I was happy seeing him because we came from the same island. "What the hell are you doing here?" I asked him.

"I volunteered for frontline duty so I can rotate home faster," was his answer. Yamane was willing to take a gamble with his life for a quick trip home.

Vicinity of Heartbreak Ridge, North Korea

I was now an assistant squad leader. We finally got word that we would be on the move again to take a hill mass just north of Bloody Ridge, a hill mass that was to be named Heartbreak Ridge during the battle for the ridge. Our company's objective was Hill 931, the midway point of the hill mass. To get to the hill we had to cross the Satae-ri Valley and move up the several spurs that led to Hill 931. Tanks were to support us from the valley.

Our squad was given the job of reconnoitering the route the battalion was to take and to find a suitable line of departure for the assaulting companies. There were four Hawaii men in the squad, Sgt. Herbert Sun, Glenwood Medeiros, another person whose name I cannot remember, and me. It was past noon when we left the assembly area. It took us all afternoon to finally find the place where Sergeant Sun had determined and located the line of departure and the finger ridge we were to climb to get to Hill 931. He marked the spot on the map. We then pulled back a couple of hundred yards to better cover.

It was going to get dark in an hour. Sergeant Sun asked for a volunteer to return to the assembly area to lead the battalion to where we were. I had that strange feeling that I was going to be "volunteered." Sure enough, someone whispered, "Angel, come over here!" I recognized Medeiros' voice in the dark. I was nicknamed Angel after a professional wrestler in Honolulu. The wrestler was a good one, but an ugly one. One of my friends, then, named me Angel, and when I asked why he said that I was the ugliest of the guys in the gang I ran around with. Anyway, I pretended not to hear and tried to be as quiet as I possibly could.

"Angel! Angel!" Medeiros again whispered. I played deaf. "Angel, god damn it! I know you're here!"

"What you like?" I finally answered. And before he could answer I said, "I know what you want. You want me to go and get the battalion."

"I didn't choose you. Sergeant Sun did!"

I was pissed and showed it. I took off my pack and the three bandoleers of ammo and threw them on the ground but hung on to my M-1 rifle.

"No act la dat," a voice hissed in the dark.

When I left the squad, it was still light. I retraced the route we took down to the valley floor, up the ridge, and to the perimeter of the assembly area where the units were waiting. It was now dark. I had a feeling I was near one of our listening posts and I didn't want to get shot by one of our men so I took a chance and whispered, "Eh, you Hawaiians there?"

"Who dat?" came the reply.

"Me, Angel."

"You damn son-of-a-bitch, I almost blew you away! Come on in," called Alfred Machado, of Honolulu. He said to be quiet and listen. I could hear water canteens rattling, apparently being filled from a nearby stream. We also knew that the French battalion was near the vicinity so I called out in my best French, "Parle vous France." The noises stopped immediately. *Shit*, I thought to myself. There were still North Koreans trapped behind our lines and the noise we heard could have been them.

I told Machado that I was to guide the battalion to the line of departure but he told me to wait at the listening post and he would bring the battalion to me. After a long while I could hear swearing and a lot of noise as they approached the listening post. If there were North Koreans in the area I was sure they heard us, too. Imagine, an entire battalion tramping in the dark and I was leading them.

It was way past midnight when we got to the place where I had left the squad. How I was able to find the same spot I'll never know. Only two men from the squad were there along with two other men from another unit. The others had already gone to the jump-off area.

As we walked down the ridge into the valley, I imagined thousands of Koreans watching us. We finally reached the line of departure about 0500 hours. It was a large wooded area at the base of a spiny spur. In the gray morning light we could see the ridge mass across the valley.

The platoon leader called the platoon together and gave us the attack order. We were to cross the valley at double time and climb the finger ridge that led to Hill 931. The ridge appeared to be quite steep and about half a mile long. From where we were, it seemed like it was 2 miles long. It was wooded so it offered us some cover.

Our platoon took the lead and I was the point man of the squad. Somehow, I always got picked to be the point man. We crossed the valley with only a few enemy mortar rounds to harass us and made it to the base of the ridge without any difficulty. With the rest of the squad behind me, I proceeded to climb up the wooded ridge. About a quarter of the way up, enemy mortar rounds began falling in the middle of the company. The rounds burst as they hit the treetops first, creating air bursts and showering the company with shrapnel. My natural instinct was to hit the ground and stay there until the mortar bombardment was over. Fortunately for my squad, the rounds were falling in back of us. "Get moving," a voice yelled from the back. I picked myself up, as did the others, and began to move quickly forward again. The North Korean mortars stopped. I looked back through the trees and saw the platoon following, but there weren't as many men as when we started. It appeared that enemy mortars had caused a few casualties.

The climb was much steeper now and our tanks, artillery, and mortars were plastering the hill ahead of us. There was still no sign of the enemy. When we started out, Muramoto, Machado, and Arnold were right behind me. They were still with me but I couldn't see the rest of the squad. We continued to climb anyway. Looking back through the break in the trees, I could see the valley floor below me and realized that we were at least more than halfway up the ridge. Man, it was hot, even under the shade of the trees. I found out later that the heat caused more casualties than the enemy mortar rounds.

I slung my M-1 rifle on my shoulder because I needed both hands to claw and grab bushes and branches to climb. I was huffing and puffing with my load of four hand grenades, three bandoleers of ammo, a cartridge belt full of ammo, and a full canteen of water. The heat made it even worse. If I ran into a North Korean, I wouldn't have time to unsling my rifle and get off a round. Whoever picked this route for the attack must have been crazy. But I kept going until I stopped for a second to catch my breath behind a tree.

I was soaked with sweat. My eyes burned from the salty sweat that got into them so I wiped them off with my sleeve. When my eyes cleared, I looked up from under the rim of my helmet and focused 50 yards up the hill and to the right. Something just didn't seem right. I then noticed a well-camouflaged bunker. I dropped quietly but quickly to the ground. Machado, who was right in back of me, pulled on my pant leg to find out what was up. I slowly turned around, put one finger to my lips, and motioned him to come abreast of me. "Look what's in front of us," I whispered, and with my finger, pointed very carefully in the direction of the bunker. I slowly started to raise myself up.

"Stay down," Machado hissed. About this time the rest of the platoon had almost caught up with us and was about 100 yards behind us. We couldn't see them but we sure could hear them.

I thought it would take more than the four of us to seize the bunker, so we decided to wait and warn the platoon. I whispered to the men down the trail to pass onward to the platoon leader that there was a bunker up ahead. I imagined that a bunker like that must have a machine gun. I wanted a better look at it so I slowly inched myself to the left of the tree and rolled into a slight depression about 3 yards to the left of Machado. Arnold and Muramoto were about 5 yards behind us. I turned to Muramoto and told him, "I ain't going to take that bunker, shit, man!"

So we just played it cool until the platoon caught up and we warned them of the bunker ahead. My BAR man, Wilson, a recent replacement, crawled up to me and asked where I wanted him to be. I told him to take his assistant BAR man and set up the BAR behind a tree about 10 yards to my left for covering fire. Instead of crawling, they both jumped up and ran to the tree. They almost made it. They were about three steps to the tree when a long machine gun burst from the bunker cut both of them down. Wilson never moved. The assistant BAR man tried to get to the tree. I yelled to him, "Don't move. Play dead. Otherwise they are going to finish you off." The North Koreans heard me and fired a burst in my direction. A concussion grenade came flying and exploded near the feet of the assistant BAR man. Wounded as he was, he got up and made it to the tree. The North Koreans fired again at the assistant BAR man but missed.

During this time not one of us fired at the bunker. Then several grenades came from the bunker. One landed on my combat pack and exploded. Lucky for me it was a small concussion grenade, which knocked my breath out of me for a few seconds. Then all was quiet and we just lay there, not doing anything for five minutes, waiting for one of us to do something. Finally, out of the bunker came a North Korean with a burp gun in his hands, apparently to survey the results of his firing. He stood in full view on the side of the bunker, confident that he had killed every one of us. I quickly raised my rifle and snapped off a couple of shots. He fell forward and rolled several yards below the bunker. That must have gotten the North Koreans in the bunker mad because their machine gun just unloaded on me for about a full minute. Bullets were flying every which way, thudding into trees, clipping branches, and kicking up dirt all around me. The depression I was in was not deep enough and I tried to squeeze my entire body into my steel helmet. One round caught me in the lower left leg and I cried out, "I'm hit, you son-of-a-bitch."

"I'm hit, too," Muramoto yelled.

"Where?" I yelled back.

"In the fucking shoulder," he shouted.

The North Korean machine gun continued firing, sweeping the area, and the bullets came awfully close once again to where I was but the small depression I was in saved my ass.

"Shit! I can't stay here. This place is too damn dangerous," I yelled to nobody in particular. But at the same time I couldn't move because the North Koreans continued to fire short bursts in my direction. All I could do was to make myself into as small a ball as possible and hug the dirt.

After considering my injury for a few seconds, I said to myself, "Fuck this shit," and rolled out of the hole and dove downhill, rolling and crawling as fast as I could, not favoring my injured leg. I passed some of the guys in my squad. I could hear the chatter of the North Korean machine gun but whether he was still trying to get me I couldn't tell. I came to a stop only when Maldonado grabbed me and dragged me behind a tree. How far down I rolled I don't know, but when I looked back up the hill I couldn't tell where I had been moments ago, nor could I see Muramoto and Machado where I had left them.

I can't remember if the platoon tried to take the bunker. The platoon medic came to me and dressed my wound, which wasn't as bad as I thought it was because the bullet did not hit any bone and had gone through the fleshy part of my calf. I limped farther down the hill and sat down at the collection point for the casualties. A couple of hours later, Muramoto joined me. The first thing he said to me was, "If you hadn't shot the commie, we wouldn't have gotten shot."

"Bullshit," I said. "They would have wiped out the entire platoon."

I asked him how he got here and he said after I rolled down the hill he stayed there until the platoon took the bunker. There were only two men in the bunker. Muramoto's wound was dressed and we both stayed there overnight along with the rest of the wounded and dead.

SEPTEMBER 1951

FLORANIO CASTILLO
Honolulu, Territory of Hawaii

The Korean War was on and all of us who were in ROTC at the University of Hawaii expected to be called for active duty after graduation. In June I received my degree in secondary education and a lieutenant's commission. Others who also received commissions were William Araki, Wilfred Leong, David Suzuki, and Tsugio Ohashi, all of whom ended up in Korea in 1952.

SEPTEMBER 1951

CPL. GARY HASHIMOTO
Baker Company, 32d Infantry
Vicinity of Punchbowl, North Korea

I received word from other members of the platoon that my buddy and classmate, Jack Hiwatashi, had been killed. I was just devastated! My best buddy, killed, after we took an oath to return home together. I never got to see Jack after he was killed. The company clerk later told me that Jack and his entire squad were in a bunker during an artillery bombardment when an enemy artillery shell came through the opening of their bunker. All were killed instantly except Jack, who was evacuated by helicopter but died on the operating table. He did not regain consciousness. From that time on I said I was going to take care of myself. One of us had to get home alive.

SEPTEMBER 1951

ALAN TAKAMIYASHIRO
Honolulu, Territory of Hawaii

The Korean War was farthest from my mind when it broke out because I had a pretty good job at the time working for International Business Machines as a truck driver and had a girlfriend who kept me occupied most of the time. But the army finally caught up with me and I was inducted on September 20, 1951, just ten days short of my twenty-first birthday.

When I told my girlfriend about my notice to report to Schofield Barracks, she told her grandmother, who gave me a pep talk about how proud I must be to have a chance to serve my country.

I reported to the parking lot in the back of the Queen Theater in Kaimuki with other inductees, from where we boarded a bus for Schofield Barracks. After we were sworn in, we were lined up in several ranks and counted off. The sergeant in charge called out, "All odd numbers, take one step forward. You are now in the marines. All even numbers, you are in the army." My number was 4.

There was a large number of haoles from the mainland who trained with us. In fact, they made up more than 50 percent of the recruits. That was my first experience with haoles. There were some minor scrapes with them but aside from that, we generally got along with them.

OCTOBER 1951

LOUIS BALDOVI
Honolulu, Hawaii

After graduating in June from Maui Technical School with a diploma in auto mechanics, I moved to Honolulu and worked at Okamura's Auto Repair Shop in Kapahulu. I shared a rented room on Lusitania Street below Punchbowl with James Yap from Haiku, Maui.

When I got back from work one afternoon my landlord handed me a special delivery letter. It was a large envelope from my dad. In it was a brown, unopened envelope addressed to me. I opened it and there was a letter that began, "Greetings." It was from the president of the United States. It was my notice to report for active military duty in November.

I notified my boss at work that day of my draft notice and told him that I had to quit my job and get home as soon as possible. He understood my situation and said I could leave at any time and wished me luck. I think he was happy to see me go because I wasn't much of an auto mechanic.

OCTOBER 1951

PFC. SUSUMU SHINAGAWA
Able Company, 34th Infantry
Chongson, POW Camp 3, North Korea

We received word that some of us were being transferred to the Chinese. Whether that was good or bad news we didn't know but we were going to find out real soon. Of the original 750 that assembled in Pyongyang in July 1950, there were only 300 of us left.

We were divided into two groups when we departed for the Chinese camp from Camp 7. The first group was composed of 170 able-bodied men—including me—who were to march 40 miles down the Yalu River in a westerly direction. The ninety-eight sick and wounded were to be transported downriver on a boat. They squeezed into the boat made to accommodate about eighty people. Each had to sit, curled into a ball, to make room for everyone. We were all given one ball of rice.

It took us several days to walk the 40 miles and it was a cold march, even for October. It rained the last day before we got to our destination and marched into Changson Camp 3 on October 19, dripping wet and cold. For some reason, those in the boat arrived several hours after us.

The group I was in was put in huts while the others were put in large buildings made of mud and straw. Tadaki, Tamaye, Arakaki, and I, all from Hawaii, were in the same hut. That same night we were issued brand-new overcoats so we discarded our lice-infested cotton pants and jackets.

For the first time we ate pure white rice. We never had white rice when the North Koreans were our captors. The rice was mixed with corn and made into a ball. We had all the rice we could eat. It was unbeliev-able! Thinking that this was the only white rice we would be having in a long while, we packed our rice bowl to save it for the next morning. When morning came, the Chinese brought us another bucket full of pure white rice. My fear of the Chinese quickly vanished with the humane treatment we were getting from them compared to what we had experienced with the North Koreans and "The Tiger." Later, I realized that we were being fattened for their propaganda and psychological war programs.

We were issued brand-new comforters and cotton padded uniforms. The Chinese encouraged us to write home and many did just that. Under the North Koreans, we were forbidden to write home. If they had allowed us to write home, I believe more men would have survived. Word from home would be an incentive to live for. At first, I didn't write home. I believed that since my mother had not heard from me for fif-teen months, she probably thought I was dead. Why give her hope again? The chance of my dying in North Korea was very high. For that reason, I first refused to write home. But once the other prisoners received letters and photos from home, that did it. I got homesick and began to write.

Many relatives sent pictures taken in front of a car or home and the men showed them to our brainwashing English-speaking instructors. The instructors would look at the pictures and say, "These are propa-ganda pictures. Your government provided the cars and homes and made the family stand in front of them." I just couldn't believe how ignorant they were of Western civilization.

One night, while a head count was being taken, several of the Chinese officers mentioned something about school. We couldn't make sense of what they meant but the next day pencils and notebooks were issued to each prisoner.

This was the beginning of an intense propaganda program. The sick and wounded got their education at the regimental hospital, which was less than a mile away. Because I was wounded I was ordered to go to the hospital but I refused. I was permitted to remain with the non-wounded.

Our classes were held outdoors. We were told to take notes. The instructor appeared to be an educated person and seemed to know his stuff. He spoke very good English and must have been their top instructor. There were also assistant instructors situated at different locations of the outdoor classrooms. On rainy days or when it was very cold classes were held indoors.

The Chinese used different tactics on us. They were very polite, treated us well, and tried to brainwash us to accept their communist doctrine. It was obvious. As far as I can remember, the first subjects were socialism and communism. The instructor told us that socialism was the trend with communism as the final goal. He said Russia was the closest to that goal but was not yet truly communistic.

The walls of the classroom were decorated with pictures of Joseph Stalin and Mao Tse-tung and flags of Russia and China. There were also posters drawn by prisoners on the walls.

Each day following the two hours of brainwashing, we were required to hold a one-hour discussion in our rooms. We were left alone and just chewed the fat until we heard the platoon instructors approaching, and then we would "seriously" get into the discussion. Two months later, our notebooks were collected and reviewed by the instructor. There were some notebooks completely blank and those responsible were reprimanded by the instructor. Later, our instructor got tired of our lackluster efforts and interest and classes became less frequent until they stopped completely. I viewed that as a victory for us.

I remember one session we had when our head instructor told us proudly how advanced the Chinese people were becoming. "Now, in China," he said, "every other family owned a bicycle." We all laughed but the instructor couldn't see what was funny. We tried to explain to him that in America, every other family owned a car and many families owned two cars.

He was flabbergasted and said, "You are all wrong. The American people are starving and there is not enough food to go around." They really believed we were lying. Yet, I thought they half-heartedly believed us and it confused them. After a while they stopped giving us lectures.

Under the Chinese, the food was much better and we were getting stronger. We had all the rice we wanted. No millet or sorghum! The good food kept coming. We were served pork and vegetables. Every day a food detail reported to the regimental headquarters and drew our rations for the next day.

In the winter months, however, there was no variety in our menu because we couldn't get vegetables and we basically had only turnip soup with rice. Sometimes, if we were lucky, we would get potato soup with rice or soup flavored with seaweed and a little pork. The kitchen detail would cook all the food and one man from each group would get the food for the group. We only ate in our rooms.

After we were turned over to the Chinese, we were allowed to manage our leisure time. One of the most popular activities was getting together and planning the menus with what was made available to us. It was like trying to make steak out of nothing, but we tried.

The wood cutting detail was the biggest task because we had to maintain our supply of wood for cooking and heating to last us through the entire winter. The detail went into the forest under guard to pick up dry tree limbs. We then cut them into sizes small enough for us to carry back to the camp. But as the months went by, we had to go deeper into the forest and farther away from camp to get the dry wood because we had stripped the wooded area near the camp. This meant carrying the wood great distances from the forest to our camp. It also reduced the amount of wood we could carry. Some of us wanted to go on this detail because it provided us with some exercise, however forced it was, and just getting out of the camp was pleasure enough.

Every Sunday was sanitation day so we all had to clean up our rooms for inspection. The blankets had to be laid on the matted floor with our overcoats neatly placed on them. At night we slept on the floor and used comforters given to us.

Bull sessions were permitted and we exchanged information with other groups and kept the rumors flying. Rumors about a cease fire and being freed kept our hopes up. The Chinese kept telling us the war was going badly for us and we wouldn't be going home for a long time, if at all.

It was during one of these bull sessions that I heard for the first time about Maj. Gen. William Dean, commander of the 24th Infantry Division. He was captured after the battle of Taejon in August 1950. It blew my mind. How can an American general get captured? Normally, the commander of a division would be several miles to the rear, conducting the division's operations. Maybe the Chinese were right. The war must be going badly for us for an American general to be captured.

OCTOBER 1951

ROBERT HAMAKAWA
Honolulu, Territory of Hawaii

I was in my second year at the University of Hawaii and attending classes regularly when several of my high school classmates from Hilo High came to see me on campus to say hello and goodbye. That day changed my life. These guys were drafted into the armed services and were to report for induction at Schofield Barracks within a few days. We grew up and went to school together and they were like part of the family. I wasn't drafted because college students were deferred from the draft. I was twenty years old then and I couldn't feel comfortable remaining in school while they put their lives on the line for our country. That guilty feeling started to nag me and I had thoughts that I might never see them again.

The next thing I did was to call the draft board to see if I could waive my deferment and get in on the draft with my friends. No problem. They were glad to take me so I took my physical, checked out of school (much to the disappointment of my parents), and reported to Schofield Barracks with my friends.

There were about a hundred of us reporting and while we were sitting in a large room, a big marine sergeant walked in and pointed to certain individuals and said, "You, you you," twenty-five times. "You are now marines," he continued. I was one of the "yous." The irony of it all was that I had waived my deferment to be with my friends only to be separated from them at induction. They all went into the army but I landed in the Marine Corps.

We were shipped to the Marine Corps Recruit Depot in San Diego the following day for boot camp for the next ten weeks, followed by an additional six weeks at Camp Pendleton for combat infantry training. The training was rugged and we local boys were longing for home-cooked meals. How we appreciated what our mothers did for us. The months flew by and we soon made our way to Korea.

DAVID LABANG
Honolulu, Territory of Hawaii

Before I entered the army I really didn't know what my future might be. I just existed, not knowing what to do with my life. I hung around with older guys who had no future. I never graduated from Farrington High School because I was expelled for gambling.

PFC. HISASHI MORITA
Item Company, 23d Infantry
Somewhere in North Korea

I figured we were nearing a permanent POW camp, which would lessen my chances of escaping, so I decided to part company with the group the first chance I got.

It was getting very cold and when we stopped at night we all had to huddle together to keep warm because fires were not permitted. So did the guards. It offered me the opportunity so one night, when we were bedded down, I simply crawled away and lost myself in a wooded, hillside area. I thought, *Wow, that was easy.*

I stayed in the hills and walked until daybreak, when I saw a village in the valley below. It appeared deserted.

I made my way down to the village and entered the first hut I came to. It appeared unoccupied so I just flopped on the floor and must have passed out from exhaustion.

I don't know how long I was asleep but the next thing I knew there was a tremendous roar and I saw that the hut was engulfed in flames. At first I stayed flat on the floor, but decided that wasn't the right thing to do so I got up and raced out of the hut, smack into a Chinese soldier without a weapon, also running for dear life. Then I heard the roar of jet engines. Hell, the village was being napalmed by our planes and was burning.

I ran for the hillside but was stopped by two Chinese soldiers with burp guns. We stood on the hillside and watched the village burn. Two other Chinese joined us. It appeared that the Chinese were part of a small patrol that had taken refuge in the village like me for the night.

My seventh and last attempt to escape was a failure. Joseph Park was damn happy to see me alive back at camp.

POW Camp 1, North Korea

We finally arrived at POW Camp 1 along the Yalu River. Richard Makua and Kazumi Arakaki from Hawaii were already in the camp. Joseph Park was still with me and together with the other two we made a foursome that took care of each other.

If one of us got sick and refused to eat, we forced him to eat and nursed him back to health. Other GIs who were ill and couldn't eat the "slop" died.

As news of the peace talks reached us, food rations were increased. We received more rice, soybeans, turnips, carrots, and cabbage. Sometimes pork was given to us, which we cooked with the cabbage or turnip. We even received one tablespoon of sugar each a month. That was a luxury. On one occasion we were given flour to make steamed buns.

During this period of "goodwill" by the Chinese, attempts to brainwash us took place. It didn't work.

I remained in POW Camp 1 until I was released in September 1953.

When I got home, my family told me that the fellow I helped to escape in the rice paddy wrote to them and told them that I was okay.

NOVEMBER 1951

CPL. GARY HASHIMOTO
Baker Company, 32d Infantry
Vicinity of Punchbowl, North Korea

We were pretty much in a static position with actions limited to patrols as both sides sat back to see what the truce talks would bring. I had about a month to go before I rotated home so I thought I'd better not take any chances and went looking for a job that would take me off the front lines. I wanted every opportunity to make it home in one piece. I heard that the CO was looking for someone to lead the chow train (hot food served once a day and carried by the Korean Service Corps up to the front lines). I thought that was easy enough so I volunteered for the job and got it. The company commander knew I was a short-timer and wanted to keep me alive, too.

The company's kitchen was located one or two hills behind the line and was considered quite safe. The meals cooked there were put in large thermos containers and taken to the back side of the hill by KSCs.

[On November 11, 1993, there appeared in the *Honolulu Star-Bulletin* an article entitled, "A Hero of the Forgotten War," written by David H.

Hackworth, a retired army colonel. He was a Korean and Vietnam veteran and the recipient of many awards for bravery, including the Distinguished Service Cross (with one oak leaf cluster) and the Silver Star (with nine oak leaf clusters). He has authored many books, including the best-sellers *About Face* and *Brave Men*. In this article Colonel Hackworth honors one of Hawaii's Korean War veterans, James G. Aguda.]

Today (Veterans Day) we honor all American veterans, for without their sacrifices we would not be free. Instead, a knock on the door in the middle of the night could lead to imprisonment, torture or death. Freedom would be replaced by fear. The liberty and lifestyle we enjoy—which many take for granted—was paid for by the sacrifices of millions of veterans since the beginning of our proud republic.

Time has taken its toll on those who survived the horror of war, and many brave comrades paid the ultimate price as teen-agers. Too often, the fallen are forgotten by the living as we celebrate Veterans Day and relive past glories from far away battlefields.

James G. Aguda, PFC, RA 10104525, Company G, 27th Infantry Regiment, 25th "Tropical Lightning" Infantry Division, died on a cold, wind-swept hill in Korea, on March 31, 1951. His heroic actions saved my shot-up platoon, which was out of ammo and running on empty. He was a special Hawaii teen-ager whose selfless belief in and care for his fellow soldiers cost him his life.

The day Jimmy died is as fresh in my mind as if it happened only yesterday. A few days before, I had told Aguda to get some Arctic boots. I told him, "You know how you Hawaiians can't take the cold." He shrugged and said, "I'm not going to be around here long enough to need them."

I had dismissed the comment; fatalistic statements were common stuff for grunts. I didn't think any more about it, nor did I then, on that rugged, fire swept hill that was marked on the map, "Objective Logfan." I thought when Aguda led a squad of reinforcements to our aid that help had finally arrived: more ammo, more rifles, more staying power so we could hold onto our newly won objective. Now, with his squad on the firing line, we just needed a little time and a lot of luck.

As the Chinese infantry launched human wave counterattacks, Aguda casually sauntered to the center of the inferno. It was like he was at the beach at Waikiki; "Hi brah, looks like big pilikia." Then he stood up. He didn't go prone like the rest of us.

He walked to the forward slope, firing his A6 Browning machine gun from the hip. He mowed the attacking Chinese ranks like Stallone in a Rambo film. His weapon sang as he fired long bursts into the enemy, knocking the Chinese attackers over like bowling pins. The whole time he was screaming to the Chinese, "Come on. . . . Come and get." I yelled, "Get down! For Christ's sake, Aguda, get down!"

But he just kept firing—a precise killing machine. Slugs were snapping all around him. I knew he was going to be killed. Then I could see slugs smack into him; in the leg, in the arm, then two more in the legs. But he just kept shooting and screaming, and I kept yelling for him to get down. Finally, he took one in the chest. It spun him around and he dropped dead. . . .

Aguda's action turned the tide of the fight. It bought us time at perhaps the most critical phase of the battle, time in which the men of Company G reinforced my platoon (we had started with 40 men and had been reduced to eight), and put down the needed fire power that broke the back of the Chinese counterattack. . . .

Afterward, the survivors of my platoon recommended Jimmy Aguda for the "Big One," the Medal of Honor. But we were grunts and could not write eloquently of his bravery and selfless sacrifice, so the brass gave his family a combat soldier's Good Conduct Medal, the Silver Star. Those of us whose lives he saved and who witnessed his heroic example felt that Jimmy Aguda was never properly honored. He should have been gotten the Big One.

There has seldom been a day since his death more than 42 years ago that I haven't thought of this cheerful Hawaii teen-ager who was a true warrior. I want him remembered and honored this day, and for his family and friends to know that he was greatly loved by all who fought at his side—those who lived and those who died.

James G. Aguda, you were a great American. May you and all the other fallen heroes rest in peace. And on this Veterans Day, let us honor all of our warriors—the living and the dead—lest none of them be forgotten.

NOVEMBER 1951

Pfc. SUSUMU SHINAGAWA
Able Company, 34th Infantry
Chongson, POW Camp 3, North Korea

The Korean system of heating the hut was a wonderful thing. Each hut had a sunken kitchen that was 3 feet or so below the level of the floor. Heat from the stove was channeled under the mud floor by way of trenches, which led under each of the rooms and heated the floor. The mud floor retained the heat well and stayed warm for most of the night.

We were allowed to burn wood for heating or for hot water only from 1800 to 2000 hours.

Once in the warm hut, I rarely ventured outside, even to use the latrine. But it got cold in the early morning hours after the heat dissipated. A cup of water in the hut would be frozen solid the next morning. Because the river was part of the prison compound, I was able to take a bath twice a week no matter how cold it was. Strangely, the guys from Hawaii took the cold very well.

NOVEMBER 1951

LOUIS BALDOVI
Wailuku, Maui, Territory of Hawaii

There were sixty-two of us, all draftees and unmarried, who assembled at the National Guard Armory in Wailuku. We were to leave that morning by air from Puunene Airport for Honolulu, O'ahu. We all wore aloha shirts and were draped in leis. I think our ages ranged from nineteen to twenty-two years. I had just made twenty in August.

Many years later my mother showed me the group picture that we had taken that day. It showed a bunch of sad-looking guys. No one smiled for the photographer.

Most of us had graduated from high school in 1949 and some were classmates of mine from Maui High School. George Matsunaga, Roy Kunishige, Yoshio Higa, Philip Yoshihara, Kaname Tamashiro, Richard Ouchi, Takeshi Yamashiro, and Wilfred Kido were classmates. Matsunaga and Kido and I were from the same small hometown of Kuiaha.

After a quick hug and a handshake from my dad I joined the others to board the bus. That was the last time I saw my dad healthy.

For all of us, it was our first trip to Schofield Barracks and our first experience of military life. When we entered the main gate, there was a large sign that read "Hawaiian Infantry Training Center" (HITC). It was one of the largest, if not the largest, training centers the army operated in the United States. It had already earned the reputation for being one of the toughest.

We unloaded at Quadrangle I, or more commonly called Quad I, one of several facilities that housed training battalions. We were the newest training battalion and were designated the 60th Training Battalion with six training companies making up the battalion, the 60th Company to the 66th Company. I was assigned to the 65th Company. Each company was made up of about 200 recruits.

The army did not waste time in getting us in tune to its routine. After drawing our gear from the supply room, we were marched to the barber shop to get our hair "trimmed." The barbers, being men of a humorous nature, asked each of us how we wanted our hair done and we would naively reply, "Just around the ears, please." In less than a minute I was practically bald.

And for the first time in our young lives, we came into close contact with haoles and blacks from the mainland on a personal basis, eating, bathing, sleeping, and all the human contacts that the military dictates.

Midway through my training a hometown friend of mine, Katsuichi Sato, whom I had not seen since the 8th grade, visited me. I was in awe when I saw him. He was a sergeant first class, a rank he earned in Korea with the 24th Infantry Division. He wore on his uniform the coveted Combat Infantryman's Badge. Months later, many of us would earn that badge.

NOVEMBER 1951

DAVID LABANG
Schofield Barracks, Wahiawa
Territory of Hawaii

The sergeant barked, "First three ranks, you are in the army, fourth rank, you are in the marines." My army career of twenty-four years began at that moment.

Basic training taught me discipline and I took advantage of it. Believe it or not, I enjoyed the sixteen weeks of basic training. It made me lean and mean. At least, I thought I was.

DECEMBER 1951

PFC. SUSUMU SHINAGAWA
Able Company, 34th Infantry
Chongson, POW Camp 3, North Korea

My elbow got infected and began to swell, with the skin stretched so thin that it began to look transparent. I refused to see the doctor. It would throb for weeks and finally I went to see the Chinese doctor. He looked at my elbow and told me that he had to make an incision to drain the pus. It worked! The swelling went down and the pain was gone. He probed the wound and took out a small piece of bone. That piece of bone was the result of the arm wound I had received in July 1950. All the doctors who treated me did not tell me or did not know that shattered pieces

FIGURE 33   Clayton Murakami of Naalehu is bedecked with leis at the
General Lyman Field prior to flying to Honolulu for induction into the U.S.
Army. November 1951. Courtesy of Clayton Murakami.

FIGURE 34   Mauians soon to be inducted into the army and marines. November 1951. Courtesy of the *Maui News.*

of bone were still in my arm. That one piece of bone had slowly moved up my elbow, causing the infection. I was not given any anesthesia and the pain was excruciating but I never cried out. There was another piece of bone the doctor tried to remove but after several attempts, he gave up. I wanted him to get the second bone out even though the probing was painful. What he did next was worse. He swabbed the wound with iodine and I yelled. I was glad to leave his office and swore that I would never go back to see him again.

There were many times when my arm hurt like hell but I refused to see the doctor. I knew that sooner or later the piece of bone would penetrate the skin and I could pull it out by myself. When I did, pus oozed out and the swelling and pain would go away. In the span of three months, I took out several pieces of bone. In the thirty-three months I was a prisoner, my wounds never healed.

We were still waiting for the good news: liberation. However, there was none and we were told that the truce talks were going well but it would be some time before an agreement would be reached and that we might have to stay a while.

DECEMBER 1951

CPL. GARY HASHIMOTO
Baker Company, 32d Infantry
Vicinity of Punchbowl, North Korea

When Norman Ahakuelo and I heard the news that we were going home in December, we were overjoyed, yet cautious. Of course, we thought of Jack Hiwatashi. Before he was killed, Jack and I had talked a few times about going home and what we planned to do. I had told Jack, "You know, Jack, I got a feeling we are going home together, no matter what."

Three months after Jack was killed, Norman and I stood on the deck of the USS *President Cleveland* in Sasebo, Japan. The ship was still being loaded with cargo so Norman and I went to the rail of the ship to watch the loading. While we watched, several trucks arrived and unloaded wooden crates. The wooden crates contained caskets. It brought me to thinking about Jack, who, by now, was buried in a cemetery back home on Maui.

The crates were now being loaded into the hold of the ship. As we stood there and watched, a crane picked up a crate and raised it to our eye level no more than 30 feet away. It hung there for a second, horizontal to us. Then, as the crane raised it a bit higher, the crate slowly swung around so that the head of the crate faced us. There, stenciled in black letters, barely visible, were the words Sgt. Jack Hiwatashi. Norman and I gasped and looked at each other. We both fought back tears.

"There's Jack," I told Norman, pointing to the crate. "He's going home with us. He waited three months for me so we could go home together."

DECEMBER 1951

PVT. ROBERT FERNANDEZ
65th Company, 60th Battalion, HITC
Schofield Barracks, Territory of Hawaii

Training began in earnest during the Christmas holidays. We were up before 0500 hours, even before the sound of reveille. Imagine the rush to the gang latrine every morning. Some guys would get up at 0300 hours to do their toiletries, dress, and lay in their bunks until reveille.

By 0630 hours we were assembled in the company street ready to march out of the quad at the command of the field first sergeant. Except for an occasional training film, all the classes were held in the field.

Getting back to the barracks early was of utmost importance because of the limited supply of hot water. Our first priority was not to bathe, but to clean our gear and weapons with hot water. We would strip our rifles and wash them in hot water, which we had been instructed not to do. It was not uncommon to see men at 0200 hours in the morning cleaning their gear. It became a habit, getting little sleep every night and training long hours during the day. The same sleepless conditions would be applied in combat.

PART III

1952 | Trench Warfare and Hilltop Battles

Aᖴᴛᴇʀ ᴛʜᴇ ʙᴀᴛᴛʟᴇs ᴏꜰ Bʟᴏᴏᴅʏ Rɪᴅɢᴇ ᴀɴᴅ Hᴇᴀʀᴛʙʀᴇᴀᴋ Ridge in the fall of 1951, the character of the Korean War changed dramatically. Mindful of the peace talks and the tremendous casualties suffered, both sides were content with improving their frontline fortifications and extending their outpost lines of resistance. An almost continuous trench line existed near the 38th parallel, extending from the east coast to the west coast of Korea. Casualties on both sides mounted, however, as pitched battles were fought on fortified hilltops north of Munsan-ni, Yokokk-chon Valley west of Chorwon, and Iron Triangle, and in the vicinity of Punchbowl.

SFC. CLARENCE YOUNG
George Company, 5th RCT
Pyoktong, POW Camp 5, North Korea

It was cold and men died on a daily basis but they weren't buried every day. The dead would be put in a shack until it could not hold any more, and when the weather permitted, a burial detail would take the bodies beyond the compound and bury them. Their bodies would be completely stiff because of the cold. The ground was so hard that we couldn't dig more than a foot or so and had to scrape whatever loose soil we could find to completely cover the bodies. We didn't need much to cover the bodies because those that died were mostly skin and bones. There were no fat dead men.

PVT. ALAN TAKAMIYASHIRO
Hawaiian Infantry Training Center
Wahiawa, Territory of Hawaii

Most of us were assigned to FECOM when we returned from our two weeks of furlough. A few were assigned to ZI or EUCOM and a few went to Officers Candidate School.

A day later we were loaded on trucks and taken to Pier 39 in Honolulu, where we boarded the USNS *General Hase*. There were more than 400 of us on ship when we set sail.

Camp Drake, Japan

We arrived at Yokohama, Japan, eleven days later and were taken to Camp Drake for processing. Camp Drake was full of GIs either waiting to go to Korea or waiting to be sent home.

We didn't sail for Pusan, Korea, but were taken to the port of Inchon on the west coast of Korea. Because of the severe tide changes of 35 feet or so, we had to wait for the tide to rise and then were transferred to flat-bottom assault boats, which took us to shore.

PVT. ALAN TAKAMIYASHIRO
Chunchon, South Korea

At Chunchon I found out that I was assigned to George Company, 31st Infantry Regiment, 7th Infantry Division. There were a number of local boys from Hawaii, but Harry Tanaka and I were the only ones assigned to George Company. We stayed at Chunchon a couple of days and then were put on trucks again and headed for the front line where George Company was dug in. After a couple of hours we knew we were nearing the front because we could hear the distant sounds of artillery fire. I was getting nervous.

Kumwha, North Korea

It was in the afternoon when we were dropped off at the company rear, which was located at the base of a ridge. A guide led us to where George Company was dug in but not until after having to climb over two ridges and getting wet in a rice paddy. On the way we passed several litter teams carrying dead men to the company rear. *Hey,* I told myself, *this is for real. I hope I don't end up like one of them.*

An officer greeted us and then turned us over to a sergeant who assigned us to platoons. I went to the 3d Platoon and was put in a rifle squad. Tanaka was assigned to another platoon. I went to the squad's bunker, where half of the squad was resting. They were all haoles. At first they thought I was a South Korean soldier until I told them that I was from Hawaii. Later I got to meet the other men in the squad. They, too, were all haoles. I was the only local boy in the squad.

MARCH 1952

PVT. ROBERT FERNANDEZ
65th Company, 60th Battalion, HITC
Schofield Barracks, Territory of Hawaii

Our training at the Hawaiian Infantry Center was in full swing. The use of the M-1 rifle, Browning Automatic Rifle, .30 caliber machine gun, carbine, and .45 pistol, all basic weapons of the infantryman, were the weapons we concentrated on. We still had to learn how to fire the 60mm mortar and 37mm recoilless rifle.

Already we were in excellent physical condition. Our instructors told us that one of the main reasons why the United States was badly beaten in the early part of the Korean War was that American soldiers were in poor physical condition. They weren't going to let that happen to us. Our company, the 65th, was called the "Running 65th" because we were always running and rarely rode trucks.

Our commanding officer, Lt. Herbert Ikeda, who was with the 5th RCT early in the Korean War, told us that we had to be in excellent physical condition or prepare to die in Korea, because most of us would end up in Korea after basic training. Actually, Lieutenant Ikeda was our second CO, who replaced our first CO after the second month of training.

APRIL 1952

PVT. DAVID LABANG
George Company, 31st Infantry
Vicinity of Chunchon, South Korea

By way of Sasebo, Japan, and Pusan, South Korea, we arrived at the 7th Division replacement center of Chunchon, which was to the northeast of South Korea's capital city of Seoul. My final assignment read, "George Company, 31st Infantry Regiment." There were about forty other local boys assigned to George Company, much more than what other units received. George Company was an infantry company that was already on the front line.

Another group of replacements arrived with more "pineapples" from Hawaii. Among them were David Labang, George Fujiwara, Kenneth Hino, Mabenis Firmino, and Albert Johiro, all assigned to my platoon. There were several more but they were assigned to the other platoons.

Vicinity of Kumwha, North Korea

It was in the early afternoon when we moved out of Chunchon by truck convoy and headed north for Kumwha. It was dark when we finally stopped at the company rear after a five-hour ride. From there our guides took us to the company's positions on line.

There were about eight local boys assigned to the same platoon. I was put in the 2d Squad and reported to the squad leader. He led me to a bunker and told me that was my "hootchie" and I'd be sharing it with two other men. A shelter half was draped over the entrance. There were two double deck bunks made of poles and commo wire. My newly found roommates were lying on the bottom bunks and got up to greet me. I found out that they had been in Korea for eight months and were due to rotate home soon. They sure were happy to see a replacement.

The next day I ran into another local boy, Alan Takamiyashiro, from Honolulu, who told me that he and I were in the same platoon. Alan had arrived at the company a couple of months before me and was a "veteran." That made me damn glad knowing that there was a local boy veteran from Hawaii in the same platoon.

One day our squad leader called us together and told us there was going to be something big taking place and our battalion was going to be part of it. We were to attack the ridge that was in front of us early the next morning.

I had a hard time sleeping that night, thinking how I was going to conduct myself in battle. I imagined several situations and how I was going to react to them. The worst one of all was if I ran out of ammunition and was confronted by an enemy with a weapon, do I surrender, or do I die fighting? I went to sleep without coming up with an answer.

At daybreak, after our artillery slammed the ridge for about ten minutes, we moved out down a finger to the valley below. We were the lead company followed by the other two companies of the battalion.

I was surprised that we were not fired upon as we made our way to the hill. The uneven terrain made it difficult to maintain visual contact with the other squads from our platoon. There were a lot of shell craters—small ones and big ones, which would afford some protection. I made up my mind that if things got hot I would make a beeline for one of the shell craters.

Less than 100 yards from the crest of the ridge I saw many objects in the air thrown from the trenches. Shit! Hand grenades by the bunches. This was followed by heavy automatic and machine gun fire. I dove into a shell crater. Man, the noise was loud! Bullets and grenade shrapnel made all kinds of noises—zinging, pinging, snapping, whirring, and churning up dirt at the edge of the crater. The cries for medics were soon heard over the noise of exploding grenades and rifle fire. I rolled on my back and looked down the hill. Our men were still moving uphill and men were yelling, "Keep moving! Keep moving!" So I got up on one knee and looked around. There were several bodies on the ground, not moving. Crouching, I leaped out of the crater and joined the others moving up the hill.

I saw a figure about 30 yards up ahead behind a small tree stump and blasted away without taking aim until I heard the ping of my empty clip being ejected from my M-1. I had fired eight rounds but didn't know if I had killed my first enemy. Probably more than a dozen of us had fired at the same enemy and claimed the same kill.

The hand grenades continued to rain down on us, and as I got closer to the trench I could see the hands releasing the hand grenades. At this point we were taking a lot of casualties, not only from grenades and small arms fire, but also from mortar fire.

There were shouts to reform at the bottom of the hill and to dig in because our artillery was going to blast the hill again. Retreating back down the hill I came across a GI in a shell crater with a busted leg. Some of the guys must have seen him but never stopped to help him. I grabbed him by the back of his shirt and pulled him out of the crater and started dragging him to the bottom of the hill. He was hurting but never cried out. In fact, he yelled, "Go! Go!" He was treated by a medic once I got him to cover.

After our artillery fire was lifted, the order came to attack the hill again. My heart was really pumping this time.

I jumped out of my hole and moved uphill, bouncing in and out of shell craters, firing uphill, and at the same time keeping my eye on the flanks for our guys. I saw several of our platoon guys fall and heard the cries for medics.

We never made it to the trenches although we were less than 100 yards from the crest. Once again the order to withdraw was given. The platoon was slowly pulling back, picking up the dead and wounded on the way down. I saw a wounded man being dragged downhill on a poncho by a buddy, bouncing along the way.

In my first combat action, we suffered a defeat. The hill was still in the hands of the Chinese.

APRIL 1952

PVT. HAROLD NAKATA
Camp Drake, Japan

Seemed like the entire U.S. Army was at Camp Drake, the major processing replacement center in the Far East. There were thousands of soldiers in transit, either returning from Korea or going to Korea. Those going home seemed to have the rank of sergeant or higher. They wore bright shoulder patches that signified the unit they were with in Korea. We were easily identified as replacements because of our short hair, no decorations, and no stripes on our arms. My orders read 7th Infantry Division.

Chunchon, South Korea

It was here I was assigned to Able Company, 17th Infantry Regiment, 7th Infantry Division. Four boys from Hawaii were assigned to the same company, one of whom was James Nakata from Honolulu.

After a long and dusty truck ride, I joined my company, which was in reserve. I was assigned to a rifle platoon and was happy to find out that James Nakata was also in my platoon. There was nothing like having another local boy in the same outfit. But with two Nakatas in the platoon, it gave everybody fits.

MAY 1952

PVT. WILLIAM ABREU
64th Company, Hawaiian Infantry Training Center
Schofield Barracks, Territory of Hawaii

We capped off our last week of basic training with a field exercise at Kahuku on the north shore. With full field packs, we left Schofield Barracks late in the afternoon for the 20-mile or so hike to Kahuku. To get there we had to make our way through pineapple fields and the rugged Koolau mountain range.

The trail was extremely narrow in the mountains. It was up a ridge, down a ridge, many times over. The mosquitos ate us up. And it rained. At about 2000 hours we took our first rest. I asked one of the cadre who was a Korean War veteran why we didn't take the trucks. "Trucks?" he growled at me. "In Korea there might not be trucks. It may rain all day, snow all day, and sweat may be running down your ass all day."

It was a good thing the shouts of "saddle up" came. Otherwise, he would have eaten me alive.

For better or for worse, we arrived at the training site at about 0800 hours and we were exhausted.

For most of the week, we trained in company, platoon, and squad tactics using live ammunition. We hardly got any sleep. I think I averaged about three hours of sleep a night the six nights we were in Kahuku.

About 0100 hours one morning one of the trainees woke me up and told me that I and a dozen other trainees had been picked for a very important mission. When I asked him what the mission was, he said he couldn't tell me until we got to our destination. Then he handed me a burlap bag.

We slipped out of the bivouac area and headed in the direction of Kahuku town. After an hour we stopped on the outskirts of a watermelon field. The mission? To steal as many watermelons as we could carry and take them back to camp. We had enough watermelons for the entire platoon.

We dreaded the last day in Kahuku because we already knew what training exercise was coming up. It was the assault on Hill 904. Every

FIGURE 35   A platoon of the 65th Training Company upon completion of basic training. May 1952. Courtesy of Louis Baldovi.

trainee who took basic training at Schofield Barracks will tell you that Hill 904 was a son-of-a-bitch. We jogged behind tanks uphill for almost a mile, and when we got to the base of Hill 904 we assaulted the hill using live ammo. It would leave everyone gasping for breath. When we completed the exercise, one of the instructors said, "This was a piece of cake compared to what you will find in Korea."

MAY 1952

PVT. CLAYTON MURAKAMI
66th Company, HITC
Schofield Barracks, Territory of Hawaii

Over a thousand men completed their training and I guessed about 90 percent of the battalion was assigned to FECOM.

But before shipping out we were all granted two weeks of leave. So I packed my small hand carry bag and went home to Pahala on the Big Island. The ten days sure went by fast. When the time came for me to leave for the airport, my mother gave me a white cloth with a thousand red dots sewn on it. She said it was called a *senninbari,* a good luck charm, which was supposed to protect me from harm because it had thousands of powers. She instructed me to wrap it around my waist before going into combat. I guess she was already convinced that I was going to Korea. I was told that the dots on the white cloth were symmetrically sewn on by females, both young and old. My mother said that she could sew only one dot. Only those who were born in the "Year of the Tiger" could sew as many dots as they wanted. There must have been a lot of females sewing on the dots because I am sure not everyone was born in the "Year of the Tiger." I found out later that some of the dots were sewn on by my future wife, whom I barely knew at the time.

It was time for me to say my final goodbye to my dad, and it was the first time in my life I noticed tears in his eyes as we shook hands. He said to take care of myself and not to be a hero. I told him not to worry and I'd take care of myself and write whenever I could and that I'd be back in no time.

Uijongbu, South Korea

The way to Korea was through Camp Drake, Japan, and Inchon, South Korea, to the town of Uijongbu, where we were assigned to our specific units.

I was assigned to King Company, 3d Battalion, 180th Infantry, 45th Division. Also assigned to the same company were Susumu Miyamoto, Jerry Sakai, and Johnny Ramos, all from Maui. I think our company was the only company with four local boys in it, at least for a while. Rosa and I were assigned to the same squad in the 3d Platoon and Miyamoto and Sakai were in another platoon but not in the same squad.

Yokkok-chon Valley, North Korea

A few days later we went on line. It was night and very dark when we relieved another company.

A few nights later Johnny Ramos and I had listening post duty. The listening post was about 100 yards below our company's position. Our job was to warn the platoon by a sound-powered telephone that was connected to the platoon CP if there was any suspicious noise or activity below us. The night was dark, and Ramos and I were sitting quietly trying to listen because we couldn't see more than a few yards in front of us.

Then we saw flashes in the distance followed by the booming sounds of artillery a couple of seconds later. The quiet night exploded! All around us the hill erupted. Ramos and I pressed against the sides of the foxhole and tried to make our bodies small, hoping that none of the shells would find their way into our foxhole. I never prayed so hard in my life. The barrage must have lasted about five minutes. When it was over, a call came over the telephone telling us to withdraw to the main line because an attack by the Chinese was expected. With Ramos in the lead, we scampered up the hill back to the trench line.

We braced for the expected enemy attack but nothing happened. Someone said to be quiet. He heard my teeth chattering.

MAY 1952

PVT. ROBERT HAMAKAWA
Item Company, 11th Marines
Vicinity of Munsan-ni

I found myself in Korea assigned to an artillery unit. I had no training in artillery and, because of that, I was assigned to the kitchen and security watch most of the time. I hated both. After having spent a month in artillery I still was not comfortable and requested a transfer to the infantry. To my surprise, my request was granted and I was transferred to the 1st Amphibious Tractor Battalion (dismounted), located northwest of Munsan-ni, fronting the Imjin River with Panmunjom to the northeast. Panmunjom was the site where the peace talks were taking place.

MAY 1952

PFC. ALAN TAKAMIYASHIRO
George Company, 31st Infantry
Vicinity of Kumwha, North Korea

I was out of the rifle squad and was now the radio man for the platoon leader. This meant where he went, I went. It was worse than being in the rifle squad because officers and radio men were prime targets for the enemy. But the position had some privileges. The bunker of platoon CP was almost the best in the platoon. I picked the best rations before they were distributed to the platoon. Best of all, I didn't have to go on patrol unless the platoon leader led the patrol.

Late one afternoon, the platoon leader told me that we were to accompany a raiding party on an enemy outpost and bring back a prisoner. The outpost was several hundred yards to our front. He had volunteered to lead the patrol because the squad was down to only five men and we were to make it seven. One of the five men was George Fujiwara from Hawaii.

The platoon leader was gung-ho and wanted to earn a medal. Before we set out, I called for our 60mm mortars to fire a few rounds at the outpost.

We crossed the rice paddies and made it halfway up the hill to the outpost undetected. I thought maybe the mortar fire I had called in on the outpost killed everyone. About 20 yards from the trench a single hand grenade landed in our midst, which brought a scream from one of our guys. That scream ignited a barrage of grenades from the Chinese outpost. Fortunately, we were so spread out that only one grenade burst near us and stunned another member of the patrol. George Fujiwara yelled at him to get moving.

Get moving we couldn't. Looking up, I could clearly see heads outlined, bobbing in the trench above me. The lieutenant yelled at me to call for 60mm mortar fire on the hill but I thought we were too close to the crest. Besides, the 60mm mortars were never accurate and I was afraid of short rounds falling on us. We had to get out of their hand grenade range so we started running down the hill. The lieutenant headed for some boulders and I followed him, but just before we reached the boulders I stumbled, twisted my ankle, and fell. I got up and hobbled to the boulders, where the lieutenant was waiting for me. He had seen what happened to me and offered to carry the radio but I told him no.

After hunkering behind the boulders and looking at the scattered patrol around him, the lieutenant decided that since there was only about an hour of daylight left it was foolish to make a second attempt. I called for our mortars and under that covering fire we made it back to our lines. Our score card read two men wounded and mission unsuccessful.

MAY 1952

Pvt. Louis Baldovi
Able Company, 180th Infantry
Pando-gol, North Korea

It was dark when we arrived at Able Company, which was in reserve. When we got off the truck I strained my eyes in the dark to see if I could recognize anyone from Hawaii. There was no one I could tell that was from Hawaii.

We were quickly hustled to the company commander's tent, where he greeted us with handshakes and the glad-to-see-you routine. Waiting outside were the squad leaders who had the names of replacements assigned to their squad. Squad leader Sergeant Conley called my name and a couple of more and said that we were in the 2d Squad, 3d Platoon, and told us to follow him.

He ushered us into a large tent dimly lit with candles and told us that it was home of the 1st and 2d Squads. Both leaders introduced their squads and asked us, the newcomers, to tell them where we were from. I was the first to speak. When I said I was from Hawaii, a GI who came in with the 1st Squad, hollered, "Eh, brah!" Man, that remark made me want to jump sky high, because here was another local boy, and we were in the same platoon, although in different squads.

I answered with a big grin and a wave of my hand. He was William Abreu, a Portuguese boy from Kokomo, Maui. I recognized him as one of the replacements on the same truck that brought us to the company but I thought he was a haole from the mainland. He thought I was from Guam because there were two or three Guamanians on the truck. I guess Guamanians and Filipinos do look alike. Now there were two of us from Hawaii in Able Company. It would be five months later before another local boy joined us.

Puhung-ni, North Korea

At 1800 hours on May 31, we left the village of Pando-gol by motor convoy for the MLR and arrived at Puhung-ni in the Yokkok-chon Valley. It took us four hours to travel 20 miles.

It was all very quiet and orders were given almost in a whisper when we unloaded. I asked the assistant squad leader, Sgt. Fred Armour from Michigan, where the front line was. "Right over that ridge," he whispered.

A nearly two-hour climb up the ridge line took us to the top of a ridge, where we were unceremoniously deposited in our fighting positions and told to be quiet and alert until morning.

When morning came, I found our platoon was positioned on the left side of a hill named Hill 347, which overlooked a valley. In the valley were dry rice paddies and smaller hills. The Chinese were in defensive positions about a mile or so beyond the valley. That was no-man's-land.

A continuous trench line between 5 and 7 feet deep, and about 3 to 4 feet wide, cut across the forward slope of hills, crests, and ridges, and ran as far as the eye could see. The trenches were heavily sandbagged on the edges, making them even deeper. There were fighting positions at irregular intervals. There were bunkers or hootchies just below the crest of the reverse slope.

Our nine-man squad consisted of a squad leader, assistant squad leader, BAR man, assistant BAR man, and five riflemen. My squad leader was Sergeant Conley, and my assistant squad leader was Sergeant Armour. They both were short-timers who had come over with the division in

December 1951 and were scheduled to rotate home in July. Two others had been there for four months. The rest of us were green.

JUNE 1952

PVT. ROBERT HAMAKAWA
Charlie Company, 1st Marines
Vicinity of Munsan-ni, South Korea

My squad leader was Sgt. Joe Quinlan from Boston, Massachusetts. I can't remember the names of the men in the squad because I decided back then not to get too familiar with anyone. It was best not to get too close with other men in the squad because it could get you killed. Nevertheless, Bill Hammond from West Terre Haute, Indiana, and I became became very close over a short period of time. Quinlan always paired Bill and me for listening post duty. Bill was a well-built, slow-talking guy, 6 feet tall, 190 pounds, rugged but gentle and a bit cross-eyed.

JUNE 1952

PVT. LOUIS BALDOVI
Able Company, 180th Infantry
Puhung-ni, North Korea

On the afternoon of June 2, Sergeant Conley called the squad together and told us that our squad had been given a reconnaissance assignment. We were to find out if Hill 275, which was about 500 yards forward of our position, was occupied by the enemy during the daylight hours. Conley emphasized it was a reconnaissance patrol and we were not to engage the enemy unless absolutely necessary. We were to leave the MLR an hour before sunup and, if all went well, we would be back before 1,000 hours.

Conley looked at us and I could tell that he was plenty worried because more than half his men were fresh out of basic training. Then he took us to the forward observer's bunker, from where we had a commanding view of the entire valley and especially Hill 275. He placed a map on the ground and traced the route we would take and told us to take turns using the powerful BC-scope in the bunker to familiarize ourselves with the terrain.

Hill 275 was shaped like a shield with gentle slopes, which reminded me of the mountain Mauna Loa on the Big Island of Hawaii. The crest of the hill, bare of vegetation, stretched about 300 yards from left to right. The lower portion of the hill was sparsely populated with trees and brush. It would not give us enough cover and concealment.

Conley said we would travel light, only rifle and cartridge belt and a couple of grenades. He said if we ran into any Chinese we would just shag ass out of there.

That night Conley shared some information with us about Hill 275. It had another name, Old Baldy, because it was bare of vegetation due to the constant pounding of mortar, artillery shells, and napalm bombs.

On the morning of June 3, an hour before daylight, Conley led the squad through the barbed wire opening of Charlie Company, through a minefield, and down a finger that led to the valley floor.

We got to the base of Old Baldy without any problem. Conley led the way with the radio man behind him. I was the fourth or fifth man in the lineup. We traversed the hill from right to left, staying just a couple of yards below the crest of the hill. At the midway point we stopped for a couple of minutes and listened. Just when Conley signaled us to continue on, we suddenly heard the thump, thump sounds of someone digging on the other side of the hill. Then we heard voices, whether Korean or Chinese we couldn't tell. The digging sounds intensified and it sounded like a group of people was digging. Old Baldy was indeed occupied by the enemy.

Conley came back to us and said very quietly, "Let's get the hell out of here!" We didn't have to be told twice. I guess he thought he had all that he needed to know. We didn't take the same path back. Instead, we took an alternate route and came in through Baker Company's positions, which had been warned by our radio man that we were coming in.

Our stay in no-man's-land took an hour longer than expected, but we were glad to have made it back without any mishap. Conley had to report to battalion for a debriefing and, when he came back, he told us that the battalion commander had commended the patrol for its efforts. Someone shouted, "What, no medals?" We all laughed.

Vicinity of Omgogae, North Korea

That afternoon we were pulled off the line and went in reserve near the village of Omgogae a couple of miles behind the MLR. I thought this was easy duty—a few days on line and then in reserve. I thought we were going to rest but was told otherwise.

In the evening our company commander assembled the company and gave us the low-down on why we were pulled off the line. He said the entire 45th Infantry Division was going on the offensive on June 6 to straighten out the OPLR. There were eleven hills in front of the division's sector, and the objective was to attack and secure all those hills and establish a string of outposts in front of the division's sector. Old Baldy, the same hill that our squad had reconned a few days earlier, was Able Company's objective. Baker and Charlie Companies would be in reserve and would relieve us after the hill was secured. The attack was to take place the night of June 6.

We were not to rest. Instead, the brass found a hill that little resembled Old Baldy and ordered us to rehearse the attack on that hill. Whoever heard of rehearsing an attack? We did that for two days and two nights.

After a short ride on the morning of June 6, we arrived at the staging area behind Hill 347.

All morning long we received briefing from our platoon leaders and squad leaders on the plans of the attack. What made our platoon pay attention to the briefing was that we had been given the assignment of leading the company in the attack. Worse still was that the 2d Squad, the squad I was in, was the point squad. The reason for that was we were more familiar with the terrain since we had been there on patrol only a couple of days before.

Artillery shells rustled overhead from time to time to soften up Old Baldy for us. Even navy Corsairs flew overhead in their bombing and strafing runs to Old Baldy. The sound of bombs and artillery shells exploding was very clear.

The afternoon was spent eating a hot meal and getting our equipment ready, especially our weapons. We were told to take food rations for a couple of days. There was a pile of C-ration boxes and we helped ourselves, breaking the boxes open and taking only our favorite rations. I took only candy bars, canned fruits, and all the toilet paper I could find and stuffed them in my combat pack. I put a packet of toilet paper in my helmet liner.

At about 1500 hours a chaplain arrived and conducted a church service in an open area. Only a handful attended the service, including me. When it was over I went to where my combat pack lay and took out the rosary my mother had given me before I left home in November and put it on my neck. I felt stronger and confident.

It took about two hours to get into position for the attack. From a connecting ridge that led to the left of the hill we watched the artillery pulverize Old Baldy. I thought, *No one could live through that.* It was now

2200 hours. When it was over, our platoon, with the company following our lead, turned right from the ridge onto Old Baldy and formed two skirmish lines, with the 3d Platoon in the first line. Since the 2d Squad was the lead squad, we found ourselves at the extreme right of the skirmish line. So far so good and it seemed that the hill was not occupied.

Then shouts of "Grenades! Grenades!" rang through the night, followed by bursting hand grenades in our ranks as we neared the crest of the hill. A heavy volume of automatic rifle fire from the top of the hill joined in and, for the first time, I heard the "brrrrp" of the Chinese submachine gun that the old-timers had warned us about. Its rapid rate of sustained fire earned it the nickname, the "burp gun."

To the left of me was Corporal Kubinski, whom I had adopted as my foxhole buddy. He was to rotate home in a couple of weeks. We flattened ourselves to the ground to avoid being hit by grenade shrapnel and small arms fire. Quickly the calls for medics came.

Flares, ours, lit the hill. I remember the flares making weird and whining sounds as they parachuted down. Each flare lasted for only about a minute.

I didn't dare get up. Conley, who was in the center of squad, yelled for us to open fire. Kubinski, who was on my left, grabbed my shoulder and pointed to the right, where several sky-lined figures were running. We both fired a couple of rounds in their direction, not knowing whether they were friend or foe. The muzzle of Kubinski's M-1 was next to my ear when he fired. It blinded me for a second and caused my left ear to ring for quite a while. The figures dropped out of sight but it was difficult to tell whether our shots brought them down.

We were still being greeted by hand grenades. From the prone position and looking up, I could see hand grenades being thrown in bunches. Many were overthrown and went sailing over our heads to explode farther down the hill into the ranks of the second skirmish line. There were screams behind us.

Burp gun bullets were kicking up dirt in our faces so Kubinski and I took several leaping steps to our right and found a small crater that gave us better cover. However, our heads were still above the ground. I carried about six fragmentation hand grenades and Kubinski had a couple so we decided to return the favor. I motioned to Kubinski to start throwing his grenades. We couldn't stand or kneel without being hit so we had to throw our grenades lying on our sides or on our backs. I could now see the crest of the hill. The problem we faced was that we were still about 50 yards from the crest and uphill. I couldn't throw a grenade 50 yards even on level ground, much less uphill. Anyway, I threw three grenades in succession while laying on my left side. I didn't even look to see where they had landed and put my face to the ground. Wham! Wham! Wham! The damn grenades must have carried only about 20 yards in the air, landed, rolled back a few yards, and exploded. The last one rolled back farther and burst just a few yards from us. Bits of shrapnel from the grenade struck my steel helmet. I let out few choice words.

I turned on my back to see if the second skirmish line was still behind us. Then I looked up and saw tracer bullets streaking above us, some orange, some yellow, some red, and some green. I had never seen green ones before. Must have been Chinese.

Sounds, like people clapping their hands in rapid succession, came from the back and right of us. Jerking my attention to the sounds, I saw muzzle flashes less than 50 yards away and figures in white clothing moving toward us. Heck, the clapping sounds were bullets cutting the air above our heads. The first thought I had was that we were surrounded! Kubinski and I fired quickly. I must have emptied two full clips in that direction. Then we both threw grenades. I didn't think we got anyone and I sure wasn't going to go down there to find out. We must have discouraged them, for we never heard the clapping sounds again.

Now men were yelling, "Fix bayonets! Fix bayonets!" At least we knew now that our people were around. "Fix bayonets?" I thought it happened only in movies. I was shaking so badly that I had difficulty taking the bayonet out of its scabbard and fixing it to my rifle. "Move out. Move out!" came the next command and I stumbled uphill with Kubinski. We ran into a wall of hand grenades and small arms fire. The charge failed and we had to withdraw to the bottom of the hill.

We were told to dig in or find a hole because in a few minutes artillery fire was going to be called in on Old Baldy. Again the hill was plastered. Watching the artillery do its job at such close range was awesome. A few short rounds burst within 50 yards of our position. The artillery support took about five minutes and we moved out again.

Kubinski and I were still together. Sergeant Conley told us to take the right side and try to outflank the enemy's position. We circled the right side of the hill not drawing any fire and found ourselves slightly behind the Chinese positions. We came upon several Chinese soldiers. One was sitting down with his back toward our advancing platoon and throwing hand grenades backward. To the right of him were three of his buddies firing their burp guns.

The Chinese grenade thrower was less than 30 feet away and was too busy to see us. I think Kubinski and I fired at the same time. I fired several rounds, which slammed the Chinese back against some sandbags. Immediately after I had shot him there was an explosion in front of him. A hand grenade he had armed must have exploded in his hands.

Kubinski was still firing after I had downed the grenade-throwing Chinese. I asked him what happened and he said that he thought he got one and missed the other two. Then we both rushed forward.

The grenadier was dead and all bloodied when I got to him. I couldn't tell where I had shot him because he was bloodied from many shrapnel wounds. I was shaking. There was a sack of hand grenades next to him. That could have exploded, too, when the grenade exploded in his hands. He had no weapon. I picked up the sack of grenades but threw it back on the ground. I didn't know at the time how to arm them.

Kubinski did get one but missed the other two. We didn't know where they disappeared to. There was a shallow trench so we stayed in it. I told him we would move back to back, he back pedaling and I facing forward. He was to cover our backs.

After a few shuffling steps his M-1 rifle roared a couple of times, and when I jerked around to see what was happening, he pointed to where we had killed the two Chinese. I didn't see anyone. I turned around and saw two figures jump out of a hole about 20 yards ahead of me and run down the forward slope. I snapped off a couple of rounds in their direction, then lost sight of them.

Small arms fire had now dwindled and there were just a few bursting grenades. Men were shouting but I couldn't tell what they were saying until I saw some of our men pointing downhill to many figures running. The Chinese were leaving in a hurry. Under the pulsating light of the flares, I emptied clip after clip of ammo at the fleeing Chinese. We had taken Old Baldy from the Chinese, but we still had some mopping up to do.

It was about midnight when we secured the hill, but far down the hill I could see figures milling around. The Chinese refused to go away.

I knew our platoon took some casualties but I didn't know how many. I think there were two missing from our squad when Conley assembled us to prepare defensive positions. Kubinski and I were paired again. We never told anyone of our encounter with the Chinese soldiers we had killed. Suddenly I remembered Abreu, who was in the 1st Squad. I jumped out my hole to look for him, which was a stupid thing to do because I could have been shot by one of our own men since we had not yet cleared the hill entirely of Chinese. I didn't know where the 1st Squad was deployed so I searched the left side of the hill, staying behind the line of foxholes and calling out, "Willie! Willie!"

"Ova heah! Ova heah!" came the reply.

Man, was I happy to hear that voice. He was as scared as I was and said he was just going to look for me. I told him to cover his ass and he said for me to do the same and I headed back to my own position.

Kubinski and I took turns improving our foxhole. It really was a small crater probably made by a Chinese 61mm mortar round. I dug first and Kubinski stood watch. When my turn came to watch, the shattered tree trunks on the forward slope in front of our hole played tricks on me. I would swear that some of them moved. Kubinski only laughed when I told him what I had imagined.

At about 0300 hours, our foxhole was only about 3 feet deep, not deep enough to stand in. We dragged several fallen tree trunks and limbs to our hole and placed them in front of it.

Then it came, at about 0400 hours, while I was still digging. Kubinski was on watch. He suddenly grabbed my arm and pointed to the distant hills. I saw many flashes beyond the mountains held by the Chinese. About a second or two later, we heard the distant sounds, like soft, rolling thunder. We heard the first few rounds whining and rumbling overhead as they overshot the hill. The ones that we didn't hear impacted on the hill without a pause. It seemed like all the commies' guns in North Korea were firing at Old Baldy. Kubinski jumped in the hole and landed on me. Times like this being small was an advantage as both of us were less than 5 feet 6 inches in height with small body frames. And the shells came crashing down. Every now and then our steel helmets would be hit by small pieces of shrapnel. Sometimes we could hear the whirring sounds of larger pieces of shrapnel as they went sailing over our heads. When a shell exploded nearby, it took our breath away. They had the hill zeroed in, and for the next fifteen minutes we just took the pasting the Chinese gave us.

From time to time we would take turns peeking out the hole to see if the Chinese were walking behind their artillery barrage. Not this time, though. For the rest of my ten-month stay in Korea, I would never again have the same experience. I must have broken the record for saying the "Hail Mary" and, at the same time, the profanities that came from my mouth would have embarrassed anyone. No one can accurately describe the fear and terror one goes through while on the receiving end of an artillery barrage.

I thought the shelling would never stop but it finally did. Both

Kubinski and I were shaken but not hurt. The hill was still smoking and the dust had not yet settled when I jumped out of the hole and ran to Willie's foxhole. He was blown out of the foxhole and was unconscious and bleeding from the nose and ear. I couldn't find any kind of injury on him. His foxhole buddy was dead, partly covered by dirt. A sliver of metal was sticking out of his helmet. Several large craters surrounded their foxhole, the edge of one crater only a few feet from theirs—probably the one that got Willie and his foxhole buddy. Willie was still unconscious when he was evacuated from the hill.

When morning came I was shocked at the amount of devastation on the hill. The entire hill was in shambles, pocketed with numerous shell craters, large and small. Hardly any part of the hill had escaped the shelling. Old Baldy was now even more bald, just a brown lump in the otherwise green, surrounding terrain. The sides of many foxholes had collapsed and some had dead GIs in them. Several were replacements like me who had been in Korea for only three weeks. Those of us who were not injured assisted the wounded down the reverse slope of Old Baldy, where litter teams from other companies took them to the aid station.

FIGURE 36   Scarred Hill of Old Baldy in the distance as seen from the MLR. July 1952. Courtesy of Glenn E. White.

FIGURE 37   A closeup view of the forward slope of Old Baldy after weeks of fighting. Two dead Chinese soldiers are barely visible at the left and the right of the photo. July 1952. Courtesy of Glenn E. White.

But there was no time to rest. We had to fortify the hill in anticipation of counterattacks and more artillery fire. With the help of combat engineers and KSCs, we began the task of building bunkers and digging commo trenches. Small TNT packages were used by the engineers to blast holes in the ground just below the crest on the reverse slope to get us started on the bunkers. KSCs collected tree stumps and logs and carried them to where the bunkers were being built. Nothing fancy. They were not living quarters but simple protection from artillery and mortar fire. We just laid the logs across the top of holes and placed three layers of sandbags on them and covered them with dirt. The holes could accommodate between two and four men. I must have filled a hundred sandbags with dirt.

The combat engineers planted mines and trip flares on the forward slope and laid concertina barbed wire the entire frontage of the hill. Later we took our empty C-ration cans, put some small rocks in them, and hung them on the barbed wire to serve as an alarm system. They would rattle if the Chinese tried to breach the wire.

We worked all day and I didn't see one goldbricking GI because we all realized that our lives depended on each other. When night came we were just dog-tired and filthy. The sweat and dirt just caked our fatigues and we must have smelled terrible.

Kubinski and I were called to dig a hole for the platoon's latrine on

FIGURE 38   Pvt. George Matsunaga of Kuiaha, Maui, cleans his Browning
Automatic Rifle before going out on patrol. June 1952. Courtesy of George
Matsunaga.

the reverse slope. Nobody gave us directions so, using our creativity, we
dug a trench about 2 feet wide, 6 feet long, and 5 feet deep, large enough
to accommodate two people at once. We laid steel pickets across the
width of the trench, leaving two openings at both ends. Those using the
latrine would squat back to back and do their business. Let me tell you,
this was no time to be bashful. Those who wanted more privacy took
their entrenching tool and went off elsewhere to relieve themselves.

Directly ahead of us was Chink Baldy, a short 400 yards away, occupied by chinks. We drew occasional sniper fire from Chink Baldy.

At about 0100 hour, the Chinese started the attack with an artillery barrage that lasted for about five minutes. Then they shot green flares in the air to signal the attack. At that moment, our forward observer called for illuminating flares and heavy mortars. We watched the chinks bunched up in front of Chink Baldy. They simply walked up to our hill in formation in spite of the pasting they were getting from our heavy mortars. No fancy fire and maneuver tactics for them.

We should have waited until the chinks got closer, but Kubinski and I started firing when we saw a group of Chinese break off to our left from the main body to outflank us. Meanwhile, our forward observer was on the ball and shifted mortar fire to the left. There were brief moments of darkness that prevented us from keeping track of the chinks' movements. Guys were yelling, "Flares, more flares." Of course, the mortar crews in the back couldn't hear them, but the guys yelled anyway.

Kubinski and I poured fire in the direction of the Chinese, who were now about 200 yards from us. Flashes from their guns were quite distinct and we could hear the sound of their rifle fire. For fear that we could both be put out of action at the same time, Kubinski leaped out of the hole and took up position in a crater about 10 feet from me as bullets struck the parapet.

Suddenly, the entire hill was lit, including the valley below. We saw searchlight beams bouncing off low-lying clouds onto the battlefield and really lighting up the area in front of us. The chinks were now caught in the open, exposed by the searchlights. Kubinski and I were yelling obscenities at the chinks as we continued to fire. They couldn't get close enough with their grenades and burp guns. Kubinski and I just hammered away until a couple of red flares from the valley shot up into the sky. The Chinese had called off their attack and were retreating to Chink Baldy.

The use of searchlights by our side was a new thing to us. We later learned that the searchlights were from the antiaircraft artillery searchlight batteries. They were mounted on trucks and moved wherever they were needed. One disadvantage, though—low-lying clouds were required for their use.

Sometime during the night our platoon leader, platoon sergeant, and squad leaders had a powwow with an officer from battalion. While they were meeting on the reverse slope, a mortar round burst several yards from the group. All received shrapnel wounds except the officer from battalion. Luckily the round was a 61mm Chinese mortar, a small one.

A lucky shot, we thought, but we all knew that the chinks were excellent with their mortars.

After midnight, green flares shot up into sky. Again, our searchlights came on, revealing a large number of Chinese forming in the valley to our right. There was a smaller group forming on Chink Baldy. At first the Chinese were massed, but as they made their way up, they began to spread themselves to our flanks. Then our mortar and artillery rounds began to drop on the mass of Chinese but that didn't stop them.

They kept coming! When they were about 100 yards away from our positions, Sergeant Conley yelled for us to beat it to the reverse slope and to take cover in the small bunkers we had built earlier. Kubinski and I took off and dove into a two-man bunker. We didn't have long to wait. We heard and felt thunderous explosions above us. There were no pauses between explosions. I curled my body into a fetal position while pieces of steel struck the top of the bunker. It was dark in the bunker so I couldn't see Kubinski. I would bet that he was as wide-eyed and scared as I was.

It seemed like forever but the explosions outside finally stopped. If the fire had not discouraged the Chinese, they would soon be throwing explosives into the bunkers. So with my M-1 rifle in hand, I told Kubinski that it would be better to go out and fight the Chinese in the open than be caught inside the bunker.

I got out of the bunker, ran a few feet, and threw myself on the ground, looking around at the same time. I saw other men also leaving their bunkers. Flares, replacing the searchlights, were still drifting down to the ground. I looked up at the crest, expecting hand grenades, but nothing came. I also expected to see Chinese bodies strewn all over the hill but was disappointed. I don't think there were more than half a dozen Chinese bodies on the hill. We could only guess that our artillery had stopped the Chinese before they could get to the crest and the survivors took back with them all their wounded and most of their dead.

At daylight, we surveyed the destruction on the hill. The first thing I did was to check the roof of the bunker that I had been in. There was no longer any dirt on it. The top two layers of sandbags were shredded and contained many pieces of shrapnel, some at least a foot long. The larger pieces of shrapnel reached the first layers of logs. One thing for damn sure, our artillery saved our asses. I told myself to be sure to thank those guys if I ever ran into them again.

And guess what? The latrine that Kubinski and I had dug was intact. Some officers were happy with the latrine that Kubinski and I had dug earlier and decided to promote the two of us to permanent latrine detail for the duration of our stay on Old Baldy. Talk about getting a shitty job.

After six days on Old Baldy, we were relieved by Baker Company. We sat at the bottom of the hill as the men of Baker Company made their way up the reverse slope of Old Baldy. As they filed by, Kubinski remarked how fresh and clean they looked. I looked at Kubinski and for the first time I saw how dirty he was. He had grown a beard and his eyes were red and sunken in from lack of sleep for five days. He had a distant look in his eyes and seemed to have lost a lot of weight. I didn't dare tell him what he looked like because I was afraid he would return the compliment.

I didn't count the number of men who were left from the original 200 or so that the company had before Old Baldy, but there sure weren't 200 when we left the hill. Of the original nine men in our squad when we started out, there were now five. Kubinski was ordered to report to the company rear and would remain there until it was time for him to rotate home. I never saw him again.

Vicinity of Pando-gol

By motor convoy, we traveled 17 miles and arrived near the village of Pando-gol at 1730 hours for a deserved rest. There were no squad tents so those who were not exhausted put up their two-man tents. I just threw my poncho on the ground and used my combat pack as a pillow and passed out.

A mobile 8th Army hot shower unit was in the area down the road a bit and we were shuttled by squads to the shower. We discarded every piece of clothing except our boots. There were towels and GI soap and even scrub brushes. There were several tables of clean fatigues, underwear, and socks. I was able to find underwear and socks to fit me but fatigues? No way. I left the shower with over-sized clothes.

When I went back to the company area after the shower, who did I see sitting in a jeep behind the wheel? Willie Abreu! He was all right! The last time I saw him he was unconscious and had been taken off the hill on a litter. He said he received some very small shrapnel wounds and suffered a concussion. The doctors recommended that he be kept off the line so now he was jeep driver for one of our company's officers. He had it made. He said if the company needed another jeep driver, he would recommend me. After all, I had a diploma in auto mechanics. "Yeah, right," I told Willie.

Tosin-ni, North Korea

On the afternoon of June 21, we were alerted to pack up and get ready to move out to a blocking position. One of our battalions was engaged in a furious battle and we might be needed to counterattack in case the hill was lost.

We left Pando-gol at 1730 hours and arrived at our blocking position at about 2030 hours. The next morning the assistant squad leader Sergeant Amour and several guys from the 1st Squad appeared in front of our bunker.

Sergeant Armour said the unit on Old Baldy almost got overrun the night before and had taken a lot of casualties. Litter bearers were needed to bring the wounded down from the hill to the forward aid station, which was just down the road from us. He also said that the Chinese now occupied part of Old Baldy. He needed volunteers, two per litter, but not two men from the same squad. We all looked at each other without saying anything. But Pfc. James Bess, from the 1st Squad, volunteered me and wanted me for his partner. Before I could get a word in he said, "Sergeant Armour, I'll take Baldy." That was the nickname he gave me when we first met. Baldy, short for Baldovi. Bess was a black from New York and over 6 feet tall. He was once an amateur boxer too, so who was I to argue?

We were warned that the Chinese still held part of Old Baldy and to be armed. The M-1 rifle was too heavy so I borrowed a carbine and Bess found a pistol.

There were more than a dozen litter teams. About 1500 hours, we took to the trail past Hill 347 to get to Old Baldy. With Bess carrying the litter, we took the lead and in less than an hour reached Checkpoint Charlie, a small knob on a finger that ran down from Hill 347. There were two large bunkers at the checkpoint. Directly in front of it was Old Baldy.

The litter teams were instructed to bring the wounded from Old Baldy to the checkpoint, where other teams of litter bearers would take them to the forward aid station.

Occasional rifle fire could be heard coming from the hill. I could see men grouped in holes or shell craters on the reverse slope.

Bess and I made two trips without any difficulty. The third and last trip almost got us killed.

Bess said quietly, "Let's go, Baldy," and we headed back to the hill, again running into other litter teams headed in the opposite direction. This time we had to go farther up because all the wounded on the lower part of the hill had been evacuated. There was no small arms fire but there were mortar rounds bursting on the forward slope. Every now and then one would fall on the reverse slope.

A medic who was tending a wounded GI called out and waved us to come to him. Both legs of the injured soldier were riddled with shrapnel. We put him on the litter and started downhill. We almost got to the bottom of Old Baldy when mortar rounds, big ones, probably the Chinese 120mm type, began falling on the hill. Bess was on the front end of the litter and he started running. I had no choice but to follow. With my short legs, I had a hell of a time keeping up with Bess. The injured GI did not cry out.

There appeared to be an increase in enemy mortar fire when we got to the bottom of the hill, several bursting on the reverse slope. Going up the hill we had problems because Bess, being taller, had the litter tilted toward me. The injured GI was in danger of falling off. I tried to raise my end of the litter to my shoulder when mortar rounds began falling near us. One was so close that the blast made both of us lose our grip on the litter and we dropped it. The wounded GI tumbled off. Through the dust and smoke I caught a glimpse of Bess as he made his way on his hands and feet to one of the bunker's entrances at the checkpoint. I was about 20 yards away from the bunkers. I began clawing my way up the hill with little progress. It seemed like I was in slow motion. I knew I wasn't going to reach the bunker, so I crawled into a fresh crater made by a shell moments before. The crater was still smoking. I had my face in the dirt when someone grabbed me by the arm and started to yank me to my feet. I saw two black hands on both my arms. I looked up and saw Bess. "You can make it, Baldy," he shouted, and he half-dragged me to the entrance of the bunker and just threw me in.

Once in the bunker Bess looked at me and shook his head. I knew what he meant. We had abandoned our man on the litter.

A few minutes later, the shelling stopped and Bess and I ran out to look for the GI we had dropped. He was farther down from where we had dropped him. He was lying face down with a wound in his back. We called a medic but the GI was dead.

While we waited, I noticed that Bess was bleeding from his back and called his attention to it. The wound wasn't serious. He said, "Hey, I'm going to get the Purple Heart." Then he checked me out to see if I was injured. All I had were bruises from rocks when I tried to crawl to the bunker.

Before his rotation home, Bess and I often talked about that one incident and we blamed ourselves for leaving the injured man out there while we sought shelter. I told Bess that he probably saved my life but he dismissed it. He said I would have probably done the same for him if I were in his position. "Don't count on it," I told him. It never dawned on me at the time to recommend Bess for a decoration.

From blocking position we moved 2 miles to the rear into division reserve to rest for a couple of days.

JUNE 1952

PVT. GEORGE MATSUNAGA
Item Company, 180th Infantry
Yokkok-chon Valley, North Korea

When I first joined the company in late May, my squad leader handed me a BAR and said I was now the BAR man in the squad. I was 5 feet 9 inches tall and was big enough to carry the 15 pound weapon. Its rate of fire was 550 rounds per minute. I thought it was a compliment but later found out it wasn't. Lives of BAR men were short because they were one of the primary targets for the enemy. The BAR gave the rifle squad its heavy fire power. I didn't mind, though, because I was very familiar with the weapon.

Pork Chop Hill, North Korea

To our company front were several low-lying hills or ridges. One was called T-Bone Hill and the other Pork Chop Hill, because they resembled the two cuts of meat, at least that's what the map indicated. T-Bone extended 2 miles into chink territory. An outpost called Eerie was on the southern tip of T-Bone, almost directly in front of our company's position.

Since our arrival, I wondered when we were really going to see some action. Not that I was gutsy but I was more curious as to what combat was really like. I finally got my wish.

On June 4, we were told that Item Company had a mission and our objective was Pork Chop Hill. The next day, we were relieved by another unit and sent to the back of Hill 347 to prepare for the attack. Other units were also in the area. From them we learned that this was a large operation in which the entire division was involved. The division was to take and hold eleven hills held by the Chinese.

I don't think anyone slept that night although we were told to get some rest because sleep would be hard to come by the next few days.

All day on June 6, we could hear our artillery booming. That night we moved to the line of departure in the dry rice paddies in front of Hill 347. We were to take Pork Chop Hill with two platoons while one platoon was held back in reserve.

We left the departure area in two columns and headed for Pork Chop. An hour later Pork Chop loomed before us in the dark. The hill was smoking from burned trees and brush from an earlier pounding by air strikes and artillery.

I was in the lead platoon. We fanned out in a skirmish with the second platoon behind us. It was an easy climb at first because of the gradual slope of the hill—until we got near the top, where the hill steepened. That was when my BAR felt like it weighed 100 pounds.

We were making quite a bit of noise, men slipping and falling and cussing. A couple of helmets fell off some heads and rolled several yards down the hill until someone stopped them. Steel helmets against rocks make a hell of a noise. Shit, we might as well let the chinks know we were there, if they didn't already.

Looking up, I saw many trails of sparks in the air coming from the crest of the hill. Immediately, I thought, *firecrackers,* because as a kid I used to throw lighted firecrackers in the air and they sparked as they fell to ground before bursting. Bullshit! They were sparks from grenades thrown by the chinks. The grenades sailed over my head and burst behind me. I flattened myself to the ground, not being able to find some kind of hole to jump in. I hadn't thought of firing my BAR. I was only concerned about dodging the hand grenades, which were now falling among the men in the first skirmish line. "Go! Go! Don't stop!" came the shouts.

The chinks now opened up with burp guns. I could see the flashes from their muzzles. We were warned of the burp gun's rapid rate of fire. Looking to one side I saw men getting up and running up the hill. Before getting up I aimed my BAR at the top of the hill and emptied an entire magazine with one long burst. I reloaded and dashed up the hill, firing in short bursts.

The hill was now lit with flares and I could see figures moving around with their arms in motion, flinging grenades. I fired in their direction and saw dirt kicked up by my rounds. There was now a lot of yelling by our men but we were still short of the crest. I must have been about 30 yards from it when the volume of fire from the Chinese increased tremendously. So did the number of hand grenades thrown by them. I was lucky to find a log and dove behind it. There was a mad

minute of firing by the Chinese. Then, as if someone had given the command to cease fire, the top of the hill became quiet. "Move out! Move
out!" came the shouts again.

The hill was absent of Chinese except for a few dead ones. They had
vacated the hill. Their dead were in a large shell crater while the
wounded were scattered throughout the hill. I couldn't get a good look
at them because the hill was now in darkness. It must have been about
0100 hours.

At daybreak, some of us were in a shallow trench waiting for our
squad leader to return after his meeting with the platoon sergeant. Our
platoon was scattered all over the hill. We didn't have visual contact with
them because of the hilly terrain. Suddenly Chinese potato masher
grenades came sailing into the trench and exploded, injuring several
men. I raised my BAR over the lip of the trench but didn't see anyone
so I threw several grenades in the direction from which the Chinese
grenades had come from. As soon as the grenades burst, I leaped from
the trench and emptied a magazine in their direction.

I wondered where the Chinese had come from because our platoon
had supposedly cleared that part of the ridge. Instead of waiting, I told
the guys, "Let's go find some Chinese before they find us." So we got
out of the trench and made a sweep of the area extending at least 50 yards
from where we were. Then we saw something suspicious. There were
pieces of cardboard that partly covered a small hole about 2 feet in diameter. When I got closer, I saw it was a deep hole, probably from where
the grenades were thrown. I told the guys if there were Chinese in the
hole they might come out, and all we had to do was wait and maybe capture a prisoner or two. We backed off about 20 yards and waited quietly.
After about five minutes a pair of hands removed the cardboard pieces
from the tunnel entrance and a head partially appeared in the opening.
Before I could do anything one of the guys blasted away with his M-1,
splattering brains and blood all over the tunnel entrance. The body disappeared into the tunnel and a couple of hand grenades came flying out
of the tunnel, forcing us to retreat to a safe distance. So there were a few
more down there, but how many I didn't know. By this time our squad
leader had returned and asked what all the firing was about. After I
explained what had happened, he told us to stand fast and to keep an eye
on the hole and left. He returned with two combat engineers with
satchel charges of explosives. They threw two charges into the open and
yelled, "Fire in the hole!" The blast really shook the hill. When the smoke
and dust cleared, the tunnel entrance was sealed. We must have buried

a bunch of Chinese. Some said a tunnel like that could hold as much as a platoon or a company of men.

The engineers, escorted by a couple of men, combed the hill for other tunnel entrances. Throughout the afternoon there was an occasional blast of explosives, which gave us some comfort knowing that the combat engineers had found more tunnels.

JUNE 1952

PVT. TARO GOYA
Baker Company, 180th Infantry
Old Baldy, North Korea

My first night on line was absolutely frightening, especially when the Chinese welcomed us over their loudspeakers. That scared the hell out of me.

We relieved Able Company on Old Baldy after it had taken the hill from the Chinese. The men of Able Company were sprawled on the side of the trail, waiting for us to get out of the way so they could leave. I cannot forget the looks on their faces. They just stared with a sort of blank look on their faces. "The thousand yard stare" they called it. Days of combat without sleep, water, and food and being close to being killed every day must have done that to them.

After I had things straightened out in my foxhole, I went looking for the other four local men in the company. I knew Louis Kaolelo was a platoon sergeant and so he wasn't hard to find. Besides, he was called Big Louie because of his size so all I had to do was ask if anyone had seen Big Louie. After I found him we went looking for Robert Toyama, William Castillo, and Andrew Fernandez. We found them and managed to spend a few minutes together wishing each other luck before it got dark.

To the front and slightly left of Old Baldy about 400 yards away was another hill smaller than Old Baldy called Chink Baldy, which was occupied by the Chinese day and night. I was careful not to stick my head out of my hole. A narrow saddle with steep sides connected Chink Baldy to Old Baldy.

At 0100 hours I heard noises at the barbed wire apron in front of my position. Empty C-ration cans filled with rocks hung on the wire by Able Company rattled at several points along the wire. Than I heard the familiar "thunk" of our 60mm mortars behind us on the reverse slope. Someone must have heard the same thing and called for flares. In less than 30 seconds our flares popped above Old Baldy, revealing shadowy figures at the wire. I heard the BAR open fire first, followed by rifle fire.

I don't know how many of us in our squad opened fired but I did. Bodies toppled on the wire. After I fired the first clip, I threw several hand grenades down the slope. The Chinese threw several grenades in return, which made me duck in my hole for a few seconds. I tried to reload my rifle with another clip, but I was so nervous that I knocked the rounds out of the clip, which fell to the ground. By the time I got another clip loaded, the firing had stopped.

Then from Chink Baldy came a sharp "crack" and then "wham" on our hill. It happened about three time s in quick succession. It was a chink recoilless rifle, a flat trajectory weapon. At that range, the round would impact almost the same time the gun was fired. But in no time our heavy machine guns brought Chink Baldy under fire and quieted the recoilless rifle.

The fire fight had lasted less than five minutes. It was only a probe by a small force to find a weak spot in our defense. We knew we had killed a few, but we were told to remain in our holes.

At daybreak two bodies hung on the wire in front of our squad. A couple of men from our squad went out to check the bodies and found them dead. The bodies were tangled up in the wire and wire cutters were needed to free them. The bodies were cut loose and dragged to the reverse slope for all to see. That was the first time I saw a dead Chinese.

JUNE 1952

PVT. ROBERT FERNANDEZ
Charlie Company, 180th Infantry
Old Baldy, North Korea

Able and Baker Companies from the 1st Battalion did their time on Old Baldy and it was now our turn. We relieved Baker Company just before dusk and quickly settled into our position.

My platoon was positioned on the right of the hill. I was paired off with a mainland haole in a foxhole that wasn't big enough for both of us so I told him that we needed to make it larger. He said the hole was good enough. I told him if that's the way he wanted it, I was going to find my own foxhole and he could stay there by himself. That shook him up a bit and he decided to help me improve the foxhole.

The first night was very quiet but there was some action on Pork Chop Hill to our right, less than a mile away. There were flares over the hill and tracer bullets streaked back and forth above it. It was too far away to hear small arms fire. The action continued throughout the night.

When morning came we laid another row of concertina barbed wire in front of us and hung more empty C-ration cans filled with small stones on it. The engineers also placed several cans of napalm between the two rows of barbed wire.

We outdid ourselves in improving our hole. From the foxhole we dug trenches to both sides of the foxhole and made a grenade sump in the middle of the hole. If a grenade was thrown into our hole, it would roll into the sump and explode harmlessly—we hoped. We dug shelves into the side of the foxhole on which to place our extra ammo and grenades. Sandbags filled with dirt two layers high surrounded our position.

One of the guys two foxholes away came by and admired our work. "All that work for nothing," he said. "We'll probably move out tomorrow."

It started innocently, like at about 2100 hours. One mortar round here, one there, maybe spaced a minute or so apart, continuing for about ten minutes. *Just harassing fire,* I thought. Then the number of bursting rounds increased slightly and then picked up noticeably. "On your toes, on your toes," came warnings from the back. "This might be an attack." Now we were getting the big stuff, 120mm mortars.

My buddy and I hunkered in the hole but peered out every few minutes to watch for advancing enemy troops. Our illuminating flares lit the hill and I could see far down the forward slope. Now I could see dark, small, moving groups about 300 yards away. Our mortars and artillery took them under fire. No one had to give the order to fire. The machine guns fired first because of the distance and then the rifles picked up the firing. I just fired as fast as I could. At 300 yards, even with the flares providing some light, it was difficult to tell if our firing had any effect on the advancing enemy. Tracer rounds from our machine guns spun crazily into the air after ricocheting off something hard.

Then someone from the back went charging down hill past our foxhole yelling like mad and firing a BAR. The guy must have been nuts. He must have gone about 20 yards past our position, slid to a stop, turned around, and raced back up the hill. I swear he was laughing when he ran back past us.

Above the noise of shell and rifle fire I could hear the rapid pings of ejected ammo clips from M-1 rifles. I don't think anyone tried to conserve any ammo. Then I heard our grenades bursting downhill even though the range was still too far for hand grenades. We had about 30 grenades in our foxhole so we started throwing them as rapidly as we could. I think everyone on the hill started throwing hand grenades, putting up a wall of steel fragments. I yelled, my buddy yelled, and I think everyone on the hill yelled. I yelled to overcome my fear. Most of the phrases were obscenities.

I believe the barrage of hand grenades we threw proved to be the turning point of the battle because the enemy started to pull back, dragging some of their and dead and wounded. We continued to fire until the cease fire order was given.

JUNE 1952

PVT. CLAYTON MURAKAMI
King Company, 180th Infantry
Yokkok-chon Valley, North Korea

On June 11, our company received word that we were going to take part in a raid on a hill named Pokkae Ridge. I didn't know it at the time but Pokkae Ridge was one of several hills located in the valley below us. It was located between Pork Chop Hill and T-Bone Hill, about a mile in front of the MLR. There were other hills in the area which became more celebrated later, such as Old Baldy, Pork Chop Hill, T-Bone Hill, Eerie, and Arrowhead.

This was going to be a tank infantry attack. The tanks led the way and we followed behind them, crossing dry rice paddies. We were getting some mortar rounds but continued to press forward until we got to the bottom of the Pokkae Ridge. The tanks laid back and fired at the ridge while we charged, firing as we went up. We were yelling and firing the way we were taught in basic training. But there was no return fire from the ridge. I made it to the trench line but found no enemy. Some guys threw hand grenades into some bunkers but all the bunkers were empty. The hill was not occupied, lucky for us. So we quickly got off the hill and made our way back to our lines with enemy mortars tracking us. We made it back to our company area on the MLR without any loss of personnel.

JUNE 1952

PFC. RICHARD MIYAMOTO
King Company, 180th Infantry
T-Bone Hill, North Korea

Eerie was a knob on the southern end of the 2-mile-long ridge called T-Bone Hill. We had relieved Fox Company of the 2d Battalion, which had taken Eerie in a slam, bang, night battle with the Chinese.

We dug trenches and foxholes and built bunkers despite being harassed by Chinese mortars that kept us scurrying around on our hands and knees. We were living like rats.

With me on Eerie were Matsuo Sakai and Isami Izawa from Maui,

Yoshi Yoshinaga from Molokai, Takeo Ebesu from Kauai, and Clayton Murakami from the island of Hawaii. I think the 3d Battalion of the 180th Infantry Regiment had the largest number of Hawaii boys in the 45th Infantry Division.

Eerie was really a small knoll but well fortified, with bunkers arranged in a semicircle around the top with trenches connecting them. Other trenches ran down to fighting positions almost to the bottom of the hill.

In the afternoon the Chinese blasted us with artillery and mortar fire. It was estimated later that in a span of twenty-five minutes 500 rounds slammed in on this tiny outpost. No one was safe anywhere. The worst place was in a bunker because if it collapsed one would be buried under all that sandbags and logs. The safest spot was in a foxhole because it was a smaller target.

About 300 yards farther in on T-Bone two squads from Love Company manned Hill 191, another outpost. It made me feel safe because now there was a friendly unit between us and the Chinese. On the outpost were two Hawaii men, Donald Yap and Kaname Tamashiro, both from Maui.

On the second night a Chinese force surprised the defenders of the outpost and quickly overran it. Our platoon went to its aid but it was too late. There were a few survivors but Yap was not one of them and was reported missing in action. Tamashiro was wounded and was last seen being brought in by a litter team. Somehow, Tamashiro was reported missing in action.

We combed the hill for other survivors. All we found were a couple of steel helmets, cartridge belts, and a damaged machine gun, all American equipment.

JUNE 1952

Honolulu, Territory of Hawaii

The *Honolulu Star-Bulletin* reported the following news item.

ISLE MAN MISSING, TWO HURT IN KOREA:
One soldier is listed as missing in action and two others as wounded on today's report of Hawaii's casualties in the Korean War.

They are:

Private Donald A. Yap, son of Stephen Apu Yap of Kahului, Maui, missing.

Private 1st Class Shigeo Otake, husband of Lillian Yurie Otake of Spreckelsville, Maui, slightly wounded.

Private Robert K. Hu, son of Wong Hu, 549-H N. School St., slightly wounded.

Casualties now total 1,118, with 271 killed, 726 wounded, 81 missing and 40 prisoners of war.

JUNE 1952

Pvt. Clayton Murakami
King Company, 180th Infantry
T-Bone Hill, North Korea

While we were on Outpost Eerie, our company was given the assignment to retake Hill 191, which was lost to the Chinese earlier by Love Company. We were to attack with a reinforced platoon.

About dusk, artillery and tanks gave the hill a good going over for almost an hour while we waited. After the support fire lifted, we formed a skirmish line with fixed bayonets and moved out from Eerie across an open area to Hill 191. We got into the lower trench system and found it empty. Using the trench we were able to get to about 100 yards from the top when enemy soldiers popped into full view and fired down on us. Then enemy mortar rounds began to crunch all around. Our squad leaders yelled for us to keep on going. I ran up the hill and fired at the trench line, where I could see heads bobbing up and down. But I was still maybe about 80 yards from the crest of the hill.

I saw a couple of our men firing from a shell crater so I joined them. After a few minutes we moved out again and came across a cave dug into the side of the hill. A couple of the guys fired into the cave opening while I worked my way to the side of the cave and threw a hand grenade in the opening. The grenade exploded and threw up dirt and smoke. No one wanted to check the inside of the cave. Instead of going straight up in the face of enemy fire, we circled the hill to the right and came across a couple more caves. Someone threw a smoke grenade in one cave and a few seconds later, smoke came billowing out from two or three different openings in the ground several yards away. The holes were connected by tunnels.

When I got closer to the top of the hill, sticks of hand grenades came floating down. Some fell short, some to the side, and some burst behind me. I made it to the trench, jumped in, and joined several others. I came to a bend in the trench and saw a hand grenade in the air coming straight at me. Before I could throw myself to ground, the grenade exploded. It was a concussion grenade and it only stunned me, or so I thought at first. I didn't know whether the Chinese who threw the grenade got away or was killed by our men.

Suddenly, two chinks ran out of a bunker but before I could raise my rifle to fire they were cut down by a BAR man. I ran past the bunker entrance and threw a grenade into the bunker without stopping. I followed the BAR man and we came upon another bunker. There was an opening at the top of the bunker so I dropped two grenades into the hole. The BAR man fired several bursts into the slit of the bunker.

We worked our way to the north side of the hill and came upon another bunker. Three chinks came running out throwing grenades. I took quick shots at them and they ran back into the bunker. I was all out of hand grenades. I told the BAR man to keep them pinned down while I went looking for grenades.

I must have run around the hill for about five minutes asking for grenades, but those who had a few refused to give up any. I went back to the BAR man, who was firing single shots into the bunker from about 40 feet away and told him I couldn't find any. He got up and did the damnedest thing. He loaded a full magazine into his BAR, walked to the bunker like he was on a Sunday morning stroll, and just blasted away at the bunker. He stopped a few feet from the bunker's opening, loaded another magazine, and emptied it into the bunker. There was no response from inside the bunker. I guess he was fed up playing games with the chinks.

The rest of the bunkers on Eerie were cleared. Now that we had the hill we were ordered to dig in because a counterattack was expected. I remember being told to dig at a precise spot. As I dug, an enemy machine gun from about 200 yards away swept our hill with fire. Bullets peppered the ground in front of me, showering me with dirt. I got out of my hole and sprinted to the top of the hill, where there was better cover. We were supposed to have dug in on the other side of the hill. Amazingly no one got hit.

I dug my hole and settled in, trying to get comfortable, when I started to feel some pain in my lower back. When I told the guy in the next foxhole how I felt, he yelled for a medic. Our medic, whom we called "Chief," came immediately. He helped me remove my flak jacket and lifted my shirt together with the *senninbari*, the sash with all the red dots. Of course, I couldn't see my back but the way Chief reacted, I could tell he didn't like what he saw. All he said was for me to go to the forward aid station, but I told him that I was okay. Besides, the battalion aid station was located behind Hill 347 and the trail leading to it was being shelled by the Chinese. Then I began to feel the pain in my back. He said for me to wait and left. He returned with our platoon leader, who ordered me to get to get off the hill.

I put on my shirt and flak jacket, grabbed my rifle, and made my way back to the aid station along with other wounded men. As we got closer to the station, I could see there was a tent set up to keep out the hot summer sun. When we got there I saw about a dozen dead men laying on the ground covered with blankets. One of them was only partially covered and I could see the upper half of the body. I moved closer to the body for a better look. He was an Oriental and looked like someone from Hawaii so I bent down to check his dog tag around his neck and it read "Shishido." He was from Hawaii. He was the first man from Hawaii whose lifeless body I saw. I silently said, "Namo Ami da Butsu," a short Buddhist prayer.

I entered the aid station and the one in charge looked at my wound. He said that he was sending me back to a hospital because the wound required an operation. A piece of shrapnel was embedded in my back but not serious enough to be called a "million dollar" wound. I was told to lay on my stomach on a stretcher and was taken to the rear and put on a truck with other wounded men and driven to a MASH hospital near Seoul.

I was operated on and, when I regained consciousness, the doctor who operated on me said I was damn lucky because the fragment had just missed my spine by half an inch. Any closer, and I would have been paralyzed for life. I believe that the *senninbari*, the sash wrapped around my waist, saved my life. I never saw it again after the operation and when I asked for it, no one knew where it was. The medics probably thought that it was just a piece of rag and threw it away. I was worried. I was without my good luck piece.

I was presented the Purple Heart Medal at the hospital. When I was well enough I was put on a train to Pusan and transferred to a Swedish hospital ship, where I stayed for a month recuperating.

There were a lot of wounded men, especially from the 45th Division, and I couldn't help but wonder what my buddies were going through. Word got back to us in the hospital that a bloody battle was going on for the hills that we had taken in June. I had mixed feelings about not being there.

JUNE 1952

Pvt. George Matsunaga
Item Company, 180th Infantry
T-Bone Hill, North Korea

We relieved King Company on Outpost Eerie. The next night at 2000 hours the Chinese attacked, preceded by a tremendous artillery barrage. I was trying to squeeze my body into my flak jacket and helmet in the trench when a shell hit just in front and collapsed the side of the trench on me, partially covering me with dirt. My BAR was also covered with dirt. I shook the BAR to get rid of as much dirt as I could, pointed it straight up, and pulled the trigger to see if the weapon would fire. Lucky for me it did.

The bombardment stopped but that was followed by heavy machine gun fire from Hill 191, another knob on T-Bone Hill, about 200 yards in front of us. That stopped, only to be replaced by rifle and automatic weapons fire just below the trench line. There were just too many Chinese. Shouts came to abandon the trenches and to dig in halfway down the hill.

Our own mortars now took the crest of the hill under fire while we tried to dig holes in the rocky hillside. About half an hour later the word came to counterattack. We charged back up the hill. Nearing the crest, we were greeted with the familiar sound of the burp guns and clusters of hand grenades. With my BAR I fired at the flashes in the trench and at anything that moved while dodging hand grenades. Of all things to happen to me, my BAR malfunctioned and could only fire single shots. I shot two Chinese that way. Then my BAR just jammed completely, probably because of the dirt that buried it earlier in the trench. I dropped it and pulled out my .45 caliber pistol and continued my attack. I was hoping to stumble across a dropped rifle but no such luck.

As I was going up I saw men running past me to the rear. "Back, back," came shouts, but I didn't believe that the orders were from officers or ranking NCOs. I turned around and joined the company at the bottom of the hill.

Some of the guys asked me why was I charging up the hill with only a pistol. I said it seemed that way only because everybody else was running in the opposite direction. I said I wasn't that crazy.

We took a lot of casualties, some from Hawaii. Among them were Kamakura from Kauai and Miyahira from Honolulu. Both were struck by mortar rounds and killed instantly. David Mau from Honolulu was reported killed but later was corrected as Wounded in Action.

JUNE 1952

PVT. ELGEN FUJIMOTO
Charlie Company, 33rd Infantry
Panama Canal, Panama

We read about the Korean War in the *Stars and Stripes* newspaper and felt lucky to be in Panama. But I was not comfortable in Panama. It wasn't a place to have fun and many of the men took to drinking, gambling, and smoking pot. I thought if I stayed there long enough I'd probably end up doing the same things so I requested a transfer to ZI or EUCOM. Both requests were disapproved but I was told that I could go to Korea if I wanted to because men were sorely needed there. That was fine with me because I'd go anywhere to get out of Panama.

Another local boy, James Karratti, was also in Panama so I called him up and told him that I was going to ship out to Korea and asked if he wanted to join me. He said, "Shoot," and got his request for transfer approved immediately.

By way of New Jersey, Illinois, and California we shipped out from San Francisco on a two-stacker troopship. There were hundreds of army personnel on the ship on their way to the Far East.

Like every soldier on the way to Korea, we were processed at Camp Drake, Japan, and assigned to our units. Karratti and I found our names listed under 45th Infantry Division. Then it was back to Yokohama for the trip to Inchon, Korea, and Yongdong-po, the 45th Infantry replacement center near Seoul. Karratti and I parted there. He went to the 279th Infantry and I went to 179th Infantry. My specific assignment was Item Company of the 2d Battalion. I was told that Item Company was in reserve at Inje and I was to join it there.

JULY 1952

PVT. ELGEN FUJIMOTO
Item Company, 179th Infantry
Inje, North Korea

The company was in the field going through extensive training when I reported to the first sergeant. I expected to be sent out to the field once I got my gear put away but the first sergeant had other ideas for me. He gave me an assignment to escort a Chinese prisoner to the 8th Army headquarters in Seoul. I was provided a jeep, driver, and automatic carbine with thirty rounds of ammo. The driver carried a .45 pistol.

It was not easy duty. This was the first time I came face to face with the enemy and it made me very uneasy. The prisoner was short, his uniform in rags. He wore no hat and had sneakers for footwear. He didn't appear dangerous or belligerent. I put him in the front passenger seat and I sat directly behind the driver so I could have a view of the prisoner from where I sat. I had made up my mind that I was going to blast him should he try to escape.

We arrived in Seoul after several hours on the road eating dust. The trip was uneventful and the prisoner cooperative. With some difficulty I found the 8th Army headquarters building and turned the prisoner over to a major. What a relief it was for me. The driver and I were offered some food but declined because we wanted to get back to Inje before dark. North Korean guerrillas were still active behind the front lines.

JULY 1952

PFC. CLAYTON MURAKAMI
King Company, 180th Infantry
Vicinity of Hwachon Reservoir, South Korea

In mid-July the entire 180th Infantry Regiment was relieved by units of the 2d Infantry Division and sent to Hwachon to recuperate and to receive replacements. At the end of July I was released from the hospital and joined the regiment there. I found many of the old-timers had rotated home while I was in the hospital. The company commander, platoon leaders, platoon sergeants, and squad leaders were gone. There many new faces, new leaders. I was told that I was now a squad leader, in charge of other men, half of whom were replacements who had just joined the company only a few days before. I was promoted to private first class.

I was again presented with the Purple Heart Medal in front of the company's formation by our new company commander, Captain Baker. Several days later, the entire 3d Battalion was presented with the Presidential Unit Citation at a parade for its performance on T-Bone Hill.

One day while we were on maneuvers, Captain Baker sent for me. He was one of those gutsy types who came from an airborne division and volunteered to come to Korea. He told me that he had gone through my medical record and saw that a "B Profile" had been noted after I was released from the hospital. It was a physical disability having to do with the lower part of my body. He said based on the medical report I was now the new company mail clerk, working under Warrant Officer Mr. Long, who was in charge of the company's clerical staff, food rations, supplies, and things like that.

I had it pretty much made when we were on line, doing the clerical stuff and distributing mail and rations to the men in the company. The company's CP bunker was always on the reverse slope a few yards below the crest of the hill, not subject to direct fire from the enemy. It was, perhaps, the strongest-built bunker. I felt damn safe in it. The one good thing was that I didn't have to go on patrols in the coming winter months.

JULY 1952

Honolulu, Territory of Hawaii

The *Honolulu Star-Bulletin* reported this story by Lt. Yale J. Kamisar.

[In the following story distributed by International News Service, Lt. Yale J. Kamisar of the U.S. 45th Division tells of the actions of two nisei soldiers with whom he fought side by side in the battle of T-Bone Hill. One of the Japanese American soldiers saved Lieutenant Kamisar's life in the fighting—toughest of 1952.]

OFFICER HAILS TWO ISLAND NISEI
FOR ROLES IN T-BONE HILL BATTLE.

BY LT. YALE J. KAMISAR
With the U.S. 45th Infantry Division In Korea, July 10 (INS)
Thunderbirds who captured T-Bone Hill will never forget their Nisei buddies. I certainly won't. One of them saved my life in that bloody June struggle on the Western front which was the toughest action in Korea since November.

Nineteen Japanese American soldiers of the 3rd Battalion, 180th Infantry, fought in the desperate two-week battle to win T-Bone Hill from the Chinese. Several paid with their lives.

The Nisei who saved my life was one of the lucky ones.

Cpl. Akira Nakata, Company K, brother of Kengo Nakata, 224 Circle Mauka St., Wahiawa, Oahu, T.H., was a star catcher on his high school baseball team. That's why he tosses grenades like a baseball peg, not the way the army taught him. During one assault on T-Bone, Nakata's automatic rifle jammed so he ran ahead of his platoon throwing hand grenades with incredible accuracy. At one point, a Red soldier had me zeroed in for the kill. Nakata heaved a grenade which hit the Chinese between the eyes and saved my life.

In Company I, nothing stopped Private First Class George Matsunaga, son of Jack J. Matsunaga, P. O. Box 28, Haiku, Maui, T.H. A shower of Chinese artillery clogged Matsunaga's automatic weapon with dirt. But he continued to fire by an awkward single shot method, killing two Chinese.

Finally the clogged rifle gave out and Matsunaga charged with his .45 caliber pistol blazing.

JULY 1952

PVT. ROBERT HAMAKAWA
Baker Company, 1st Marines
Vicinity of Munsan-ni, South Korea

A young Puerto Rican by the name of Pedro was assigned to our platoon as a replacement. I was told to take him under my wing and orient him to the rules of combat. He was eighteen or nineteen, and stood 5 feet 5 inches and had arrived in Korea a week before.

One day while patrolling in an open field we were spotted by the Chinese from across the Imjin River. The sun's reflection off their scopes or binoculars gave them away. I knew we were in trouble so I yelled to the patrol to hit the ground. A tank took us under fire, and at 1000 yards, the direct fire from a tank would take but a couple of seconds before the round impacted. Even before I hit the ground, one round exploded several yards away. As I was going down, I felt something hit the heel of my left combat boot, tearing the heel off but not injuring my foot. A piece of shrapnel had struck my foot. We waited for the tank to fire again but after several minutes it appeared that the tank had gone into hiding, fearing our artillery. We made it back to the company without any further incidents. When I took off my flak jacket in my bunker, I found several holes in the back containing small pieces of fragments. I didn't get a scratch.

Pedro was not as lucky. He caught some fragments in the neck area but could walk without any assistance. One week in Korea and already he earned his first Purple Heart but had yet to see the enemy. He was sent back to the battalion aid station for the removal of the fragments. In three days he was back with me.

We went out again several days later to reconnoiter a village to see if the Chinese occupied it. These daylight patrols were okay if we could get immediate mortar or artillery support when we called for it. We drew fire again. Pedro was struck again in the neck and although not seriously, it was enough to shake everybody up. Off he went to the aid station again. This time I talked to Sergeant Quinlan to see if he could get Pedro transferred to a rear echelon unit because the third time might be fatal to Pedro. The sergeant argued that Pedro was on a lucky streak and wouldn't take my suggestion. He was firm on his decision so there was no sense in arguing.

Unbelievable as it may sound, Pedro was back with us again. During some harassing Chinese artillery fire, he got hit for the third time in the upper shoulder and neck and earned his third Purple Heart. He finally was transferred out of Korea. Maybe Sergeant Quinlan was right. Pedro was on a lucky streak. But Pedro was not of the same mind when he left. Who can blame him? That must have been some kind of a record. How many guys can say they spent less than a month in Korea, got wounded three times in three weeks, and got back to stateside in less than a month and never saw a single commie. Anyway, we missed the little guy.

JULY 1952

PFC. ALAN TAKAMIYASHIRO
George Company, 31st Infantry
Vicinity of Kumwha, North Korea

One morning my platoon sergeant and I got out of the trench to bury our empty C-ration cans about 5 yards down the forward slope. I dug the hole while he held the empty cans. While he was watching me, a sniper's bullet struck the ground between the two of us. The platoon sergeant threw the cans down the slope and we both scrambled back into the trench. That shot was fired from more than 500 yards away. The shaken platoon sergeant, who was soon to be rotated home in a few days, told me that he would never, ever leave his bunker again.

JULY 1952

PFC. LOUIS BALDOVI
Able Company, 180th Infantry
Alligator Jaw, North Korea

My foxhole buddy, Kubinski, had already rotated home and I never had the chance to say goodbye to him. Sergeant Conley and Sergeant Armour were still with us but were due to rotate before the end of the month. Those two really made me feel I was valuable to the squad and took care of me.

In our new position, we quickly got into the routine of improving the trench and bunkers, and checking on the barbed wire, mine field charts, and trip flares. I was now the assistant BAR man to James Bess, who had joined the 2d Squad. The problem being an assistant BAR man was that I had to carry extra ammo for Bess, as well as ammo for my M-1 rifle. I was promoted to private first class.

After a few days on the MLR we relieved the 1st Platoon on Alligator Jaw. It was so named because its features were not those of a typical hill. It was two fingers jutting out to the valley floor for almost a mile. The fingers looked like the long snout of an alligator with its jaws agape. About 100 yards separated the tips of the jaws. The tip of the lower jaw was manned by a platoon from the Philippine Battalion. Beyond the jaws 300 yards away was T-Bone Hill, a Chinese stronghold.

The 1st Platoon drew the first assignment to Alligator Jaw. Everyone in the company took a very special interest in the 1st Platoon because we knew that our turn would soon come. Being stuck out there alone about a mile from the MLR and close to the Chinese was scary, and the thought of being surrounded and cut off by them and killed or captured passed through my mind often.

For three days and nights the 1st Platoon reported no enemy activity. The squad-size patrols it sent out drew nothing but blanks, which reassured us that it was going to be a snap. Maybe it wouldn't be so bad after all. Maybe the Chinese just wanted to take it easy, too.

We finally got the word that we were going to relieve the 1st Platoon the next evening. Our platoon was relieved on line and sent to the company area for some hot chow and to prepare for outpost duty. We were allowed to sack out that night and all through the next day.

I decided to take as much ammunition and as many grenades as I could carry and an extra ammo can for the light.30 caliber machine guns. I tried to stuff three boxes of rations in my combat pack but there wasn't enough space for them so I broke them apart and packed only what we could carry, along with socks, underwear, and such. The rest we gave to the KSCs. The KSCs were to carry water cans and more rations and were to return with the relieved platoon.

At about 1700 hours we put our gear together and waited for dusk to make the long walk to the outpost. I think I had at least 60 pounds of equipment to carry, maybe more. When we got to the outpost we were exhausted and sweaty. July in Korea was probably the hottest month of the year and a few minutes into our walk I was dripping wet.

We made the exchange with the 1st Platoon in the dark without any difficulty. We were told that it was a snap and we shouldn't worry. They were happy to leave us all their ammo and hand grenades.

The outpost was on a very small knoll at the end of the jaw. There were no bunkers but there was a network of trenches around and down the knob leading to firing positions. There was a main trench that circled the knob about 30 yards from the top and a secondary trench about 20 yards below the main trench. The two circular trenches were connected with trenches. From the secondary trench, there were trenches that spidered out to two-man foxholes farther down the knob. There were three two-man LPs located about 50 yards below the foxholes. The command post, heavily sandbagged, sat on top of the knob. It had a commanding view of the entire outpost and the valley.

From T-Bone Hill, about 300 yards away and at a higher elevation, the Chinese could easily watch our movements. Whenever we had to move during the day we had to keep our heads down or get them shot off by snipers from T-Bone Hill. We had to keep our movements to a minimum. Every now and then a Chinese sniper would fire, not at anyone in particular, but just to keep us honest. I crawled on my hands and knees whenever I wanted to go anywhere. At night we could move while upright.

The first night was quiet until about 2200 hours, when we heard singing and saw lights coming from the direction of the lower jaw and moving in the direction of T-Bone Hill to our front. The lights were from lanterns and flashlights. This was reported to the company on the MLR. Their answer was that the Filipinos had a patrol out that night so be on the alert. Singing and lights on a patrol? They were looking for trouble! This continued for almost an hour, like some crazy guys having a party in the rice paddies. Then the singing stopped and all was quiet.

At 0100 hours, a terrific fire fight broke out near the area where we last saw the Filipinos. We could hear the Chinese burp guns, our own slow automatic weapons, and the bursts of grenades. We could see the muzzle flashes from weapons clearly. The fire fight took place less than 200 yards away and lasted for about ten minutes.

Half an hour later, we heard the same singing and saw the lights, headed for the lower jaw outpost. We thought we saw something very unusual and weird.

Soon, a radio call explained what had happened in the rice paddies that morning. Much earlier, just after dark, another patrol had gone out to set the trap. The lights and singing were from a Filipino decoy patrol sent out to lure the Chinese out and draw them into an ambush. It worked.

On the second night, Bess and I had listening post duty and drew the midnight to 0300 hours shift. The LP was on the right of the outpost. Bess and I had about three hours to kill before relieving the LP, so we laid down in the trench to sleep, hoping no one would step on us. We couldn't sleep so we talked about ourselves and our hometowns until it was time to relieve the LP.

The listening post was connected to the CP with a sound-powered telephone. If the CP wanted to contact us, normally every half hour, the person on the other end had to whistle very quietly to get our attention. The LPs would do the same to call the CP. Bess said he would take the first hour and I should try to get some sleep. I sat down, curled my body, and closed my eyes.

About 0200 hours Bess shook me hard and said the CP was calling in all LPs because there was some movement in front of the other LPs. Then our flares lit the outpost and surrounding area. Man, did we welcome the light. Our mortars were on the ball.

We didn't need a repeat of the message. Heads down, Bess and I started to leave the LP when several grenades burst just below our LP. We scrambled up the trench to the first firing position, which was about 50 yards above the LP. From there, Bess poured fire in the area of the LP and I threw a grenade as far as I could in that direction. A figure tried to climb over the sandbags to get into the LP but a burst from Bess dropped him into the LP. Then there was movement to the right, to the rear of the outpost. I emptied a clip and threw a grenade in that direction. I could now hear firing and bursting grenades on the other side of the outpost. Firing then came from the rear of the outpost to the right of us, which indicated that I missed the chinks that I had seen moving to the rear of the outpost. Our platoon sergeant was now shouting orders for men to cover the back side of the outpost. Help came in the form of two men with rifles. A figure jumped into the LP and sprayed our position with his burp gun, forcing us to duck down into the trench. I was out of hand grenades so I motioned to one of the guys for a grenade but instead of giving one to me he threw it himself. It seemed like a long time until finally, the grenade went off with a whining blast. I saw another figure racing from the LP up the trench making for the secondary trench line. I fired several times and the figure dropped out of sight. Bess was firing, at what or whom, I didn't know. The other two GIs were firing to the rear of the outpost.

Bess took off for the secondary trench line on his hands and knees and we all followed. He yelled for us to keep our heads down. Hell, no one had to tell us that. The outpost was now alive with the sounds of rifle and automatic weapons fire. Most of the platoon had formed in the secondary trench and was blasting away. I don't think more than five minutes had gone by since the fire fight began.

Several red flares went up in the rice paddy and the firing from below the outpost decreased gradually until it stopped completely. A cease fire call went out and we stopped firing. Someone threw a couple of "just in case" hand grenades down the hill, hoping to nail some chinks. We moved up to the main trench line, where we counted heads and casualties. Except for a couple of men wounded by hand grenades our platoon came out without any serious injuries.

We anxiously waited for dawn. When it came, the 1st Squad was given the task of sweeping the bottom of the hill and the rice paddies for any dead or wounded Chinese. The 2d Squad checked all the trenches below the main trench and the LPs. Bess and I checked out our listening post and found only a cap and a burp gun left behind by the Chinese. There was a small red star sewn onto the cap. The other squad found one dead Chinese in the rice paddy. The Chinese left us alone the next two nights and we were relieved by the 2d Platoon.

When I got back to the MLR I was told to go the company CP and report to the first sergeant. I got a wonderful surprise! I was to go on TDY to the 45th Division 700 Ordnance Maintenance Company back in division rear for three weeks effective July 12. When that day came, I went down the hill where a jeep was waiting for me to take me to the rear. Guess who was the driver? Yep, Willie Abreu. It was about a 10-mile ride and Willie told me there was a rumor that the division was going to Japan. It was only a rumor, but it raised my morale for a while.

I had it made at the ordnance company. No one told me anything and I didn't ask. I did absolutely nothing for a week—just slept most of the time until someone wised up and reported me to the first sergeant. After a chewing out he sent me packing back to the company, which was still on line.

The day after I arrived back at the company, I was told that the 2d Infantry Division was going to relieve the 45th Division the next night. Just before we were relieved we heard the booming sounds of artillery and could see flares lighting up the night to our left in the direction of Old Baldy and Pork Chop Hill. We quickly gathered our equipment and started walking off the hill, happy that we were not on Old Baldy. Much later in reserve, we learned that while the exchange was taking place between the 2d and the 45th Divisions on Old Baldy, the Chinese attacked in force and knocked the 2d Infantry Division off the hill.

JULY 1952

PFC. SUSUMU MIYAMOTO
King Company, 180th Infantry
Chungosong, North Korea

I was busy cleaning my rifle late one morning when I heard explosions coming from the front of our company's position. Everyone came out of their bunkers to see what was happening. It was Fox Company from the 2d Battalion returning from a morning raid on T-Bone Hill. They were being fired upon in the valley by Chinese mortar and long-range machine gun fire. We could easily see the mortars bursting and tracer bullets plunging into the company's formation as they tried getting out of the range of the chinks' guns.

Most of the men double-timed through the curtain of fire to the base of our hill, where there were bunkers. But there were others who froze, unable to run to safety. The chinks were aware of that and concentrated their fire on them.

I don't know what got into me. I said to the men around me, "Let's go help those guys." I leaped from the trench, not bothering to see who might be following, and ran through the barbed wire opening downhill, passing and sometimes almost knocking down the men from Fox Company as they made their way to safety. They must have thought I was nuts. Maybe I was.

Now enemy mortars took the trail under fire, forcing me to hit the deck a couple of times but I continued my run to the trapped men. Later I was told I had covered over 500 yards.

Mortar and machine gun fire still rained down on the trapped men but I managed to get to one whose right leg was shattered. He couldn't run and was left behind.

Here I was, all of 120 pounds, and an injured GI who must have weighed over 160 pounds. I didn't think I could carry him 500 yards to safety even if he had one good leg. Looking around for help, I saw two men cowering in a shell crater about 30 yards away who didn't appear to be injured. I ran over to them and pulled one up to help me. He had a dazed look on his face. I grabbed him by the arm and practically dragged him to the wounded GI. The other followed, not wanting to be left behind.

I told the two to pick up the wounded soldier and carry him while I carried their weapons. The machine gun stopped firing but the mortar rounds were still bursting around us. We had to run, stop, run, stop, sometimes half dragging the poor wounded GI, which made him holler like hell. We finally outdistanced the mortars and got to the safety of the bunkers, where we turned the wounded GI over to a medic. I received slaps on my back and handshakes on my way back to my bunker. When I sat down, I shook for about twenty minutes.

AUGUST 1952

PFC. ROBERT HAMAKAWA
Baker Company, 1st Marines
Vicinity of Munsan-ni, South Korea

Baker Company was situated on a low hill, maybe 50 or 60 feet above the flats, and spread out along the south bank of the Imjin River.

Affected by the coastal tide, the river rose and fell by as much as 30 feet or more. One day the river could be 300 yards wide and the next day it could be a small channel of water only a couple of yards wide, revealing an expanse of mud flats. Really interesting. But we were concerned when the tide was low because it gave the Chinese the opportunity to cross the river on a dark night and infiltrate our lines.

Sometimes when things were quiet, it gave me a chance to think about the war and ask myself what the heck I was doing in Korea. I had a draft deferment because I was still in college in 1951 but waived it to be with my buddies who were drafted in October of that year. I would now be on summer break and enjoying all the privileges that went with civilian life. Those lucky dogs back home. But like the rest of the men who were eighteen to twenty years old, I had to put everything on hold. Finishing college, getting married, and having a family would have to come later, if I survived the war.

I was twenty years old and the teenagers considered me to be old except for Sergeant Quinlan, who really was an old marine at the age of twenty-three. He was a graduate of MIT and was drafted right after graduation. I asked him why he didn't become an officer with his qualifications and he said he just wanted to put in his time and get out. As we talked he really surprised me when he told me he knew of a Hamakawa who attended Springfield College in Springfield, Massachusetts. They met when they served on their respective schools' debate teams. Was he a relative? Heck, he was Kio, my older brother. After the initial shock at how small the world was, we got along really well.

There were several outpost battles along MLR of the 1st Marine Division but not much movement where I was. It was basically to defend our piece of real estate and conduct patrols out in no-man's-land.

Living on the front lines we lacked the comforts of home, especially the hot shower. We had a shower but certainly nothing that resembled what I had given up months ago. A 55 gallon drum was perched several feet above the ground and was filled with water carried from a nearby well. A valve controlled the gravity-fed water. Bathing had to be in pairs. One guy showered while the other controlled the water from the top.

One day while I was showering and completely soaped down, I could hear our artillery firing and the rounds whistling overhead. A round exploded prematurely in the air about 100 yards from the shower unit. Before we could duck or throw ourselves to the ground, steel fragments went whizzing overhead. The round was timed to burst above ground over enemy territory, but this one burst too soon over friendly territory. Fellow marines were not concerned if I got injured but were more worried that the water drum had been punctured by shrapnel. Fortunately, it wasn't.

There was this seventeen-year-old Irish kid named Malloy. We all wished we could get him back to his mama in New York because he was a wise kid and should never have been put on the front lines. One day, just for excitement, like we didn't have enough of it, he stripped completely naked and hopped on top of a tank and waved his "skivvies" to the enemy. I don't know if he had been observed by the enemy but when he did that, we got some incoming rounds. Sometimes we wished that he would catch a piece of shrapnel and get sent home.

The end of July was the beginning of the monsoon season in South Korea and it continued into August. We tried to pick a bunker that had good drainage but there was one occasion when our platoon was short of bunkers and our squad had to build one. One of the men had studied to be an engineer in college but dropped out to get into the war. He helped us build a very sturdy bunker with good drainage. The materials for the bunker came from the engineers and KSCs. We built two triple-deck bunks with a lot of space between them. He scraped up some materials to make a stove, complete with an exhaust pipe. We were the envy of the platoon and after a while our hootchie became the meeting place for the squad leaders and platoon sergeant.

Sleeping in bunkers really took some getting used to because of the constant moisture. It was warm in the winter if the stove was working and very cool in the summer, although outside of the bunker it might be 90 degrees.

Then the monsoon came. Talk about rain! I thought it would never let up. It rained for an entire week, but our bunker was dry. The only problem was the mud we brought in whenever we came in from the rain. There were reports that a couple of bunkers collapsed during the rainy period.

There were no hot meals for a couple of weeks because the muddy roads made it impossible for the jeeps to bring the food up. Most of the guys skipped eating one or two meals rather than eat the ever so present C-rations. I think the higher-ups anticipated all of this because we were never in short supply of C-rations. Guys were getting sick with bad colds and dysentery. Dysentery came from unsanitary mess kits and utensils because there was no hot water to sanitize them. The platoon medic was busy treating men who reported to sick call.

One afternoon, the enemy decided to harass us with mortars when I was returning from the platoon CP. I made a dash to a foxhole, which was occupied by Bill Hammond. I yelled for him to make some room for me and jumped in beside him. The hole had about a foot of water in it. If I had known that he was sharing the hole with about 100 or more little green frogs, I would have taken my chances out in the open. Bill said the little frogs were there when he jumped in.

We continued to get a few incoming rounds so we decided to stay in the hole and bail the green frogs out. We threw out as many of the little creatures as we could.

A jeep drove up, dodging bursting shells. About 20 yards from our hole, this GI stopped his jeep and dashed up the hill toward us. There was no room for a third party so when that body made a flying leap into our hole, Bill and I kind of moved to one side to make room for him. Instead, he landed on top of us. That pissed us off. Using both our shoulders, Bill and I heaved the guy out of the hole. Whoever it was, got up, got into the jeep, and took off. Later, we were asked if we had seen Lieutenant Colonel Blatti, CO, 1st Amtrak Battalion. Bill and I shook our heads and after a safe distance from everyone, we said in unison, "*That's* who it was."

SEPTEMBER 1952

PFC. ELGEN FUJIMOTO
Item Company, 179th Infantry
Vicinity of Punchbowl, North Korea

We were in blocking position on a ridge line behind the MLR. One night we heard bugle calls and small arms fire. The firing stopped at the sound of one single bugle. The bugle call gave me chicken skin.

I was taught how to use the metal detector in one, quick easy lesson and found myself in a mine clearing detail to clear the evacuation trail of mines and booby traps. Because of the many small steel fragments on the ground, the metal detector beeped constantly, giving false alarms. After a couple of days we gave it up because it was too slow; we used our bayonets to probe for mines. No easy task because I kept thinking one was going to blow me all to hell. We never found any.

OCTOBER 1952

CPL. DAVID LABANG
George Company, 31st Infantry
Triangle Hill, North Korea

Except for patrol actions, things were pretty quiet from May to September and the brass kept shuffling our division around, moving us here and there on the front line and sometimes sending us back in reserve for a rest. We didn't want to be sent back in reserve or blocking because it would take longer to accumulate the required 36 points to rotate home.

During this period I was promoted twice, to private first class and to corporal, and finally got my wish to be in the weapons squad. The squad leader made me an assistant machine gunner. A few days later the machine gunner went on R&R to Japan for a week and I became the acting machine gunner. My voluntary training in the weapons squad months before finally paid off.

A few days later the company clerk told me that I was due to go on R&R and where would I want to go, Japan or Pusan, South Korea? I chose Japan because many of our men who had gone to Japan came back with unspent Japanese currency so I thought I would ask them for it since there wasn't any use for it in Korea.

I felt pretty good, knowing that I would be taking a rest away from the hills of Korea for a while. However, there was talk that our division was going to be part of a big operation and all R&Rs were canceled. That was no talk— it was for real!

In preparation for the attack I made sure that I was loaded with ammo and grenades. I carried about six hand grenades. When I put on my equipment, it must have weighed a ton. I don't know why but I oiled my bayonet, not that I wanted to stick a chink with it, but at the time it was the thing to do.

I opened a can of fruit cocktail and drank only the sweet juice. I tried to rest on my combat pack but I was just plain nervous. I thought, *If I had to make a will today, who will I give what little I had in my possession?* If I got killed, my parents would get my GI Insurance. I hardly slept that night.

The objective was a hill complex called Triangle Hill. The reason why it was called Triangle Hill was because the hill complex had three dominant peaks that formed a rough triangle—Hill 598, Pike's Peak, and two smaller peaks, Jane Russell and Sandy Ridge. The 1st Battalion was to take Sandy Ridge and the 3d Battalion, Hill 598. The 2d Battalion was to remain in reserve on Hill 604 less than a mile to the south of the triangle. We would give supporting fire and be committed only if the 1st and 3d Battalions failed to take their objectives. We had box seats to watch the entire attack.

Before the attack the hills were plastered with artillery and napalm bombs from navy Corsairs. The entire hill complex was covered with smoke and dust. As soon as the navy and artillery did their job, our mortars and heavy machine guns laid down a protective fire while the companies of the 1st and 3d Battalions began their climb up the hills.

I grabbed a pair of binoculars and trained them on the 3d Battalion. What I saw made me choke. It was taking heavy casualties but still continued its attack. I could see men falling or being blown into the air by mortar rounds while others were pinned down by enemy machine gun fire. Others were waving their arms forward, urging their men to go on. A few men managed to work their way into the outlying trenches. It was less than an hour since the battalion started its attack but it never got near the top of the hill. Then the men began falling back to the bottom of the hill.

The 3d Battalion made another attack and this time gained the crest. Night came and the battle for Hill 598 raged on. We could hear the battle but couldn't see much.

On the third day both battalions had to withdraw for some reason. Later some survivors told me that they had almost run out of ammo and couldn't be resupplied because their ammunition carriers were getting killed on the way up.

On October 15, it was decided by regiment that our battalion, the 2d, must be committed to take Hill 598. We would attack in a column of companies, with Easy Company leading off, followed by Fox and George Companies. I breathed a sigh of relief after I found out that George Company was last in the attack order. After artillery and mortar prepped the hill mass, Easy Company moved out. This time we encountered only light enemy artillery and mortar fire and gained the crest without any difficulty. We followed Fox Company to the top and cleaned out the bunkers and trenches.

After mopping up Hill 598, our company pushed through Easy Company to take Pike's Peak. The hill was pounded with artillery fire for about fifteen minutes, followed by supporting fire from our heavy mortars. We didn't know it at the time but the chinks on Pike's Peak were entrenched in deep caves and tunnels, safe from our artillery and mortars.

We got three-fourths of the way up, but met the same fate as the 1st and 3d Battalions. There was just too much Chinese fire power, so we pulled back down the hill a bit with heavy casualties. Again the artillery was called to pound the hill. This time George Company was in the lead with Easy Company behind us. Seeing what happened to the 1st and 3d Battalions, I felt that this was going to be my last day alive. Pessimistic, but if I came out of it alive it sure would be a wonderful surprise.

My machine gun crew followed behind the rifle squads. I carried the tripod while my assistant carried the machine gun. We each carried a can of ammo while the ammo bearer carried two cans. Each ammo can weighed about 18 pounds. I also carried a carbine and a .45 pistol.

The point of our attack almost got to the trenches but was hurled back almost halfway down the hill. Too many hand grenades. I couldn't find a spot to put my gun into action because there were too many men in front of me. Small arms fire seemed to have slowed down, but men were still falling from it. With my gun crew following me, I dove into a crater and set up the machine gun on the edge of the crater. As soon as it was loaded I started firing at the trench line. Then my helmet went ping! I lost the grip on the gun and slid to the bottom of the crater against the ammo bearer. I thought I had been hit. I took off my helmet and looked at it. There was a deep dent on the side of it, probably from a spent bullet, which didn't have enough velocity to penetrate my steel pot. I shoved my helmet back on my head and scrambled back to my gun. I kept the helmet as a reminder until I rotated home.

I could see our guys, dodging hand grenades and shooting at any movement on the crest and trench line. Small groups of men would make a charge, only to be thrown back. Two men walked down the hill past us dazed, paying no heed to all the exploding grenades and rifle fire.

Suddenly, the grenade and small arms fire trickled down to a complete halt. No mortar fire, no grenades, nothing! It was quiet. No one moved except to seek better cover. It was like someone pushed the "pause" button to halt the battle momentarily. I think it was about five minutes later that the men in front of us got up and walked to the top of the hill without any shots fired at them. We got up and joined them. The chinks had given up the hill and had taken their wounded with them. We could see a few of them running down the hill in the distance but no one paid any attention to them. Then someone called for our mortars and soon we could see our mortar shells falling among them. The hill was littered with Chinese dead.

It had been five hours since we started the attack. I was still alive! Maybe being pessimistic was the right call after all. My machine gun crew was lucky. No one got killed or wounded. The only casualty was my helmet. And when I looked around, it appeared that we did not lose many men but there was a bunch of wounded being tended to by our medics.

We got the dead chinks out from the trenches and piled them up farther down on the forward slope. Many had been burned to a crisp from napalm strikes by our planes. Someone suggested that we use the dead chinks as sandbags to improve our firing positions but we nixed the idea because they would begin to smell in a couple of days.

Most of the bunkers and parts of the trench line had caved in from the air and artillery pounding so we had to repair them as best we could. "Repair the bunkers! Get the trench line fixed! We'll be getting chink artillery pretty soon," squad leaders and platoon sergeants were shouting. I set up my machine gun at a damaged section of the trench and began shoveling dirt out the trench.

That evening, KSCs brought rations, water, and ammo up the hill. My ammo bearer was able to scrounge about six cans of machine gun ammo for our gun and some hand grenades.

OCTOBER 1952

2D LT. FLORANIO CASTILLO
Charlie Company, 27th Infantry
In transit, South Korea

After stops on the west coast and Japan, I arrived in Pusan, South Korea, in mid-October, where we embarked on a long, slow train ride north that was interrupted on several occasions by North Korean guerrillas. Train security and UN troops along the way had to clear nearby hillsides while we waited. Some of the troops took cover under the train cars. The war was more than two years old and I didn't quite understand why there were guerrillas in South Korea.

Along the way, I was touched by the scores of young, dirty, and ill-clothed children crawling out of dilapidated, cardboard lean-tos and rushing to the troop train begging for food. We gave them whatever leftover rations we had. Even when the train was under way, they followed for a considerable distance before tiring and just watched us until we were out of sight. They were scenes I have never forgotten.

When we finally arrived in Seoul at first light, I saw a city devastated and leveled to the ground. Buildings that were left standing were so heavily damaged that they were beyond repair. Then we continued by truck to the northeast to a replacement center, where we stayed for a couple of days. I received my assignment to Charlie Company, 1st Battalion, 27th Infantry Regiment, 25th Infantry Division.

OCTOBER 1952

PFC. ELGEN FUJIMOTO
Item Company, 179th Infantry
Hill 812, North Korea

We carried full field packs to the top of Hill 812, which was located several miles near the east coast. It was the longest climb I had ever made in Korea. The terrain in that part of the MLR was high, rugged, and steep. Pine trees dominated the landscape.

I think I was the skinniest one of all in my platoon, and my platoon leader took pity on me and offered to carry my pack. I declined the offer because I had too much pride, but I suffered and tried not to make it noticeable.

Two days after we got to Hill 812, my platoon sergeant came to our squad and asked for volunteers to go on an early morning mission into enemy territory. It was a raiding party to get a prisoner. No one volunteered. He left, apparently, to ask the other squads. He came back and asked our squad again. I figured the other squads also said no to him.

I guess he was bucking for a medal or promotion or begging to get himself killed. I asked him if he had been on Old Baldy and he said yes. Well, if anyone came off Old Baldy he certainly must know what he was doing so I said I'd go with him. "Fuji is going," he told the squad. "Anyone else?" I don't think the others wanted this Japanese from Hawaii to show them up so they all volunteered, even the squad leader. Because I was the first to volunteer I was made the assistant patrol leader, much to the disgust of my squad leader.

Our objective was an enemy outpost at the bottom of a finger directly in front of the MLR. We left our trench line just before dawn and took the well-beaten trail down the ridge line that must have been used hundreds of times by other patrols. My position in the patrol was the tail end to keep the men moving.

We got to the bottom of our ridge and crept to about 50 yards from the base of the enemy outpostundetected. Just as we began the climb to the outpost the point man stepped on a mine and was blown into the air. No cry came from him so we assumed he was killed. This alerted the outpost defenders, who poured automatic fire into our ranks. I found cover behind a small mound of dirt and returned their fire. A bullet struck the forearm of my rifle and made it useless. Miraculously, I wasn't injured. Then I heard someone yell, "I'm hit." It was the platoon sergeant. I yelled to the guy nearest the platoon sergeant to toss me the sergeant's carbine and ammo. I told the GI next to me to cover me, and I made a run up the hill firing the carbine at full automatic. The others followed me. Two North Koreans leaped from a foxhole to the rear so I gave them a burst but missed them completely from less than 100 yards. As I neared the top several hand grenades came sailing down the hill but exploded several yards from me. I felt it was time to get out of there so I ran back to where the platoon sergeant lay and told him that we should abort the mission. He agreed.

Someone took a chance on stepping on another mine to drag the body of the GI who had stepped on the mine to where we were. He was dead. We put him in a poncho and took turns carrying him. The sergeant was able to walk so we retreated into the dense underbrush and to the bottom of the ridge and stopped to see how we fared. We had one KIA and three WIA and no prisoners. It took us two hours to get back to our lines.

OCTOBER 1952

CPL. HAROLD NAKATA
Able Company, 17th Infantry
Vicinity of the Iron Triangle, North Korea

Over several months I was promoted to private first class and then to corporal and managed to work myself into the weapons platoon, where I eventually became a machine gunner on a light .30 caliber machine gun. This was easier than being in a rifle squad or rifle platoon because I didn't have to go on patrols often, unless a patrol needed more fire power, which hardly ever happened.

On October 5, my machine gun team was attached to a platoon that relieved another platoon on an outpost almost 1,000 yards from the MLR. The outpost was located at the end of a spur that ran down from our hill position. It took us almost an hour to get there and we made the relief in the dark. During the walk down to the outpost, we were harassed by enemy mortars but we did not sustain any casualties although there were some pretty close ones.

The gun position that I took over was at the top of a draw, commanded a good view of the platoon's sector, and had a clear field of wire. There were about twelve cans of machine gun ammo left behind by the gun crew we relieved. They must have been too lazy to take it with them. Including ours, there were eighteen cans of ammo for my gun. In the back and to the right was a solidly built bunker that doubled as sleeping quarters and shelter from enemy artillery.

From morning to dusk we received a steady diet of Chinese artillery and mortar fire so we stayed in the bunker most of the day, venturing out only to do our private business. The Chinese mortars were the big ones— 120mm—and they sure made huge craters. A direct hit from one of those would demolish a bunker. Our platoon was not without casualties and our medic was kept pretty busy. In the late afternoon we were really pounded and we felt certain that this was in preparation for a night attack. At 1800 hours, the barrage lifted and we all ran to our firing positions, anticipating an attack. It never came but we were put on 100 percent alert for the rest of the night.

After being on alert all night, we wanted to sleep but it was impossible because there was a repeat of the previous day's shelling. I tried calling the CP but the phone was dead, probably from a round that severed the lines. Then at dusk the Chinese really poured it on. Sometime later one of the guys who was watching the shellacking from another hill told me that he could barely see our outpost because of the dust and smoke caused by the bombardment. He said the Chinese also brought under fire the supply trail that ran down from the company to the outpost. Then the platoon runner came busting into our bunker out of breath and told us to get out there now because it sure looked like the Chinese were going to attack. All that shelling must have meant something. He then took off to warn the rest of the platoon. He was one brave son of a gun, running around like that.

Something told me to get out of there so I peeked from the entrance of the bunker and the first thing I saw were a couple of orange or red flares shot into the sky. I turned to my buddies and shouted, "They're coming!" And not waiting for a response, I took off into the darkness and ran to my gun pit, getting there just in time to see, no more than 75 feet away, a Chinese looking the other way. He didn't see my gun in the dark. Several yards behind him were more Chinese. I pulled the trigger. Nothing happened. The gun was only half loaded so I had to crank it once more to fully load it. And just as I did that the Chinese turned my way and pointed to my position. I gave him and the men behind him a long burst, not letting up on the trigger and kept them under fire, hoping that my gun crew and the rest of the platoon would get out of the bunkers.

The Chinese did not wait for the shelling to stop. They walked right into it. Then the shelling stopped and our mortars lit the night with illuminating flares. I could see some of them in the draw so I swept the gun from left to right, right to left, not aiming, just pointing. My gun crew finally joined me. My assistant shouted that I was firing too fast but I didn't pay any attention to him because I was too scared and excited as hell.

Hand grenades burst in front of my gun so I fired in that direction and kept a continuous stream of bullets in front of me. I was so intense with my own situation that I couldn't hear other guns firing. I heard a loud thump above me and saw someone land in front of my gun and disappear into the night. It was a Chinese! He had come from the backside, which meant part of the outpost was overrun.

"Grenade," somebody shouted, and before I could react, the grenade exploded in the gun pit and knocked me from my gun. I felt excruciating pain in my face and eyes. I cried out, "My eyes! My eyes!" I touched my face with my hands and felt the sticky wetness of blood. I couldn't see out of my right eye and my left eye was blurry. I yelled, "Get the gun," but nobody answered. With my blurry left eye I could see my gun crew down in the hole, dead or injured.

The pain in my eyes was unbearable but I pulled myself up to the gun and just fired it downslope until the left eye focused. I was worried that the Chinese who threw the grenade must have been several yards away, so I just swung the barrel in a sweeping motion and fired long bursts. When I ran out of ammo I had to feed the gun myself with some difficulty. This went on for at least an hour or more until two of our guys seeking cover jumped into the gun pit. I told them to take over the gun and I slumped to the bottom of the pit, covering my face with my hands. I still couldn't see with my right eye.

The two took over the gun until red flares shot up into the night. The tempo of the firing slowed down until the hill was quiet. The flares were the signal for the Chinese to withdraw.

I could still walk and two men helped me to the reverse slope of the hill, where my platoon leader came to see me. He asked why I didn't call the CP to warn them of the Chinese. I told him the phone line was dead, and besides, who had time to call when a Chinese is only 75 feet away? He laughed. He said I saved the platoon and he was going to write me up for a decoration. Much later I was awarded the DSC (Distinguished Service Cross), the nation's second highest award.

I was taken to the forward aid station, where I found I had metal fragments in my arms, chest, face, and right eye. My right eye was heavily bandaged and I still couldn't see too well with my left eye. That same day I was taken to the 121st Evacuation Hospital in the rear by helicopter.

121st Evacuation Hospital, South Korea

I was treated at the 121st Evacuation Hospital until October 9 and then was flown to the 343d General Hospital in Zama, Japan, where I received more treatment. My next stop was Tokyo General Hospital for a few days and then on to Tripler Army General Hospital in Hawaii. On November 21, my right eyeball was removed and my eye fitted with a prosthesis. I remained at Tripler until March 31, 1953, and was medically discharged shortly after.

OCTOBER 1952

PFC. ALAN TAKAMIYASHIRO
George Company, 31st Infantry
Vicinity of the Iron Triangle, North Korea

I was told that I was eligible for R&R because I had been in Korea since February. I was now regarded as one of the old guys because the men who were in the company long before me had since rotated home. I told the company clerk that I wanted to go to Tokyo because my kid brother was with the air force and stationed at the Tachikawa Air Force Base near Tokyo. My request for Tokyo was approved.

Tokyo, Japan

I went on R&R with two boys from Hawaii. I have forgotten their names, but I remember one was from Oahu and the other was from the Big Island. We flew out of Kimpo Air Base to Japan and landed at an airport near Camp Drake, where we were given Class "A" uniforms and fed a steak dinner. From Camp Drake we caught a taxi to Tokyo.

We had such a great time that we joked about not going back to Korea. I had $400 with me because I had saved $50 a month just for R&R. I spent it all in Tokyo. I never felt guilty having a great time in Tokyo because I don't think others felt guilty when they were on R&R. The fact of the matter was that I might get killed when I got back to my company so I might as well enjoy my last days on earth. The only regret I had was that I never got to see my kid brother.

Triangle Hill, North Korea

After I returned from R&R, our division moved slightly north of Kumwha. Directly in front of us was a hill complex called Triangle Hill. This sector was mountainous compared to the area where we were before. We were told that this sector was heavily fought over sometime in June and July.

One afternoon, the Chinese threw a lot of shells at us. I was in the platoon CP near the crest and below me were two Hawaii men, Shimabukuro and Suda, who were the best of buddies and really took care of each other. Suda was on my right and down a little about 30 yards away and Shimabukuro was 50 yards down the slope in front of me. I had a clear view of the two local boys. The shells were coming in like mad and once in a while I would peek from my foxhole to see what was going on. On one of my peeks, and much to my amazement, I saw

Shimabukuro leave his foxhole and race uphill to where Suda was and disappear into Suda's foxhole. *What the hell is he trying to do?* I said to myself. *Get the "million dollar" wound so he can go home?*

After the shelling was over and fearing the worst, I raced for Suda's hole to find out why that crazy Shimabukuro had gone to Suda's hole in the midst of the artillery barrage. When Shimabukuro came out of the hole, I asked why he did a stupid thing like that. He said he was worried about Suda and wanted to see if he was all right. When he dove into Suda's foxhole he found Suda reading a paperback. Suda came out of the foxhole and explained that if he was going to die, he may as well die happy, and reading made him happy. Besides, what else could he do, anyway? In a stream of four-letter words, Shimabukuro told Suda he wouldn't be looking out for him anymore which, of course, was a lie.

Our company was given the job of taking a hill called Pike's Peak after our battalion had just taken Hill 598. I was still the radio man for the platoon. When George Company was ordered to move out, my legs wouldn't move. My legs refused to move no matter how hard I tried to get them to work. They were paralyzed. I wasn't injured and I wasn't scared. Finally, after seeing the rest of platoon pressing forward and my platoon leader shouting at me to bring the radio up, I moved one leg with my hands, then with other until both legs responded. The guys told me later that it was all in my mind.

George Fujiwara has ahead of me by a couple of yards but in the confusion, I lost track of him for a few seconds until I stumbled over him. He was on the ground, his M-1 rifle broken in two. I had to follow my platoon leader so I yelled for a medic and continued up the hill. I passed several bodies on the ground—ours mostly—and stumbled over a couple more. I got to the trench, jumped in, and came upon a dead GI lying on his back with his helmet covering his face. A GI ahead of me accidentally kicked the body, causing the helmet to fall off his face. He had no face. It was blown away. He probably was someone from the 1st Battalion.

While the rest of the platoon prepared for a counterattack, I decided to take a break in a shell crater until my platoon leader needed me. Four or five men thought that was a good idea and joined me. The shell crater became the platoon CP, and I stayed there until it got dark.

Not a good move. A mortar round burst on the edge of the crater, spraying shrapnel into the crater. When the smoke and dust cleared, it appeared that everyone in the crater was injured. One GI had a badly mangled leg and was moaning for help. Someone made a weak cry for a medic.

My helmet lay a few feet from me so I reached for it, only to cry from a pain that shot up from my backside. I tried to get up but my lower body wouldn't move. I was paralyzed from my waist down. This time it was for real. I still had the radio on my back and wanted to take it off but any movement to my lower body made me swear in pain so I left the radio on my back. Just as well, because it offered some protection.

I had to get out of the crater but I still couldn't move my legs. The radio on my back restricted my movement but I finally took it off with a great deal of difficulty and feeling a lot of pain. Then I reached out with one hand to the edge of the crater and luckily got hold of a metal stake used to anchor barbed wire. I tried to pull myself out but couldn't. One of the KATSUSAs who often mixed with local boys from Hawaii saw me struggle and went for help. Soon I felt someone grab my field jacket by the arm and try to pull me out of the crater. It was dark so I didn't know who it was. I yelled, "Who's that?"

"Me, Labang," was the answer. It was Sgt. David Labang, another local boy, who was in the same platoon as me.

"This Alan," I answered in pain.

Labang pulled me out and started to drag me by the field jacket down the hill. I screamed in pain and he let me down. Someone yelled at Labang to leave me alone and to get back to his position. Labang swore at him and said that I was a friend and he was going for help. "Hang on, I'll be right back," he said. In a few minutes he came back with a litter and four KATSUSAs. They put me on a stretcher and Labang told them to take me to the forward aid station.

There were many wounded men waiting to be treated at the aid station. There were also many dead men on the ground lined up, some covered with ponchos or blankets, others without covers, face up. I must have been one of the most severely wounded because I was immediately put on a jeep and taken to a field hospital several miles behind the MLR. It must have been one of the MASH hospitals. All this time I didn't know how badly wounded I was and exactly where I got hit. All I knew was that I got hit somewhere in the back and was in great pain.

At the hospital a nurse gave me a bath and cleaned my wound. She told me exactly where my wound was. In the ass! I was put on the operating table next to a GI who was covered with blood. A nurse came with a hypodermic and told me not to cough. I passed out when she put the needle in me.

When I awoke, I was in a bed with all kinds of tubes hooked up to my body. It was so uncomfortable that I began pulling on them, trying to take them off. A nurse saw me and told me if I wanted to suffer to go ahead and pull them off. She scolded me for a few minutes and made me promise not to do that again. After that I was so heavily sedated that I didn't know what was going on half of the time.

OCTOBER 1952

PFC. WILLIAM ABREU
Able Company, 180th Infantry
Hwachon, North Korea

I was sitting in my jeep ready to drive the CO to battalion headquarters when a truck drove up loaded with replacements for our company. When it stopped, I saw nothing but Oriental faces. My first thought was, *Local boys from Hawaii.* There must have been about twenty of them. I got out the jeep and ran to the truck to welcome them to the company. As I got closer, I heard jabbering, not in pidgin English, but in Korean. They were KATUSAs assigned to our company. Was I ever disappointed!

OCTOBER 1952

SGT. CHARLES CHANG
Able Company, 180th Infantry
Hwachon, North Korea

After almost two years of training recruits for the Korean War at the Hawaiian Infantry Training Center, Schofield Barracks, Hawaii, the

FIGURE 39 Sgt. Charles Chang and Pfc. Louis Baldovi on Hill 854 after early morning patrol. October 1952. Courtesy of Charles Chang.

FIGURE 40   A train stop enables Pfc Louis Baldovi to stretch his legs on his way back to the front after a week of R&R in Japan. Courtesy of Louis Baldovi.

army decided I had enough surf, sunshine, and garrison duty and ordered me to Korea. Maybe it was because they wanted me to find out how good a job I did preparing men for combat.

When I got to Korea I was assigned to Able Company, 180th Infantry Regiment, 45th Infantry Division, a National Guard division

FIGURE 41   Thunderbirds Pfc. William Abreu and Pfc. Robert Fernandez in reserve at Hwachon. October 1952. Courtesy of William Abreu.

from Oklahoma called to active duty. They were known as the Thunderbirds. It arrived in Korea in December 1951.

I joined the company in October when it was in reserve in Hwachon, North Korea. I was made a platoon sergeant, replacing the one who had already rotated home. I was happy as hell to find out that there were two local boys in the company. There was Pfc. Willie Abreu, a jeep driver, who was wounded on Old Baldy, and Pfc. Louis Baldovi, a BAR man in one of my squads. They had been in Korea since May and were considered veterans of the company. I had to depend on those two guys, especially Baldovi, who was in the rifle squad for five months.

As soon as I could, I put in for a promotion for Baldovi. In November he was promoted to squad leader and to the rank of corporal.

Not long after I arrived, the 1st Battalion was sent up on line to relieve a ROK battalion at night on Hill 854, a few miles from the east coast. It was raining like heck when we arrived in the area. The trucks unloaded us near a 105mm howitzer gun battery, which was firing rapidly. I noticed the tubes of the guns were pointed up at a very steep angle, meaning that they were firing at very short range. Directly ahead was Hill 854. I wondered what the situation was all about.

We found out soon enough. The North Koreans in force had

attacked Hill 854 a couple of hours before we arrived, forcing the ROKs off the crest of the hill. The ROKs had called artillery fire on their own positions and that was why the gun tubes we saw were pointed almost straight up. We were told to drop our packs and be prepared to counterattack with the ROKs in case the hill was lost to the NKs. It was still raining and we were told to fold our ponchos and tuck them under our cartridge belts behind us. We were given an extra bandoleer of ammo.

The CO called all platoon leaders and platoon sergeants for a meeting to discuss the attack order in case we needed to counterattack. This was my first time on line and I wasn't sure how I was going to react when the bullets started to fly.

I called all my squad leaders and briefed them on the attack plan. I asked Baldovi what he thought, and he said all we had to do was go straight up the hill and hope for the best. There went our best-laid plans.

About midnight, the artillery went silent and the fire fight on the hill slackened and died down. Two hours later, we were told that the ROKs had counterattacked and had kicked the NKs off the hill and were in control of Hill 854. It was time to relieve them.

Slipping and sliding in the rain and in the dark, we passed ROK soldiers on their way down. Once in the trench we took a left where it ran downhill. Again, we ran into ROK troops heading in the opposite direction. The trench was slippery and narrow so we had to stop to let them through.

I dropped off the squads at their respective sectors and told them it was 100 percent alert until morning and I wanted everyone in the trench with their weapons locked and loaded. Beyond the last squad on our left were the Filipinos from the 19th Battalion Combat Team that tied in with our left flank.

I went back up the trench to look for the platoon CP and found platoon leader 2d Lt. Wayne Seeley in the bunker with a frustrated look on his face. He was bent at the waist slightly, his head almost touching the roof of the bunker and standing in a foot of water. The bunker was deep enough for the ROK soldiers, who must have been midgets, but not deep enough for Seeley, who was 5 feet 8 inches, and me, at 6 feet 2 inches. The roof leaked. It was the beginning of a miserable night.

At 0500 hours our mortars, probably the 81mm from the battalion's weapons company, began registering their guns. I could hear the shells bursting in the valley and some on the forward slope. One short round hit somewhere near our bunker and caved in part of one wall, bringing down mud, sandbags, and logs. My weapon and field telephone were buried under the debris. I dug them out and waited for daylight.

I sent my platoon runner to look for a vacant bunker at a higher point of the trench line and he reported back that there were a couple that looked all right. The one we chose was certainly better than the one we had earlier.

I checked on the platoon to make sure the squads were cleaning their weapons because I knew they were caked with mud and inoperable. I told them it was 50 percent alert so half of them could clean their weapons and the bunker. The rain had stopped, but we were all wet and muddy. When we walked in the trench we were weighed down with about 4 pounds of mud on our boots.

I finally got to survey the terrain we were on and in front of our position. We were not on the very top of Hill 854. We were on a ridge to the left about 200 yards from the top. The ridge sloped down to the left but I couldn't tell where it ended. But there was a little brown spot almost the same height as our hill more than a mile to the west. When I asked about it later I was told that it was Hill 812. It came under attack the previous night, too.

The ridge we were on ran east to west. The forward slope was gentle but marked with many small draws leading up to our trench line. There were no rice paddies because of the rugged terrain. Where Hill 854 ended at the bottom, the terrain beyond climbed to a ridge that was called Napalm Ridge. Beyond that was a series of high ridge complexes occupied by the North Koreans.

The weather finally cleared several days later and we were able to get ourselves and the bunkers cleaned up. Lieutenant Seeley told me to be sure that all the men had dry socks and foot powder and for them to take care of their feet. What little water was available was for drinking and washing our feet. He said never mind shaving—to the delight of the men—and forget about brushing our teeth. Our feet were most important.

I sent a patrol out one night to capture a prisoner on Napalm Ridge. The mission failed. One man was missing and several were wounded when the patrol returned. The missing man was the BAR man. The next morning the naked body of the missing man was spotted on the forward slope of Napalm Ridge about 50 yards below the trenches. When the battalion commander heard about it, he was furious and came to the hill. He told our CO we didn't leave our dead behind and ordered him to retrieve the body.

Because the missing man was in our platoon, Lieutenant Seeley and I had to come up with a plan to retrieve the body. We decided to have the mortars really pound the trenches and throw up a heavy smoke screen just before we made the climb to the body. Two squads were to make the attempt, with Corporal Balajadia's squad getting the body and the other giving covering fire. He cussed me like hell when I told him what he had to do. Sergeant First Class Ashby, another platoon sergeant and recent replacement from Hawaii, volunteered to accompany me.

When we got to the base of Napalm Ridge, the mortars plastered the trenches with high explosives and laid down a thick smoke screen,. Balajadia's squad moved through the smoke screen to get to the body. The North Koreans poured fire into the smoke screen, halting his advance. At that moment the smoke began to drift to the west, partly exposing Balajadia's squad. I just knew that this wasn't going to work and I wasn't going to leave any more dead men on the hill so I yelled for him to get his squad back down the ridge. Taking advantage of what little smoke there was, he was able to get his squad back with only one of his men slightly wounded.

I radioed Lieutenant Seeley and told him that we couldn't get the job done and we were returning. I was the last one to get back into our lines. We were debriefed by the battalion commander and he accepted the results of the mission.

For two more days, the bleached body of the BAR man lay exposed on Napalm Ridge. One of the tanks was given a fire mission to destroy some bunkers on Napalm Ridge. The next day the BAR man's body was missing. Whether the North Koreans removed the body or the tank's fire had mistakenly blasted the body off the ridge was left to speculation.

OCTOBER 1952

SGT. GEORGE MATSUNAGA
Item Company, 180th Infantry
Hill 854, North Korea

I was now assistant platoon sergeant. My platoon was to relieve a platoon of Able Company, 1st Battalion, when it was just about getting dark. I was leading my the platoon into the trench line and had turned a corner when I bumped into a GI leaving. I mean we almost went helmet to helmet. Words of "endearment" flowed from his mouth. In the the graying light I recognized my hometown buddy, Louis Baldovi. He also recognized me immediately. We slapped each other on the back as if he and I were the only ones on the hill until someone said, "What the hell's going on up there?" We parted with a quick handshake and he was gone. That was the only time we had seen each other in Korea.

OCTOBER 1952

PFC. ROBERT FERNANDEZ
Charlie Company, 180th Infantry
Hwachon, North Korea

Except for living in squad tents, sleeping on cots, and eating hot meals twice a day, reserve duty was for the birds. We were constantly in training.

One afternoon after returning from the field, I immediately went to my tent to lie down on my cot. There, at the head of cot, neatly placed on the blanket, was the Combat Infantryman's Badge, the same badge that Sergeant Walea, my training platoon sergeant, wore when he first talked to us in basic training. Boy, was I a proud son-of-a-gun. I rushed out of the tent waving the badge to those who had not yet seen it. They all ran to their tents to see if the CIB was on their bunk. Those who had fought at Old Baldy got their badges. We all put on our badges and walked around the company area like proud peacocks.

NOVEMBER 1952

PFC. ALAN TAKAMIYASHIRO
George Company, 31st Infantry
Camp Zama General Hospital, Japan

From the field hospital, I vaguely remembered being put on a train and flown to Taegu, which was halfway between Seoul and Pusan. When I reached Taegu I was put on an air transport ambulance with other casualties and flown to Haneda Airport, Japan, where we were loaded on an ambulance bus. Our driver was Japanese. If I had a gun I would have shot him because he drove like a mad man, never slowing down, hitting every pothole he could find. I was hurting.

I thought we were going to be taken to the Tokyo General Hospital but instead we were taken to the Camp Zama Hospital. The doctor who treated me first was Dr. Fukushima, a regular physician at the hospital. I remember him because he had an "Ike" jacket on and I wondered why he wore an "Ike" jacket instead of the familiar white lab coat that doctors normally wear while on duty. At first I wasn't too happy being treated by a Japanese doctor, but later he told me that he was from Hawaii, which put me at ease. He said he would be my personal doctor until I was ready to be transferred to Army Tripler General Hospital in Hawaii.

Every other day I had surgery. The surgeons continued to take out shrapnel and did a lot of skin grafting. It was here that I found out the details of my injury. I had lost most of my buttocks. There was damage to my anus and my lower vertebrae were exposed. To relieve the pain, I was given daily shots of morphine and since I didn't have an *okole* any more, I had to take all the shots in my arms. My arms were full of holes. One shot relieved my pain for only two hours at a time and I needed several in the course of the day. I started to become an addict and wanted more shots to ease my pain as the days passed. Doctor Fukushima realized what was happening to me and ordered all shots stopped. Going cold turkey was rough and I had to endure the pain until my condition improved.

I wanted to go home to Hawaii but I was in no condition to travel and remained at Camp Zama for a month. Then when I thought I was going home, I was taken to Yokohama General Hospital, where I was treated for three more days. Finally, I was given the good news that I was well enough to fly home. With other injured Hawaii boys, I was flown home and admitted to Army Tripler General Hospital, where I was treated for several months until my discharge from the army.

DECEMBER 1952

Honolulu, Hawaii, Territory of Hawaii

By Sarah Park, *Honolulu Star-Bulletin* Reporter

SOMEWHERE IN KOREA, DEC. 21—Korea is a bleak, tired looking country. It looks like a weary old man, dried up and emotionless, listless and worn. The country side is padded with rolling hills, sharp peaks and mountains the color of pinkish taffy . . . and dotted with pines and scrub oaks. . . . On Christmas Eve and Christmas Day, Hawaii soldiers will join United Nations forces in . . . guarding Korea's taffy like hills. These are the men who sit by their guns, go on patrol on nights when the mercury slides below zero. To them, Christmas is just another day. It's a day of extra vigil, just in case the enemy decides to try and take advantage of American sentimentality about the birth of Christ.

DECEMBER 1952

PFC. ROBERT FERNANDEZ
Charlie Company, 180th Infantry
Inje, North Korea

Our battalion, if not the entire regiment, had been kept in blocking position or division reserve since early November and was just taking it easy.

It was too cold for field exercises so we spent the time visiting other local boys, drinking beer, and gambling, mostly shooting craps.

One day, word went around for all Hawaii men in the battalion to assemble near battalion headquarters for some kind of a meeting. Shit, it was cold. I think it was near 20 to 30 degrees. Anyway, it was an order so I put on my parka and pile cap and walked to the battalion headquarters, where the Hawaii guys were already gathered around a tiny lady dressed in army clothing. From the edge of the group I heard her say that she was Sarah Park from Hawaii, a newspaper reporter from the *Honolulu Star-Bulletin,* and she was here to write about the men from Hawaii. She said she would be in Korea for at least a month and would interview other local boys from the other divisions. She would like to talk to a few of us and take group pictures and send them back to Hawaii.

She took several group pictures and the one that I was in included Jitsuo Higa, Henry Yoshihiro, Isaac Malag, Tetsuo Igawa, Louis Baldovi, Susumu Fukugawa, Gilbert Kihara, Calvin Hiraoka, Seizen Tamashiro, Yukio Tanaka, and Robert Hu. I never saw the group photo

FIGURE 42 SEND SOME HAWAIIAN WEATHER! Hawaii's men in Korea realize more than ever how wonderful Hawaiian weather is. *Left to right, front row,* Cpl. William Castillo, Pfc. Shinichi Sakuma, Pvt. Douglas Waterhouse, and Pvt. Ervan Sardinha. *Second row,* Cpl. Johnny Ramos, Cpl. Clayton Murakami, Sgt. Matsuo Sakai, and Pfc. William Abreu. *Third row,* Sfc. Donald Suyat, Cpl. Takeo Ebesu, Pfc. Yoshi Yoshinaga, Sgt. Richard Miyamoto, and Pfc. Toki Ansai. December 1952. Courtesy of the *Honolulu Star-Bulletin.*

until 1990, when it was brought to my attention by Louis Baldovi at our 45th Division reunion in Honolulu.

Miss Park finally asked me why was I in Korea. I told her that I was drafted, had no choice, and was sent to Korea. She walked away. I guessed she wanted a more philosophical or patriotic answer.

DECEMBER 1952

1ST LT. FLORANIO CASTILLO
Charlie Company, 27th Infantry
Vicinity of Munsan-ni, South Korea

Our battalion relieved a South Korean battalion two weeks prior to New Year's Eve. The ROKs left behind a lot of old and poorly maintained ammunition—mortars, bazookas, machine guns, and hand grenades. They were tested and many were found to be defective.

On New Year's Eve, our battalion commander ordered a "mad minute" of firing along our battalion front using all the ammunition left behind by the ROKs. At the stroke of midnight, we ushered in the New Year of 1953 with five minutes of uninterrupted fire to the north. Just before midnight our sector was lit with thousands of tracer bullets criss-crossing over enemy territory. You might say 1953 came in with a bang.

PART IV

1953 | Truce Talks, Patrols, and Artillery Duels

THE FAILURE OF BOTH SIDES TO AGREE ON THE ISSUE OF IN-voluntary repatriation of prisoners of war slowed down the peace process at Panmunjom. Meanwhile, men died while negotiators stared at each other across the conference table. Hilltop battles and artillery duels, usu-ally ignited by the communist forces, blazed across the Main Line of Resistance, with both sides attempting to strengthen their final position before the cease fire was reached. Outpost Reno, Pork Chop Hill, Christmas Hill, and Old Baldy were some of the many hills bitterly con-tested until the end of hostilities on July 27.

SFC. CHARLES CHANG
Able Company, 180th Infantry
Inje, North Korea

We spent December and most of January either in reserve or blocking because of little activity on the MLR. I suppose the Communists, like us, decided the weather was not suitable for large-scale operations.

The town of Inje was located southeast of the Hwachon Reservoir and along the Soyang River, which made our camp even colder. A couple of mornings, the temperature dropped to below zero. Even with winter clothing and snow pack shoes that we called Mickey Mouse boots (they resembled Mickey's big feet), it was still extremely cold.

While the winter clothing provided warmth, it also created problems when we had to take care of our bodily functions. Getting out of the several layers of clothing in time to urinate or defecate was very difficult, to say the least. Sometimes men couldn't get out their clothing fast enough and would suffer the humiliation of doing it while partially or fully clothed.

The few tented gang latrines were never enough to accommodate the long lines of men. There were outdoor urinals made of empty artillery shell casings behind the clusters of tents. When the ground was frozen the urine would not drain through the sump and would freeze almost instantly. When the weather warmed up just a bit, the frozen urine thawed and created a mess, not to mention producing a terrible odor.

I was promoted to sergeant first class in December. You might say it was a Christmas present.

We finally got orders to return to the front. All the platoon sergeants in the battalion left a day earlier so we could be briefed by the units we were to relieve and find out the exact locations for our platoons.

The ride from Inje to Heartbreak Ridge was through mountainous terrain and it took us several hours in the cold to get there. Although the trucks were covered, the bitter wind whipped through every opening, cutting into our winter clothing. I had never been in this kind of cold before.

It was dark when we arrived in the vicinity of Heartbreak Ridge. The driver dropped the tailgate and I was the first off the truck. The truck bed was almost 4 feet off the ground, and, not thinking how brittle my bones were from the cold, I leaped off the truck. Talk about being jarred. As soon as I hit the ground pain shot up both my legs and up my spine. I thought my bones would snap in two. Some of the guys were already jumping off the truck before I could warn them and they yelled in pain as they made contact with the frozen ground. The truck driver, seeing what happened, yelled for the rest to climb, not jump, off the truck.

Our guide came to get us and the first thing he said was, "What the hell was all that noise about? I could hear you guys from the top of the hill. There's North Koreans all over the place." No one tried to explain to him what had happened.

The guide told us to follow closely behind one another because of the narrow and slippery trail. It was a switched back trail because of the steepness of the hill and it took us a long time getting to our position.

I was greeted by the platoon sergeant I was to relieve and he led me to the platoon CP, my future home for the next three months. He briefed me on his platoon's assignment and the placement of each squad. Since it was cold, he said that he would show me the platoon's frontage in the morning so I might as well get some sleep. I didn't have to be told twice.

In the morning I got a good look at Heartbreak Ridge. The damn hill scared me. Heartbreak Ridge was a huge ridge complex that extended south to north; the highest point was to the north, and was in North Korean hands. I was told that the ridge was about 7 miles long. There were three dominating peaks well over 800 feet in elevation. On both

FIGURE 43　Heartbreak Ridge. March 1953. Courtesy of David Suzuki.

sides of the ridge were two valleys. To the left was Mundung-ni Valley and to the right was Satae-ri Valley, each with a small village at the head. There were many steep subridges or spurs running down to the untended rice fields of the valley floor.

JANUARY 1953

CPL. LOUIS BALDOVI
Able Company, 180th Infantry
Heartbreak Ridge, North Korea

Back in November while in reserve, Sergeant Chang wanted to promote me from BAR man to squad leader, a position that I did not want because it meant being responsible for other men. When Abreu was injured in June 1952, I told myself just to worry about my own butt. But because Chang and I were from Hawaii, I felt obligated to take the squad leader's position, but with the condition that I could give it up whenever I felt like it. He agreed. After all, Hawaii guys had to take care of each other. But he screwed me up by having me promoted to corporal in November because with rank came responsibility. When I went to complain to him about it, he only laughed and said that he would make me a sergeant before I left Korea.

We left all bundled up for the cold for the front lines on trucks late in the afternoon. Sergeant Chang had gone ahead the day before.

We carried a full field pack, which included a sleeping bag, blanket, extra set of fatigues, socks, and all the rations we could carry. On the way, all of us kept pounding the bed of the truck with our boots to keep the blood circulating. We made a hell of a racket.

It was very dark when we arrived at our destination. Sergeant Chang, along with the other platoon sergeants, was there to greet us. The platoon sergeants told us not to jump but to climb down from the truck.

Someone said, "Where the fuck is this place?"

"Heartbreak Ridge," Sergeant Chang said.

"Looks more like Assbreak Ridge," came the the reply, which brought a little laughter.

We started our climb following the 1st Platoon. It was the climb of all climbs. There was snow and more snow the higher we got. Halfway up the climb, I bumped into the GI in front of me. It had an accordion effect. The clanking of equipment and swearing filled the night as men bumped into men ahead of them.

After more than an hour, Sergeant Chang called a halt and told us that we had reached our position. He said to get off the trail so the other platoons could pass by.

"Squad leaders up front," Sergeant Chang called out quietly. I was paired off with the squad leader I was to relieve and followed him into the trench with my squad behind me. He pointed out the fighting positions to me and I assigned my men to each as we went by. The problem was I had nine men in my squad and he had twelve. He had more positions than I had men so I had to leave three positions vacant.

He pointed out the bunkers for my squad and then took me to the squad's CP bunker, a large one that could accommodate about six men. A couple of candles dimly lit the bunker.

The squad leader said he would leave everything except his weapon. There was a field telephone already hooked up to the platoon CP, several cases of fragmentation hand grenades, bandoleers of .30 caliber ammunition, and a couple cases of rations. He was going to travel light when he left. He gave me a crude, hand-drawn map that showed the minefields in front of my position and the patrol routes.

I asked him how long he had been on Heartbreak Ridge and he said almost two months. Because of the weather, enemy activity was light, with only patrol clashes in the valleys. His squad averaged about a patrol every week. A quick calculation told me that he must have pulled about eight patrols while he was on the hill. That was too much to suit me. Since I arrived in Korea I must have already been on at least a dozen, four as patrol leader.

Casualties in his squad numbered three or four men slightly wounded from mortar rounds.

He was anxious to leave. He shook my hand and said good luck. When we stepped outside the bunker, his squad was waiting, ready to leave. He took the lead quietly and his squad followed until they disappeared around the bend of the trench.

I quickly went to check on my men, two KATUSAs, three Puerto Ricans, and three haoles. One of the Puerto Ricans, a college graduate, was my assistant squad leader. When I got to the last fighting position on the right, I found a gap of 50 yards between my squad and the squad to my right. I talked to the squad leader and I asked him if that gap was his responsibility. He said no.

I quickly went back to my CP to call Sergeant Chang to notify him of the problem but before I could ring him on the field telephone, it rang. It was the sergeant. Before I could say a word he said 100 percent alert tonight and hung up. Who could sleep in this damn cold, anyway? I went back into the trench to make sure that every one of my men was awake and in the trench.

When morning came I assigned the two KATUSAs to one bunker, two Puerto Ricans to another, and the two haoles in another one. Three of us, the assistant squad leader, a haole who was my runner, and I shared the CP.

Having to communicate with Koreans, Puerto Ricans, and haoles was confusing. My Hawaiian pidgin English added to the confusion, sometimes bordering on the comical. Fortunately, while in reserve, I had conducted some sort of language classes for my squad so everyone could understand a few basic English words. Using gestures and basic words of the different languages, we were able to come to an understanding of what was said. The KATUSAs could also speak Japanese, which delighted me because I could understand and speak a little Japanese I learned from my Japanese American friends where I grew up.

On several occasions the KATUSAs and Puerto Ricans got into arguments. Hearing them jabbering at each other in their own language, not knowing what was said, was very funny.

The sky was overcast, it was cold, and there were patches of snow on the ground. Now I could see where we were. My squad's position was halfway up the hill and facing northeast, with the Satae-ri Valley below us. Beyond it was a terrain feature called "Punchbowl" because of its shape.

The terrain before me was steep and wooded. A commo trench wound its way the length of the ridge, disappearing and appearing with the uneven terrain and up another ridge complex to the south known as Bloody Ridge. My CP was just below a very prominent rock outcropping. The ridge was very rocky, the reason why the trenches were of varying depth and width.

Several mornings later, I got a call from Sergeant Chang and our conversation went like this.

"Baldovi, Chang here. Your squad has patrol tomorrow night."

"Get somebody else who hasn't gone before, one of the new guys. I've got 30 points and six more I'll be rotating home."

"Cannot."

"Why not?"

"Lieutenant Seeley from S-2 requested that you take the patrol."

"Fuck Lieutenant Seeley."

"Put it this way. He called the CO."

I wanted to say fuck him, too, but thought better of it.

First Lieutenant Wayne Seeley was my platoon leader when we were on Hill 854 near the east coast back in October. He didn't like the way I handled a patrol and chewed me out for it.

In the morning, my assistant squad leader and I reported to the platoon CP. Lieutenant Seeley was there with my CO. He asked me how I was doing and I said fine. He never told me why he wanted me for the patrol and I didn't ask.

Lieutenant Seeley said that the battalion needed a prisoner for interrogation and was desperate for one. According to previous recon patrols in the valley, NK patrols had been sighted in the valley almost nightly between midnight and 0300 hours. The enemy patrols were consistent in their routes and had been setting ambushes at the end of the finger that ran down from our company's position. They wanted prisoners, too.

The plan was to set up an ambush at the end of the finger well before the enemy patrol got there. To be sure we got there before the enemy, it was suggested that we get to the ambush site between 2200 and 2300 hours. That would mean sitting out there in the cold for a long, long time.

I asked for white winter camouflage suits but was told that none were available, although I had seen battalion personnel visiting the front wearing them. I also asked for M-2 automatic carbines and was told to borrow them from men in the company.

At 1300 hours I assembled my squad at the chow bunker and briefed them on the patrol. The thing that I impressed upon the men in my squad was that if we got into a fire fight, I expected everyone to fire his weapon, even if the enemy was not to their front. I said I would check every weapon when we returned to see if they had been fired. I told them that we would carry automatic carbines and four hand grenades each and to put on as much warm clothing as they possibly could because we would be out in the cold a long time.

I told my assistant squad leader to go to the weapons platoon and scrounge enough automatic carbines and banana magazines for everyone in the squad. I wanted six banana clips per man. While he was doing this, I took my binoculars and checked the patrol route from three different positions. I figured it would take me about an hour and a half to get down to the valley floor. The spur was a steep one and it was covered with snow at least halfway down to the valley. It looked slippery and it appeared that we would have difficulty negotiating the trail, especially on the return climb.

My assistant squad leader came back with only four automatic carbines. I went to the platoon CP and confiscated two more from the assistant platoon sergeant and radio man. I don't think any of my men knew how to fire the automatic carbine so I had to instruct them on its operation.

I told my squad to get some rest in the afternoon and to meet me in front of my bunker at 2100 hours. I had decided to leave at 2130 hours.

At 2100 hours my squad assembled outside of my bunker. When I saw them, I burst out laughing. I told them they looked a bunch of penguins waddling around with so much clothing on. They must have had the same thoughts about me.

We maneuvered through the barbed wire gate and through the minefield, and started down the trail. We had to grab tree branches and shrubs to avoid falling. Every five minutes or so I stopped the patrol just to listen. Our huge Mickey Mouse boots made crunching sounds in the snow.

It was about 2300 hours when we reached the end of the spur. I set the defense in a semicircle facing the valley floor just inside the tree line. Each man took cover behind a tree, log, or rock. I told the men on the flanks to throw hand grenades when the firing started to discourage the enemy from flanking our positions. Then I told my radio operator to let the company know we were in position.

There was no snow at the bottom of the finger so we were able to blend in with the dark surroundings using the trees as cover. It wasn't as cold as when we started out.

The minutes went by very slowly. I could feel the perspiration in my boots, generated by walking, turn to ice. My men had difficulty keeping still in the cold and I could hear them moving around.

It was now midnight and I was hoping that the enemy patrol would choose to stay home in their warm bunkers. I figured another half hour and I would head back to our lines. Ten minutes, twenty minutes, and finally the half hour went by and in my mind I said, *Hooray*.

Kim Bok-ki, who was on my left, tugged me on the arm and whispered, "North Korean," and pointed to his left. I didn't see anyone and I strained my eyes to see when a dark figure loomed up about 30 yards in front of us. That son-of-a-bitch was huge. It couldn't have been a North Korean. I think it was Kim who fired first. At the same time, a sparking hand grenade arched toward us but hit a tree branch, fell to the ground, and exploded. I yelled, "Fire! Fire!" The noise from six automatic carbines and three M-1 rifles was deafening. I thought that the figure which appeared would come crashing into our perimeter but it fell 10 yards short of us. Then burp gun fire mixed with our own fire. Our automatic carbines were just smoking, keeping up a steady rate of fire. I yelled for my squad to keep on firing even though we couldn't see the enemy.

After a couple of minutes I realized only our carbines were firing, so I yelled for the patrol to cease fire. I saw several figures running and disappearing to the left. The fire fight lasted no more than three minutes. The crisp night air mixed with burned powder and smoke stung my nose.

"Anyone get hit?" I called out.

"Me, Angel," someone cried out.

It was one of the Puerto Ricans.

I got to him and asked where he was hit. He said his left arm was numb but he didn't how bad it was because of all the clothing he had on. I told him to hang on.

I waited five minutes. There was no movement so I decided that the NKs had left. I sent half the squad out about 20 yards from the perimeter to see if there were any wounded or dead Chinese. Kim ran to where he had seen the NK disappear in the underbrush. The others came back and reported there was no sign of the enemy.

Kim was still out there. Then I heard someone thrashing in the bushes ahead and told everyone to get down. Kim stumbled back to us, holding up a quilted NK jacket in his hand for us to see. That son of a gun had stripped the dead NK of his jacket. I told the radio operator to report that we were returning and there was no prisoner but we accounted for one dead NK, which we could prove.

The wounded Angel was helped by the KATUSAs and they started the climb first. The rest of us leap frogged behind them, watching our backs. It took us nearly three hours to get back to our lines.

Sergeant Chang, our platoon leader, and Lieutenant Seeley were at the barbed wire gate when we entered our lines. We were taken to the platoon bunker, where we were debriefed over hot cups of coffee. Lieutenant Seeley was not too pleased that we couldn't get him a prisoner but was delighted that we had one kill.

FEBRUARY 1953

PFC. ELGEN FUJIMOTO
Item Company, 179th Infantry
Vicinity of Punchbowl, North Korea

I finally got promoted to private first class but, as squad leader, it carried a rank of sergeant.

It was my squad's turn to go out on patrol, so my new platoon leader and I went to battalion for the briefing. When we got there, the briefing officer told me that my platoon leader, who was going to accompany me for the experience, was going to be the patrol leader. I would be his assistant but would run the patrol. Since I was not officially the patrol leader, I asked if I would still be given credit as the patrol leader. He said no. A major happened by and heard the discussion. He told the briefing office that since I was a sergeant and was going to lead the patrol, I should be credited as the patrol leader. He was shocked when I told him that I was only a private first class. He told my platoon leader to find a sergeant to lead the patrol or to lead the patrol himself, experienced or not. But I still had to go on the patrol.

FEBRUARY 4, 1953

Honolulu, Territory of Hawaii

The *Honolulu Star-Bulletin* reported this story by Sarah Park.

KAUAI CORPORAL ASSUMES JOB
OF PROTECTING SQUAD'S FLAG:
On the eastern front in Korea-High upon one of the American forces' northernmost positions, an American flag flutters defiantly in the face of Communist soldiers—a symbol of the bravery of her fighting men.
   Flying within only 15 yards of enemy soldiers, the flag has one of its most ardent protectors, a baby faced soldier from Kilauea, Kauai. . . .
   "I can look down on it from my bunker," says Corporal Henry U. Tamura, 21, son of Mr. and Mrs. Usaburo Tamura. . . . Corporal Tamura is leader of a machine gun squad on Sandbag Castle, a windswept, frozen ridge. . . . eight miles above the 38th parallel. . . .
   "The enemy fire at our flag all the time," Corporal Tamura said. "But every time they get smart, we answer back with everything we got. It usually makes them shut up."
   This is the second flag put up by Corporal Tamura's company. The first one was a white turkish towel on which were painted red stripes and a blue corner. There weren't any stars except for holes from enemy bullets. . . .

FEBRUARY 1953

CPL. LOUIS BALDOVI
Able Company, 180th Infantry
Heartbreak Ridge, North Korea

Since our arrival at Heartbreak Ridge in late January, I had been on three patrols and was scheduled to go out again early the next morning at 0100 hours. At noon I went to the platoon CP to be briefed. While we were waiting for the platoon leader, Sergeant Chang offered me a canteen cup of coffee. I held the cup while he poured. While he was pouring, my right hand began to tremble so I set the cup on the ground. Chang asked why I did that and I said that the canteen cup was hot. After he filled the cup I picked it up. My hand shook so violently that I spilled the coffee and dropped the cup.

"Are you okay?" Chang asked.

"I don't know," I replied.

I stuck both hands out and they were trembling. I put them in my parka pockets but they continued to shake. Then my body began to shake. I thought it was the cold but I wasn't feeling cold. Assistant platoon Sgt. Robert Reed took a blanket and wrapped it around me. I finally calmed down, and when the platoon leader arrived, I was all right. Chang and I never told the platoon leader what had happened to me.

When the briefing was over, Chang pulled me to the side and asked if I wanted to be replaced. He could assign another squad to take out the patrol. I said no—I was all right.

It was about 2200 hours and I had already briefed my squad for the 0100 patrol and was putting my gear together. The phone rang. It was Sergeant Chang.

"Louie, pack up."

"What?"

"Pack up, you're going home."

"What?"

"Special orders. Get your ass here, now!"

I didn't know what to do. Then both my hands shook again. I put them in my pockets. I looked at my assistant squad leader for a moment, not knowing what to tell him until he asked what the call was about. "I'm going home," was all I could say.

I suddenly realized that I couldn't leave my squad, not with a patrol coming up in a few hours. We had been together for almost three months and had formed a strong bond despite our differences in race and in language. The word "home" struck me again and I regained my composure. I told my assistant squad leader he was now the squad leader and he had to take the patrol out in the morning. He muttered something in Puerto Rican, which I didn't understand, and hugged me. I shook the hand of my radio operator and wished both of them luck.

I put on my parka and my steel helmet, rolled up my sleeping bag, slung my M-1 rifle, and walked outside. I dropped in on every squad bunker and fighting hole and said goodbye to my men and wished them luck. The last men I said goodbye to were my two KATUSAs. They cried and begged me not to go. Kim Bok-ki refused to let go of me. The other KATUSA pulled Kim away.

"You lucky dog," was the first thing Chang said to me when I walked into the CP. The platoon leader shook my hand and wished me good luck. I asked Chang the reason for my going home but he didn't know what the special order was about. He said I'd find out at the company's CP down the hill. I asked him if I could do anything for him back home, he said no. The next time I saw him again was three years later in Hawaii.

With my sleeping bag and rifle, I went down the trail. Halfway down I realized I had forgotten my .45 pistol that I had loaned to Sergeant Reed. I thought of going back but nixed the idea. One stray artillery round could be my downfall and what's one pistol, anyway. My life didn't depend on it. I continued down the hill to the company CP.

Willie Abreu was waiting for me outside the CP. He had stayed up to wait for me. I asked him if he was going home too, but he said no.

The company clerk gave me the orders that got me off the hill. It was from the Red Cross requesting an emergency leave for me to return home. My father was gravely ill but the papers didn't say the kind of illness he had. I wondered what had happened to my dad because when I last saw him nearly a year ago he looked fine and had not complained about his health.

Abreu and I stayed up all night talking. He said for me to call his parents up and to tell them he was okay. At 0400 hours, he walked me to the truck, where about a dozen others were getting on board. I told Abreu to watch himself, hugged him, and got on the truck. He waved until we disappeared into the night.

Then we went on this crazy ride because the driver, who was also going home, wanted to get the hell out of there. He drove like a mad man. A couple of the guys pounded on the cab to make him slow down but he wouldn't have any of it.

It took us several hours to get to Yongdong-po, the 45th Division rear, where we were processed. That evening, while walking to my tent after chow, Sfc. Wallace Oshiro, a high school classmate of mine who worked in division headquarters, handed me a set of orders. It was my promotion to staff sergeant. How do you like that? I recalled Chang saying that I would leave Korea as a sergeant. The orders also read that Chang was promoted to master sergeant.

FEBRUARY 9, 1953

Honolulu, Territory of Hawaii

The *Honolulu Star-Bulletin* reported this story by Sarah Park.

HAWAII SOLDIERS IN BATTALION CITED FOR T-BONE HILL THRUST:
With the U.S. 45th Infantry Division In Korea. Medals, awards, cita-
tions—these hardly atone for the brutality of war, the loss of lives, or
the wounding of the flesh.

But they are the symbols of this country's gratitude and its deep
founded respect for the young men who must bear arms for the rest of
us, for what we believe in—for what we hope will one day be a world
free of brutality and aggression.

Such a symbol was presented on a chilly afternoon by a river side
in the eastern hills of Korea.

The thousands of men of the 180th Infantry Regiment gathered
there to see units of the Third Battalion of the regiment receive the
Presidential Unit Citation. They include 50 men from Hawaii. . . .
"Outstanding performance of duty and extraordinary heroism. . . ."—
can you realize the significance of these words?. . .

On June 13, 1952, units of the Third Battalion assaulted the hill, and
took it. Two other battalions had been hurled off the hill with heavy
casualties. With the coming of darkness, the enemy poured intense
artillery fire on our men. Waves of enemy troops charged up the hill,
but were forced to tumble back again. . . .

The enemy suffered more than 2,000 casualties in that action,
according to the citation.

MARCH 1953

PFC. ELGEN FUJIMOTO
Item Company, 179th Infantry
Vicinity of Punchbowl, North Korea

Nothing changed. I was still ordered to take out patrols even if I were
only a private first class. This sure was a foul-up outfit. I received a
sergeant first class as a replacement in my squad who outranked me
many times over. This was his third tour in Korea and he volunteered to
serve in an infantry outfit so he could earn the Combat Infantryman's
Badge. He had served with rear echelon units on his previous tours.

Although he had enough rank to be a squad leader, he was made my
assistant. I told the platoon leader that the sergeant should be the squad

leader because he had to earn his pay. The platoon leader said the sergeant needed some time to be broken in and denied my request. I then went to the company commander and told him the same thing. No dice. He also said no.

My squad's turn came again to go out on patrol so here was the chance for the sergeant to get some experience. It was just a recon patrol so it was an easy mission as long as we didn't run into any commies.

About a mile out from the MLR, I had the squad take a break before we headed back to our lines. I noticed that the sergeant, who was about 20 yards in back of me, had covered himself with his poncho. Then I smelled cigarette smoke. The damn fool had lit a cigarette. Man, was I teed off. I went over to him and, in a muffled voice, told him, "You want to get us killed? Put that damn thing out."

My squad got ready to move out immediately because that fool of a sergeant may have alerted the commies who might be in he area.

When we got back, I told the CO that what that stupid sergeant had done could have jeopardized the patrol. I wanted him out of my squad but my request was denied.

APRIL 1953

Pfc. Susumu Shinagawa
Able Company, 34th Infantry
Chongson, POW Camp 3, North Korea

I was heating water to take a bath when a guard came into the kitchen and ordered me to gather my personal belongings. "You are going to the hospital," he said. I never asked to go to the hospital because my wounds were not infected, nor was I ill. Besides, I hated going to the hospital. I wondered what was up.

There were fourteen of us who were ordered to the hospital. We were kept there for four days without being told why. It really played hell on our minds. Of course, there had been talk about some of us going home, but I had been disappointed too many times for me to believe that rumor. One of the men said that we might be sent to the city of Paekton, where better medical facilities were located. That made a little sense because most of us needed it.

On the fifth day we were served sake, fried meat, vegetables, and bread. We were also given candies and cigarettes. We all wondered what we had done to deserve this treatment or if this was another one of their psychological strategies to brainwash us. Maybe this was their final attempt to break us. After we had eaten, a Chinese officer appeared and asked if we had enjoyed the farewell party. "Farewell party?" we all gasped. "Where are we going?" several asked.

"There will be an exchange of wounded and sick prisoners of war and you have been selected. You are going home."

I was dumbstruck. I didn't believe him. I really thought he wanted to bring us to a high and later lower the boom on us by telling us that it was all a mistake.

He asked each of us what was taken from us at the time of our capture and said he would try to replace the items. I told him that $140 in American currency and a watch were taken from me. And would you believe it? I was given $140 in American money and a Russian wrist watch. That convinced me I was going home. Yet, there was no jubilation among us when we realized that we were going home because we still didn't trust the commies. The mood was somber.

I had mixed feelings about going home, probably because of the many friends I was leaving behind. I was glad but also sad.

Panmunjom, South Korea

I never had a chance to say goodbye to my buddies. From Chongson, we were taken to Paekton, the assembly point for the exchange of prisoners of war. There were eighty of us in the truck convoy when we left Paekton at 5:00 A.M. on April 17. Each truck was marked with a red flag in the back and a red cloth over the hood for the benefit of our air force.

Many hours later, we reached Pyongyang, the North Korean capital. The city had been flattened by bombings and only a few buildings were left standing. We stayed in the city for two days, getting cleaned up and fattened for the exchange. The Chinese wanted us to look good so they could say that we were well treated as prisoners of war. We left Pyongyang on the morning of April 21 and arrived at Panmunjom shortly before noon.

There was a bridge before Panmunjom that the trucks could not cross. It was called the "Bridge of No Return." Once the bridge was crossed, there was no turning back into North Korea.

The convoy stopped just short of the North Korea side of the bridge. A North Korean dropped the tailgate of the truck and motioned us off the truck. There were some shouts as we piled out. Some of us ran, some walked, like me. My leg, although healed by Chinese medical standards, still bothered me.

As I crossed the bridge I saw the American flag. I got chicken skin when I saw it. For all those people who get a thrill in burning and stomping the American flag—if only they knew what it stood for. I wished they were there with us when we crossed the bridge. With tears rolling down my cheeks and my head high, I walked to freedom.

We were whisked away to an army camp a couple miles away, where we were issued new uniforms and allowed to meet the press. I was given a Camel cigarette and although it wasn't my brand, it tasted great after thirty-three months smoking the terrible kind we made out of whatever we could find resembling tobacco. Next came a cup of coffee, a glass of milk, a milk shake, and a stick of chewing gum—all bad for me following my prison camp diet.

These things reminded me of another life. It seemed so unreal, yet it was real. I was in a daze and couldn't comprehend the fact that I was no longer a prisoner of war—after thirty-three months and sixteen days.

That afternoon I went to a Holy Communion service. I felt much better and the perspective on my new surroundings and freedom came into better focus.

A helicopter took us to a hospital at Yongdong-po near Seoul, where we stayed overnight. From nearby Kimpo Airfield, a Globemaster flew us to Tokyo, where we were taken to Tokyo General Hospital for several days of testing, interrogation, and a physical check-up.

APRIL 1953

CPL. ELGEN FUJIMOTO
Item Company, 179th Infantry
Vicinity of Punchbowl, North Korea

After sixty-three days on line, I finally got to take a hot shower. My squad was ordered off the line and to report to regiment to get cleaned up. The bottom of the hill to the 8th Army shower unit was a long way and we had to walk to get there. My first hot shower in two months. I stayed under the shower until I got yelled at by the long line of naked GIs waiting for their turn.

When I got through, I went to the stacks of clothes to find clothing that would fit me. I found a set of fatigues that fit me, but they had holes in them, probably bullet holes. I told the attendant about the condition of the clothes and he told me that several truck loads of laundry had been hijacked a couple of weeks before on their way to division. He said to come back in about a week and he might have a better selection of clothing.

Back on line, I felt somewhat refreshed after the hot shower even though I perspired a lot climbing the hill back to my position.

Just before dark a patrol from another platoon left the MLR through my squad sector. They had gone only about 200 yards down the finger when they were ambushed by the commies. Ambushed right in front of our lines. That sure shocked everybody.

Right away there were cries for medics. Since my squad was nearest to the action, I got half my squad and rushed down to the ambush site. My platoon leader followed me. I could hear the burp guns and our own BAR firing. Instead of moving directly into the perimeter of the ambushed squad, I led my men to the right of the perimeter to outflank the commies. I saw figures moving about in front of the perimeter and told my men to fire in that direction. I fired two banana magazines with my automatic carbine until it malfunctioned, and threw a couple of hand grenades to the right of the perimeter.

From our lines, a couple of machine guns opened up fire on the trail the commies used. That's when they broke off contact and disappeared among the trees and dense undergrowth.

Two men in the patrol were killed. Both of them were in my squad two months before and had transferred when they returned from R&R. My squad came out of it without a casualty and was commended by the company commander for reacting so quickly to the situation.

I was considered a short-timer, as I had been in Korea since July 1952. I started to take great precautions in what I did, like wearing my helmet and flak jacket at all times. I did not venture far from my bunker unless I really had to. I never walked upright in the trench. I made my bunker more secure by scrounging sandbags and filling them with dirt and putting two more layers of sandbags on the roof of the bunker. The guys thought it was silly for me to take all those safety measures. I wasn't taking any chances.

MAY 1953

PFC. SUSUMU SHINAGAWA
Able Company, 34th Infantry
Honolulu, Territory of Hawaii

After a few days in the hospital, I boarded another Globemaster and flew to Hawaii. It was a long flight so we had to make a refueling stop at Midway Island. The next stop, Hawaii.

As the aircraft descended for its approach to Hickam Air Force Base, its flight path took us directly over the island of Kauai, my island. I could see the island very clearly. In fact, I could see my hometown of Eleele. I kept telling myself, *I'm home. I'm home.* Only a few days before I was a prisoner of war in some forsaken place in North Korea, and now I was flying over my hometown.

My mind wandered and images of the men still in North Korea floated through my mind. I could see what they were doing. The river was just thawing out when I left. That meant winter was gone and "wood details" were going out to gather firewood. They were going about their hopeless daily routines. There were burial details. It seemed unfair.

We finally landed at Hickam Air Force Base. I was surprised to see a large crowd gathered when the aircraft taxied to the terminal. A flight attendant came to me and said to get off the plane first since I was from Hawaii and the first Hawaii prisoner of war to be repatriated. Someone told me to stop at the top of the ramp, wave to the crowd, then walk slowly down the ramp. I don't remember doing that. I also don't remember if a band was there.

Nearby was a parked bus. I entered the bus through the rear door and walked to the front. I looked out of the bus and there, to my surprise, was my mom, waving to get my attention. With tears streaming down my face, I ran out of the bus to her and hugged her with all my strength. She grabbed my right arm and kept rubbing it. Later, I found out that someone had told her that I was wounded in my right arm and she thought that it had been amputated.

After meeting my family and friends, all of us, now former prisoners of war, boarded the bus for Tripler Army General Hospital. I stayed there for three months and the wounds that I had received in July 1950 finally healed.

JUNE 1953

Sfc. Clarence Young
George Company, 5th RCT
Pyoktong, POW Camp 5, North Korea

We heard that peace talks were going well and the war might end soon and some prisoners would be released on a prisoner exchange program. Men who corroborated with the Chinese were rounded up and taken away. We never saw them again.

CPL. ELGEN FUJIMOTO
Item Company, 179th Infantry
Vicinity of Punchbowl, North Korea

I was waiting in line at the chow bunker when one of the cooks brought me a note from the first sergeant. The note read, "Fujimoto and Kaplan, get your asses down the hill, now." The word "now" was underlined. My first reaction was, "Shit, another dirty detail." I felt really discriminated against. Anyway, I grabbed my carbine, and Kaplan and I went down the hill to the company CP.

When we got to the CP the first sergeant was smiling. Maybe the detail wasn't going to be so bad or he was relishing the thought of making it rough on us. When I got close to him I noticed that his eyes watered. Still smiling, he said, "You're going home. You're going home." Man, I wanted to jump in the air and click my heels but all I could say was thanks. Kaplan broke down and sobbed.

We were scheduled to leave in a couple of days and were told not to go back up the hill unless it was absolutely necessary. I asked about our gear on the hill and the first sergeant said to leave it there. I had some personal things that I needed so I told him that I was going to go back in the morning to get them.

Back on the hill the next morning, I picked up my things and put them all in a waterproof bag and said my goodbyes to most of the men in the platoon, especially the men who were with me when I was a squad leader. The sergeant I had trouble with came to wish me well and told me how he appreciated my getting on his butt. He realized how tough it was being a squad leader. I heard later that he became the assistant platoon sergeant.

The truck ride from Punchbowl to Yongdong-po was a long and dusty one. From there we took a train to Inchon. Every once in a while the train would come to a grinding stop due to guerrilla activities ahead of us. On one occasion, I climbed into the overhead baggage compartment for cover.

Camp Drake, Japan

We went by ship from Inchon to Sasebo, Japan, and got on a train to Camp Drake, where I stayed for twenty-one days processing guys on their way home. I don't know why I got picked for that job while many of the other Hawaii men were being sent home.

It was a pleasant duty and I enjoyed my off-duty hours so I asked the first sergeant if I could extend my stay in Japan by enlisting for another three years. He said to put in a request. I did, but it was disapproved.

I finally caught a plane to Hawaii with other local boys, refueling at Midway Island and landing at Hickam Air Force Base. We were processed at Schofield Barracks and sent to Fort Shafter, where we waited out the rest of our service time. I was discharged on July 9, 1953, eighteen days before the Korean War Armistice was signed.

JULY 1953

1ST. LT. IWAO YOKOOJI
Military Intelligence, 2d Infantry
Along the DMZ, Korea

The final days of the shooting war were filled with talk of an imminent cease fire agreement. That drew elation and our immediate thoughts were (1) no more artillery shells with the possibility of our names on them will find their way into our foxholes, (2) no more nightly fears of the communist forces overrunning our positions.

The order to cease fire before 2200 hours on July 27 was a welcome one and a cause for a thunderous celebration. Fireworks may have been used back home but in the war zone live ammunition was plentiful and available for use and use it we did—to the max. Normally, we were constrained by the practice of supply economy but, what the heck, the shooting was about to end.

The night of July 27, 1953, was literally turned into day when both sides fired their weapons to get rid of their ammunition, either attempting to kill one or more of the enemy or rejoicing over the end of the three-year slaughter of soldiers and civilians. The shooting frenzy kept up to one minute before the 2200 hours deadline, with both sides mindful of not wanting to violate the cease fire agreement. While we were elated over the end of the shooting war, an uneasy calm fell over the area after the firing.

JULY 1953

SFC. CLARENCE YOUNG
George Company, 5th RCT
Pyoktong, POW Camp 5, North Korea

It was in late July when we were told that an armistice agreement was signed. While there were some celebrations, the overall mood of the camp was rather calm.

The Chinese began sorting out prisoners to decide who should leave first. The wounded and my friends Verano, Defontes, and Tupa were among the first group. But before they left, I asked them to tell my family that I was alive and well and, should I not return, it was not because I didn't want to but because I was kept back by a certain Chinese general as punishment for my behavior in camp. I also told them to check the POW list to see if I was scheduled to return. If I was not on that list, I asked them to check the MIA list. I really believed that I would never return home.

SEPTEMBER 1953

SFC. CLARENCE YOUNG
George Company, 5th RCT
Pyoktong, POW Camp 5, North Korea

It had been several weeks since the first group left and little by little the camp became deserted. I kept saying goodbye to my friends, giving them same message I gave the first group. We were now down to the last fifteen prisoners of war in the camp. I was the only enlisted GI; the rest were officers. It reaffirmed my belief that surely I would remain in North Korea.

Late one afternoon, we were called out in formation and told we were finally going home. While the officers were congratulating each other, I waited for the camp commander to say, "All of you are going home, except Young." Those words never came.

After a change of clothing, we picked up what few possessions we had and boarded the truck. I was the last one to board. After a couple of hours we reached a train station and took a train south. Many hours later we stopped at a town and got off the train and waited. A group of officers from another POW camp joined us. I struck up a conversation with one of them and found out that, he, like me, was a troublemaker in camp and gave his Chinese captors fits.

Our truck finally arrived. As we prepared to board I heard a voice call out, "Sergeant Young." It was a Chinese general who called me. He pulled me aside and said, "Do you remember me?" Shit, how could I forget? He was the one I refused to stand up for who told me that I would be the last to leave.

"Sure, I said," and left it at that.

"Good. I kept my promise to hold you until the end."

He was polite and I decided to be civil. I was complimented by the fact that he remembered me and made a point to see me off. After a few pleasant remarks, he said, "Goodbye, comrade," and saluted me. I returned the salute and boarded the truck.

On the ride south I didn't know what the others were thinking, but I thought about my three attempted escapes and my crazy antics in camp and wondered why I was still alive going south to freedom. I should have been shot several times. It was crazy.

Many, many hours later we came to a small bridge. We had arrived at Panmunjom.

When I got off the truck a full bird colonel came to my side and told me a chaplain was available if I wanted to see one. I said okay and after the session with the chaplain I was taken to a shower unit. I showered, was fumigated, then showered again. I could have stayed under the hot shower all day.

After I was cleaned up and dressed in clean fatigues, an officer led me to the mess tent and sat me down at a table. He said I could have anything I wanted. "You order what you want and I'll get it for you," he said. I asked for an ice cream sundae with banana and pineapple topping and a big, juicy steak. He left and after a while he returned with exactly what I had ordered.

Half an hour after I had eaten, I gagged and couldn't breathe. I was rushed to the aid station, where they pumped my stomach. After I recovered I was told that the food I had eaten was too rich for me and too soon after my POW diet. I should be more careful the next time I ordered any food, they said. Hell, they should have warned me about it before I ordered my food.

I was fine the next day and was told the next leg of my journey home would be to Kimpo airfield, where we would be flown to Japan.

In Japan, we were taken to the Tokyo General Hospital Annex, where all former POWs were interrogated as part of the process before being sent home. In the hospital, it finally dawned on me that I was free, never to face my communist captors again. I never felt this way when I got to Panmunjom. Tears started pouring down my face and I began crying like a baby. I just couldn't help it. I just let myself go.

I waited two days before my turn came to be debriefed because officers were interrogated first and, besides, my name was Young, almost last on the POW list. I was asked how many POWs I knew had died for certain, their names (if I could recall them), and how we were treated. When it was over, I was told that what was discussed was highly classified and I was not to share details of the interrogation with anyone.

I was given a pass and went to the NCO club in Tokyo, where I ate frog legs and chicken. When I got back to the hospital, I felt a sharp pain in my throat and had difficulty breathing. I coughed up blood. My first thought was that I had contracted tuberculosis in the POW camps.

Fortunately, I was able to see a doctor who examined me and found that I had piece of shrapnel lodged in my chest near my lungs. That piece of shrapnel had never bothered me while I was in captivity. I was operated on the same day and the shrapnel was removed successfully. I recovered quickly, and within a week I was able to have meals in the hospital cafeteria.

One morning, when I was in the hospital cafeteria having a late breakfast, someone called out, "Ten hut!" which made everyone in the dining area jump to attention.

"At ease," a command followed. I was standing next to the aisle. I looked down the aisle and saw this tall, thin, white-haired officer walking down the aisle shaking hands with some of the former POWs. He wore two stars on each shoulder. When he came to where I was, he came to a stop, looked at me for a second, and said, "Hi, Sergeant." I wondered how he knew my rank because my stripes were not on my fatigue uniform.

"Good morning, General," I replied.

He continued down the aisle shaking hands and finally sat down to eat breakfast. I was still eating when the general got up to leave. He walked straight to where I was seated and stopped. I tried to stand, but he put one hand on my shoulder and said for me to keep my seat.

"Sergeant, don't you remember me?" he said in a quiet voice.

"No, sir."

"The old man by the well? You're the jet pilot, right?"

I said to myself, *Oh, my God.* He resembled that tall, thin GI at the well who told me he was the commander of the 24th Infantry Division and I didn't believe him. He was General Dean!

I finally blurted out, "Yes, sir."

"If you're not doing anything this evening, come to my room. I would like to talk with you."

"Yes, sir," I answered. I stood up and saluted him. He turned and walked away.

That evening I went to the building where the general was quartered and entered the hallway, which opened up to several rooms. A guard refused me further entrance even though I told him that General Dean had ordered me to report to him. I raised my voice until the general's aide appeared and asked the guard what the commotion was about. I told him that the general had invited me to see him but the guard refused to let me in. The aide told me to wait while he checked with the general. The aide returned and told me to follow him to the general's room.

The general welcomed me and pointed to a chair for me to sit in. We talked for about an hour about our prison experiences and at the end of the meeting he asked me when I was leaving for home. I said I didn't know and I was still waiting for the first available plane to Hawaii. He said he was bound for Hawaii in a few days and wondered if I would like to join him. Me, a poor Chinese boy from Hawaii, being offered a plane ride by a general? That almost floored me.

I said I would like very much to fly home with him. He asked if I had a uniform and I said I hadn't been issued one yet but in due time I would get one. He called his aide, a colonel, and told him to take me to a tailor in the morning for two uniforms with all the decorations that I was entitled to.

The next morning, the aide took me to a tailor shop and had me measured for two sets of fitted, gabardine uniforms. He came back the next day with the uniforms and all the decorations on them plus a pair of highly polished shoes. My stripes were sewn on. I was a sergeant first class when I was captured but the stripes on the sleeves were those of a master sergeant. I had received a promotion while I was a prisoner of war.

The next day I stuffed what few belongings I had into a small handbag and joined the general in the lobby for our ride to the airport. With other POWs, we boarded a hospital plane, a C-54 transport. Most of the passengers were officers.

Aboard a Hospital Plane

I was seated at the rear of the aircraft by myself. General Dean came and sat down next to me and we began talking again of our time in the prison camps. We talked as if we were old friends. Maybe we were, looking back at the time we met at the well. I tried to apologize for my behavior at our first meeting, but he just laughed and said not to worry about it. If there was anything I needed, anything, just ask him. He was assigned to Fort Ord, California, and if I needed anything, I could call him there.

It was a long flight to Hawaii. I was napping when the crew chief woke me up and told me I was wanted in the cockpit. When I reached the cockpit, General Dean was there. He pointed to the left and said, "Look, there is your island." I stretched over to the window of the cockpit and, sure enough, there was an island below—Kauai, as I understood later. General Dean turned to the pilot and asked him if we could have a quick tour of the island of Oahu for my benefit. The general was reminded that there was a reception waiting for him and the POWs at Hickam Air Force Base and he would need permission to extend the flight. The co-pilot called and permission was granted and we took a look of Oahu from the air.

Hickam Air Force Base

It was late in the afternoon when we landed at Hickam Air Force Base, almost an hour past our scheduled arrival. There was about an hour of daylight left. When the plane came to a complete stop, I looked out the window and saw a huge crowd behind the fence line. There were VIPs all over the place. A band was playing and an honor guard stood at attention. General Dean came to me and said, "I want you to step out of the plane first."

"But sir, they are waiting for you," I said.

"Never mind me. This is your home and I want you to be my personal aide for this moment. When we are on the ground, just follow me and stay on my right."

I had my handbag in my hand. He called his aide, a colonel, to carry my bag. We walked to the door of the airplane and I stepped out ahead of the general. Immediately I was hit with a barrage of flashes from cameras and other lighting equipment and I almost stumbled down the steps. There were generals, admirals, and other high-ranking officers in their dress uniforms. Behind them was the Honor Guard.

When we got to the welcoming party, the general introduced me to them by saying that I was his personal aide. After a few questions, he gave a short speech. Admiral Stump asked General Dean and me to inspect the Honor Guard. As we were trooping through the Honor Guard, I heard my wife calling from the crowd but dared not turn my head because the general was my responsibility.

When we finally passed the last rank of Honor Guards, I asked the general if I could join my family. He said by all means and to give my family his regards. He shook my hand, we saluted, and I ran to my family and hugged my wife, daughter, and son, who draped me in leis. My son had an extra lei so I went back to the general and gave it to him.

My family had to return home without me because I had to undergo tests at Tripler Army General Hospital. My leave started the next day and it was wonderful to be home again with my family.

In my captivity I wrote over 100 letters to my wife but she received only one. The letters probably never left the prison camp but were trashed by the prison camp commander. When she received this one letter, the army had to verify it to confirm my POW status because I was previously listed as missing in action. After the battle in April 1951, my field jacket with my name on it, which I had used to cover a wounded GI, was found at the battle site. Others, who thought I was blown up in the half-track vehicle, reported me killed and, because my body was not found, I was listed as missing in action until the Chinese reported me as a prisoner of war.

Years later when I read about General Dean's actions in the battle for Taejon, I realized why he had this rather unique relationship with me, although only briefly. He was the infantryman's general. He did not command his division from miles back of the front but fought alongside the men he commanded. He had a genuine interest in his men.

SEPTEMBER 22, 1953

Honolulu, Territory of Hawaii

The front page of the *Honolulu Advertiser* carried the following article written by reporter Jack Burby:

FIGHTING GENERAL BACK. Maj. Gen. William F. Dean, the hero of Taejon, came to the United States from a Communist prison last night, arm-in-arm with one of Hawaii's own.

The tall silver haired soldier, the prize prisoner of war of the Reds for 38 months, marched down the ramp of a hospital plane at Hickam at 7 p.m. with a broad smile on his face. At his side was M/Sgt. Clarence Y.K. Young, 28, of Honolulu, who spent 29 months as a Communist prisoner in Korea and who was freed 18 days ago with the general.

As the two men stepped into the glare of the arc lights, the general's grin faded, his face sobered. He took the sergeant's arm. "This is one of Honolulu's own," he said in a low voice. "One of Hawaii's own . . . a real hero."

Then he kept the sergeant by his side to share the spotlight as an honor guard snapped to attention and a brass brand blared a greeting. After the salute, the general moved toward the welcoming party. That was too much for Sgt. Young. He pulled away and ran across the parking ramp, out of the arc lights and into the arms of his family.

Roll Call of Killed in Action

Aguda, James G.; 3/30/51
Aguinaldo, Benito R.; 8/12/50
Ah Let, Louis; 8/12/50
Akazawa, Kazuaki; 9/16/51
Aki, Clarence H.; 12/08/50
Akina, Frederick K.; 6/17/52
Alexander, George R.; 8/12/50
Alfaro, Eddie Carvalho; 11/04/50
Amis, Alfredo; 7/20/50
Apao, George; 3/01/51
Apo, August L.; 9/26/52
Arai, Tatsuo; 10/14/51
Arakaki, James Seifuku; 1/08/53
Arakaki, Seichi; 9/26/52
Arakawa, Wilfred H.; 9/26/52
Arioli, Peter; 12/03/50
Asada, Hiroshi; 1/04/51
Asato, Thomas T.; no date
Asau, Albert H.; 3/08/51
Aspili, David; 8/10/52
Asuncion, Julian; 8/23/50
Atkins, Elroy J.; 7/24/53
Auyong, Clarence K. E.; 10/10/51
Bacarro, Florentino; 6/24/51
Baduria, Daniel, Jr.; 8/29/50
Balalong, Jose; 2/11/50
Bannister, Norman L.; 11/28/50
Barreto, Jamie; 2/15/51
Bedoya, Vincent V.; 8/12/50
Belarmino, Wedro C.; 10/03/51

Berasis, Ignacio M.; 10/15/52
Bergau, John H.; no date
Blackley, Charles E.; 11/28/50
Brillantes, Mac; 5/18/51
Brown, Daniel K.; 4/25/51
Bruckner John A.; 12/31/51
Buhisan, Philemon S.; 2/12/51
Burke, Douglas A.; 10/15/51
Burnett, Anthony L.; 12/06/50
Burton, Walter A.; 9/26/50
Cadiz, Liberato B.; 9/03/50
Calaustro, Antonio; 11/15/52
Calhau, Ernest M.; 3/23/51
Camacho, Louis C., Jr.; 8/13/50
Camillo, Anastacio F.; 8/12/50
Canyon, Peter; 6/18/53
Cardoza, Robert R.; 9/16/51
Chang, Albert S.; 11/27/50
Chinen, Harry M.; 1/03/51
Chong, Marchmont T.; 7/04/52
Chun, Wilfred Y. W.; 7/31/50
Chung, Raymond C. S.; 11/04/50
Coelho, Allan A.; 11/12/52
Correa, Benjamin M.; 7/21/52
Costa, John, Jr.; 9/11/51
Cowart, Carey S.; 3/22/51
Delu, Emil William; 1953
Demello, Justin M.; 9/18/50
Demello, Stanley C.; 8/16/50
Duitilen, Bruno C.; 8/17/51

Enaena, Richard; 1/29/51
Enoka, Henry P.; 4/26/51
Eshima, John S.; 8/13/50
Estrella, Benjamin B., Jr.; 11/24/52
Eum, Timothy T. S.; 2/19/51
Evans, William J.; 8/10/50
Palani, Matagisa S.; 8/12/50
Faris, Harold; 7/20/50
Farmer, Robert W.; 9/16/50
Faulkner, Robert C.; 9/05/51
Ferreira, Gerald J.; 9/16/50
Figueroa, Julio; 9/16/50
Finnegan, Thomas J.; 10/02/50
Flores, William Billy; 6/08/52
Friel, Ernest D.; 11/20/51
Fujimoto, Junichi; 2/15/51
Fujita, Hitoshi; 11/21/51
Fujita, Takeshi; 8/29/50
Fukamizu, Haruo; 8/12/50
Fukumoto, Ralph T.; 11/29/50
Fukumoto, Yoshimi; 5/18/51
Funakoshi, Thomas Y.; 12/14/52
Furtado, Walter C.; 11/01/50
Gajeton, Alfredo; 7/27/50
Galius, Rosalio; 1/30/51
Gampon, Alfredo M.; 8/28/52
Ganal, Pedro A.; 6/03/51
Ganeku, Seiken; 3/07/51
Garalde, Rufino; 9/06/51
Gaylord, William A.; 9/16/50
Gomes, John H., Jr.; 9/03/50
Gomes, Robert; 9/20/50
Gonzales, Donald P.; 3/26/53
Goto, Raymond T.; 6/19/53
Goto, Satoshi; 8/23/50
Gouveia, Donald J.; 1/07/51
Goya, Masao; 3/08/51
Gramberg, Bernard M.; 7/25/50
Gushiken, Gilbert M.; 7/19/50
Gusukuma, Yoshinobu; 7/10/52
Guzman, Rodrigo Q.; 11/24/51
Hagino, Hiroshi; 5/17/52
Hagiwara, Yoshio; 1/31/51
Haili, Raymond A.; 4/08/53

Hale, Isaac K.; 7/12/51
Hamada, Mitsuo; 11/29/50
Hamada, Patrick K., Jr.; 8/26/51
Hamaguchi, Rodney M.; 7/05/50
Hayakawa, Richard Y.; 4/17/53
Hema, Thomas E.; 9/04/50
Hernaez, Paulino E.; 5/30/51
Heu, Herbert Fah Yen; 12/11/50
Heu, William M.; 11/02/50
Hewlen, Richard D.; 11/07/50
Higa, Sadayasu; 10/06/51
Higa, Yutaka; 10/13/51
Higashida, Walter W.; 9/20/51
Hirakawa, Edward K.; 7/20/51
Hiraoka, Rin; 12/06/50
Hirokane, Jiro; 10/21/51
Hiwatashi, Jack A.; 9/07/51
Hiyane, Shigeo; 9/03/51
Ho, Everett A. E.; 9/02/51
Hoapili, Moses K., Jr.; 7/16/50
Hokoana, Paul H.; 7/20/50
Homawan, Alfredo C.; 9/05/50
Hookano, Peter M.; 8/25/50
Hookano, Vernard K.; 9/17/51
Hung, Robert D. T.; 10/10/51
Hussey, Wilfred K.; 12/12/50
Iaea, Alvin H.; 7/08/50
Ikeda, Yoshio; 8/12/50
Ishibashi, Edward M.; 10/12/51
Ishida, Mitsuyoshi; 12/07/50
Ishikawa, Wallace K.; 7/20/50
Ishimoto, Albert A.; 8/11/50
Ishimoto, Robert S.; 4/02/51
Ito, Yukinobu; 10/28/52
Itokazu, Yeikichi; 4/05/51
Ivy, Emmit M.; 8/12/50
Iwami, Osamu; 8/09/50
Izu, Isamu; 7/12/50
Izuo, Franklin Naruaki; 12/27/52
Jernigan, Vernon; 8/27/50
Joseph, David J.; 8/03/50
Kaaihue, Michael C.; 10/07/52
Kaakimaka, John K.; 12/12/50
Kaapana, Basil K.; 9/18/50

Kahoohanohano, Anthony T.; 9/01/51
Kahue, Arthur Cecil; 10/29/52
Kailianu, Robert W.; 7/16/50
Kaiuwailani, Howard W.; 3/26/53
Kalama, Clarence L.; 8/12/50
Kalawe, Albert; 6/08/52
Kaleo, William K.; 4/24/51
Kalepa, Lewellyn K.; 6/23/53
Kalino, Herbert K., 8/25/50
Kamai, Herman B.; 9/10/50
Kamakaokalani, William M., Jr.;
   10/17/52
Kamekona, William W.; 2/15/51
Kamoku, Benjamin S.; 7/20/50
Kanekura, Fred T.; 8/02/50
Kaneshiro, David T.; 8/12/50
Kaneshiro, Harry Y.; 2/20/52
Kaneshiro, Hayato; 9/20/51
Kaneshiro, Jack S.; 7/20/50
Kauahi, Alexander K.; 9/01/50
Kauhane, Samuel K.; 7/19/50
Kauhini, Leroy S.; 6/24/51
Kaui, Sidney K.; 12/02/50
Kawahara, Masayoshi; 10/09/51
Kawahara, Suyeo; 7/17/52
Kawamura, Masami; 10/08/51
Kawashima, William M.; 9/17/51
Kaya, Minoru; 7/20/50
Ke, Hiram L.; 11/28/50
Ke, Robert W.; 11/30/50
Kealalio, Daniel; 7/20/50
Kekiwi, Nelson; 10/16/52
Kekoa, Joseph K.; 7/12/50
Kelii, Matthew K.; 9/18/50
Keliikuli, David K.; 1/31/51
Kenolio, Arthur; 2/01/51
Keomaka, Samuel K.; 8/21/50
Kihara, Masayuki; 8/15/52
Kilar, Robert; 8/12/50
Kim, Albert W.; 9/09/51
Kim, Chan J. P., Jr.; 7/08/50
Kim, Charles C. S.; 8/06/50
Kim, John Chung June; 2/05/52
Kim, John L., Jr.; no date

Kim, Richard Bo Kil; 6/13/52
Kimura, Seiki; 10/03/51
Kinoshita, Richard; 10/14/51
Kiriu, Hiroshi; 10/13/51
Kiyohiro, Tetsuo; 10/12/51
Knobloch, Carl F.; 8/11/50
Kobashigawa, Robert; 10/03/51
Kochi, Takashi; 5/21/51
Kojiri, Satoru; 6/30/52
Kono, Richard Y.; 8/12/52
Koo, Young C.; 11/13/52
Koshimizu, Muneo; 10/05/51
Koyanagi, Sueo; 10/16/52
Kuhns, Homer K.; 9/24/50
Kuikahi, David A.; 3/30/52
Kumakura, George M.; 6/09/52
Kumashiro, Masaru; 9/08/51
Kuni, Moses E.; 9/24/50
Kunieda, Minoru; 2/28/51
Kupau, Leonard; 3/23/53
Kupau, Richard; 9/02/50
Kurosawa, Susumu; 7/12/50
Kutsunai, Kiyomitsu; 4/26/51
Kwock, George A. N.; 4/17/53
Labogen, Jimmie D.; 7/25/52
Lacro, George; 8/03/52
Ladao, Edward; 7/16/50
Lagansua, Teofilo; 5/18/51
Lagrimas, Fernando; 8/31/51
Lam, David W.; 1/01/51
Laping, Faustino; 10/27/52
Largusa, Bonifacio; 9/27/50
Lasua, Lawrence P.; 11/28/50
Lau Hee, Walter K.; 11/30/50
Le Blanc, Oreste I.; 8/12/50
Lee, Charles S. A.; 7/07/50
Lee, Elvin M.; 10/30/50
Lee, Sunnie Say Mun; 11/28/50
Lee, Yuk Kay D.; 2/14/51
Long, Jac E.; 1/03/51
Louis, Edward D.; 5/28/53
Lum, Chew Wung; 10/14/51
Lum King, Alfred; 5/05/53
Mabang, Pacifico; 6/20/51

Mabenis, Firminio; 10/15/52
Machado, Henry B., Jr.; 8/10/52
Machida, Lawrence K.; 9/04/50
Mackey, Robert K.; 4/16/53
Maeda, Hanford K.; 7/30/50
Maeda, Haruo; 7/29/50
Maguire, John J.; 8/09/50
Makaena, Charles K.; 8/11/50
Maldonado, Daniel; 4/22/51
Manuel, Franklin; 4/25/51
Martin, Horace E., Jr.; 4/22/52
Martin, Nicholas; 4/05/51
Martin, William R.; 8/23/50
Masatsugu, Ralph S.; 11/10/51
Mateo, Aurelio; 5/18/51
Matsuda, Heishin; 4/26/52
Matsuda, Kumaji; 7/20/50
Matsunaga, Joseph J.; 11/02/50
Matsushige, Jun; 11/13/52
Matthews, George M.; 8/13/52
Matutino, Gregorio; 8/23/50
McWhorter, Vance B.; 11/09/50
Mendonca, Leroy A.; 7/04/51
Mendoza, James J.; 4/04/51
Mew, Raymond K. W.; 10/12/51
Misaka, Kenneth A.; 4/06/53
Mitchell, John, Jr.; 1/12/51
Miyahira, Alan T.; 6/14/52
Miyahira, Samuel S.; 4/23/51
Miyajima, Donald S.; 8/16/50
Miyamoto, Robert K.; 6/23/51
Miyasato, Wilbert Y.; 10/14/51
Miyashiro, Daniel T.; 7/16/50
Miyashiro, Tamotsu; 5/18/51
Miyashiro, Tamayoshi; 10/02/50
Miyata, Harry Y.; 11/26/50
Miyazaki, Shigeo; 11/27/50
Mizusawa, Tsunematsu; 9/03/51
Mokiao, Raymond T.; 8/09/50
Molina, Benjamin; 7/01/52
Mooiki, George; 7/16/50
Moranti, Barbartine; 4/26/50
Morinaga, Akeji; 9/12/50
Morisako, James M.; 8/18/52

Morishige, Eiji; 2/04/51
Moriwaki, Kiochi; 9/20/50
Moriyama, Fumio; 5/18/51
Moriyasu, Haruo; 5/23/51
Murakami, Tadao; 3/07/51
Muraoka, Tsukasa; 6/22/52
Murata, Yukio; 12/23/52
Nagai, Ernest A.; 10/04/52
Nagamine, Hiroshi; 11/28/50
Nakama, Hideo; 7/19/50
Nakama, Seiso; 8/12/50
Nakamura, Noburo; 9/18/51
Nakasato, Satoshi; 7/20/50
Nakasato, Yeichi; 12/11/50
Nakashima, Roy T.; 4/22/51
Nakata, Shinichi; 5/25/51
Nakatani, Seinojo; 9/01/50
Namba, Raymond J.; 10/08/51
Naone, Philip R.; 7/31/50
Navarro, Julio Q.; 7/19/50
Ng, George K. S.; 10/15/51
Nihei, Lawrence Y.; 12/03/50
Nihei, Richard K.; 3/11/53
Nishida, Richard K.; 1/30/51
Nishimura, Charles; 8/12/50
Nishiyama, Kenichi; 10/22/51
Nitta, Frederick M.; 9/08/51
Ogasawara, Neil N.; 9/30/52
Ogata, Suetoshi; 9/19/51
Ogusuku, Takeo; 8/26/51
Okamura, Arthur I.; 10/14/51
Okimoto, Hisao; 10/06/51
Okinaga, Clifford H.; 8/15/52
Oku, Hiroshi; 10/09/51
Ono, Jitsuo; no date
Onomura, Milton T.; 6/25/52
Opulauoho, William K., Jr.; 9/12/51
Orig, Bruno R.; 2/15/51
Ortogero, Antonio; 8/13/50
Oshiro, Alfred E.; 1/05/53
Oshiro, Paul H.; 8/31/51
Ota, Mitsuyuki; 7/16/50
Otaguro, Thomas N.; 8/13/50
Pacheco, James F.; 10/24/52

Pacleb, Pontolion M.; 7/16/50
Palcat, Elpedio P.; 9/01/50
Palenapa, James; 10/07/51
Palamores, Amado, Jr.; 3/13/51
Panela, Esmenio; 12/02/50
Pang, Hoover T. H.; 9/19/51
Park, Raymond; 11/02/50
Park, Wilson; 8/09/50
Parungao, Tom; 8/09/50
Pele, Maika; 11/03/50
Perio, Daniel B.; 9/19/50
Pestana, Frederick; 2/09/51
Peters, Fred H.; 9/24/50
Peters, James M. E.; 8/12/50
Petroff, John, Jr.; 5/18/51
Pililaau, Herbert K.; 9/17/51
Pineda, James W.; 6/27/51
Ponciano, Benjamin; 9/16/50
Popa, Crisanto N.; 10/09/51
Pua, Raymond Kauinohea; 10/26/52
Purdy, William U.; no date
Purugganan, Mariani; 7/16/50
Queja, Edward K.; 9/17/50
Quittlen, Bruno C.; 8/17/51
Rainalter, William John; 4/22/51
Ramos, Lawrence; 9/11/51
Remers, Raymond Edwin; 10/21/52
Reyes, Ildefonzo; 11/24/51
Rivera, Fernando, Jr.; 7/20/50
Robinson, John L. P.; 5/30/51
Roman, Raphael; 11/07/50
Runnels, Frank J., Jr.; 12/03/53
Sagadraca, Fausto; 7/03/51
Saito, Masaki; 5/01/50
Saito, Masaya; 8/22/50
Saito, Tsugio; 7/08/50
Sakamoto, Allen T.; 10/15/52
Sakamoto, James N.; 8/12/50
Sakamoto, Masami; 10/26/52
Salomon, Richard; 4/9/53
Sandobal, Albinio; 12/04/53
Santiago, Gilbert; 11/07/52
Sasaki, Takeshi; 8/28/52
Sato, Shoji; 10/06/52

Sator, Gonzalo; 9/28/51
Schreiner, Allen W.; 11/17/52
Senaha, Henry T.; 9/20/51
Shibao, Nobumi; 11/25/52
Shima, Lawrence Y.; 4/07/51
Shimabukuro, Robert; 8/15/52
Shimabukuro, Shingo; 2/14/51
Shimogawa, Kenneth K.; 9/20/50
Shimoya, Toshio; 9/19/51
Shishido, Nobuo; 6/14/52
Shishido, Takashi; 8/11/50
Simbre, Rofino; 8/12/50
Sniffen, Edward M.; 6/10/52
Snyder, Charles E.; 8/12/50
Suzuki, Herbert H.; 8/07/50
Sweezey, Robert J.; 8/12/50
Sylvia, Adrian J.; 9/22/50
Tabangcura, Elpido; 3/24/51
Tabusa, Horace S.; 7/20/50
Tahara, Charles S.; no date
Tai, Calvin; no date
Takafuji, Theodore; 12/02/50
Takahashi, Edward; 12/03/50
Takamatsu, Herbert T.; 9/07/51
Takeshita, Nobuyuki; 7/22/51
Takeuchi, Harry Fumio; 12/06/50
Tamaru, Charles Y.; 11/04/50
Tamasshiro, Kaname R.; 6/14/52
Tanonaka, George H.; 7/20/50
Tanouye, Kiyoshi; 2/15/51
Tengan, Shinji; 7/28/52
Tenn, Francis H.; 1/30/51
Tokunaga, Richard R.; 10/15/52
Tom Sun, Celestine H.; 10/02/50
Toma, Daniel Takashi; 10/12/50
Torikawa, Casey; 7/28/50
Toro, George; 8/15/50
Torres, Robert R.; 2/12/51
Tosaki, Sadato; 8/22/50
Travis, Gilbert M., Jr.; 10/07/52
Tsuji, George Terumi; 1/29/57
Tsunoda, Sueo; 5/19/51
Tsuruoka, Harry N.; 11/14/52
Uehara, Noboru; 4/25/51

Uejo, Seiho; 10/09/51
Uemura, Mitsuo; 11/16/50
Ujimori, Yukio; 9/21/50
Ura, Konomu; 6/29/52
Urro, Faustino; 9/11/51
Uyeda, Robert T.; 2/14/51
Uyehara, Takeo; 9/07/51
Vallesteros, Juan B.; 2/12/51
Velles, Richard G.; 11/27/50
Vierra, Harold A.; 9/25/50
Vincent, Raymond M.; 10/13/51
Waiwaiole, Louis E.; 11/29/50
Warner, Leonard P.; 4/23/51
Warrick, Raymond P.; 11/03/52
Watanabe, Richard M.; 7/10/50
Watkins, Albert; 2/23/51
Wilkins, Joseph H.; 9/29/50
Williamson, Charles; 8/28/50
Wong, Kan Wah; 9/16/51

Wright, Benjamin H.; 11/25/50
Yaka, Muneo; 10/15/52
Yamagata, Nobuji; 10/04/51
Yamaguchi, Tsugio; 10/14/52
Yamaguchi, Yeiji; 8/09/51
Yamakawa, Timothy S.; 10/15/53
Yamane, Taketo; 10/09/51
Yamasaki, Harold S.; 1/04/51
Yang, Edwin D. S.; 10/04/50
Yap, Donald S.; 6/10/52
Yasunaka, Gary K.; 4/25/51
Yokomichi, Thomas H.; 9/07/51
Yokooji, Tetsumi; 9/28/51
Yokotake, Katashi; 7/19/52
Yoneshige, Itsuo; 10/16/52
Yoshida, Kanji; 5/25/51
Yoshikawa, Toshiharu; 8/11/50
Yoshino, Tatsuno; 9/13/51
Young, William T. C.; 10/18/52

Source: Office of Veterans Services, State of Hawaii.

APPENDIX B

Basic Combat Organizations

Rifle Squad: The basic combat unit of the army in the Korean War. A squad leader, assistant squad leader, BAR man, and six riflemen make up the nine-man squad.

Rifle Platoon: Three rifle squads and a weapons squad make up the platoon of thirty-six men. The platoon leader is a lieutenant and is assisted by a platoon sergeant.

Rifle Company: Commanded by a captain, the company is made up of three rifle platoons and a weapons platoon. The weapons squad consists of a 60mm mortar section (three guns) and a 57mm recoilless rifle section (three guns).

Infantry Battalion: A battalion has three rifle companies and a weapons company. It is commanded by a lieutenant colonel and has approximately 1,000 men. A heavy .30 caliber machine gun section, an 81mm mortar section, and a 75mm recoilless rifle section are its heavy weapons.

Regiment: Three battalions comprise a regiment, which is commanded by a colonel. Its heavy firepower comes from a 4.2-inch heavy mortar company, an artillery battalion, and, sometimes, a heavy tank company.

Division: Three infantry regiments make up an infantry division commanded by a major general. Main support includes three 105mm howitzer battalions, one 155mm howitzer battalion, an antiaircraft artillery battalion, and a tank battalion.

Basic Weapons Used by American and Communist Forces

United States

1. *U.S. Rifle, Caliber .30, M-1 (Garand):* The basic weapon of the infantry squad. It is semiautomatic, weighs 9.5 pounds, and fires an eight-round clip.

2. *U.S. Carbine, Caliber .30:* Fires lighter ammunition than the M-1 rifle and can be fired semiautomatic or full automatic but has less range and killing power than the M-1 rifle. Can be used with a fifteen-round magazine or thirty-round "banana" magazine.

3. *Pistol, Caliber .45:* The standard side arm or pistol of the army. It has great stopping power at a range of 25 yards.

4. *Browning Automatic Rifle* (BAR): The primary automatic weapon of the rifle squad. The rate of fire is 500 rounds per minute. It weighs 16 pounds or 20 pounds with a fully loaded magazine.

5. *U.S. Machine Gun, Caliber .30:* It is fully automatic, and uses the same cartridge as the M-1 rifle and BAR. It is the platoon's machine gun. There are two models.

6. *Rocket Launcher (Bazooka), 3.5 inch:* The 3.5 replaced the 2.36 bazooka. It weighs 15 pounds and fires an 8.5 pound charge.

7. *Recoilless Rifles:* The 57mm and the 75mm recoilless rifles are the artillery for the infantry companies. The 57mm is a shoulder weapon and the 75mm is fired from a tripod. They are flat trajectory weapons and are effective against fortifications.

8. *Mortars, 60mm, 81mm, and 4.2 inch:* Simple weapons consisting of a base plate and a smooth tube. They fire high explosive shells at very high angle capable of reaching targets that are in defiled. The 60mm mortar is carried by a company's weapons platoon and the

81mm mortar by the battalion's weapons company. The 4.2 mortar has great range and is carried by regiment.

9. *Quad .50s:* Four .50 caliber machine guns mounted on a half-track vehicle that are fired simultaneously. It was developed as an antiaircraft weapon but found to be most effective against massed ground attacks. It was in great demand by infantry companies in the Korean War.

10. *Artillery:* The artillery used in the Korean War was of World War II vintage.

—105mm howitzer. Has a range of nearly 7 miles.
—155mm howitzer. Has a range of 10 miles.
—155mm gun (Long Tom). Has a range of 14 miles.
—8 inch (202.2mm) howitzer. Has a range of 10 miles. It weighs 15 tons and requires a special utility vehicle to tow it.

11. *Hand Grenades:* Three basic types of hand grenades were used by UN forces in Korea: concussion, fragmentation, and chemical. The most commonly used one was the fragmentation or pineapple grenade. After the safety lever was released, the grenade would explode, after a four- to five-second delay. It had a kill radius of 5 to 10 yards and could inflict wounds in a blast radius of 50 yards.

The Communist Nation

1. *Infantry Rifles:* The communist forces relied upon a hodgepodge of shoulder weapons from the Russians and captured Japanese rifles. The most common were the Russian 7.62mm carbine and the Japanese 7.7mm Imperial Army rifles.

2. *Submachine Gun, 7.62 PPSH 41 (Burp Gun):* Designed by the Russians and later by the Chinese, the gun delivered a rate of fire of 900 rounds per minute, from whence the nickname, "burp," was derived. Its rate of fire was almost twice the rate of American automatic weapons and was most effective at close range.

3. *Mortars:* The Communists possessed 61mm and 82mm mortars that could fire American 60mm and 81mm mortar rounds, which the Communists captured in great quantities. Their longest-range mortars were the 120mm and 122mm mortars.

4. *Artillery:* Long-range artillery used by the Communists was the Soviet-made 122mm rifled cannon and the 152mm howitzer.

5. *Hand Grenades:* A grenade shaped like a small bottle was the most common form of grenade used by the Communists. These were made of explosive-filled metal heads mounted on wooden sticks. Similar-shaped grenades with thin metal canisters designed to stun rather than kill were the concussion grenades used almost exclusively by attacking communist troops. A favorite tactic of the Communists was to arm the first wave of attackers with only hand grenades, hoping to stun the defenders. The second wave would follow with automatic weapons.

Source: Michael J. Varhola, *Fire & Ice* (Mason City: Savas, 2000).

SELECTED BIBLIOGRAPHY

Alexander, Bevin. *The First War We Lost.* New York: Hippocrene B. Books, 1986.
Appleman, Roy E. *South to the Naktong, North to the Yalu.* Washington, D.C.: U.S. Government Printing Office, 1961.
Ballenger, Lee. *The Outpost War.* Washington, D.C.: Brassey's, 2000.
Berebitsky, William. *A Very Long Weekend.* Shippenburg, Pa.: This White Maine, 1996.
Blair, Clay. *The Forgotten War.* New York: Times Books, 1987.
Dvorchak, Robert J. *The Battle for Korea.* Hong Kong: Combined Books, 1987.
Ent, Uzal W. *Fighting on the Brink.* Paducah, Ky.: Turner, 1996.
Fehrenbach, T. R. *This Kind of War: A Study in Unpreparedness.* New York: Macmillan, 1963.
Franks, Kenny. *Citizen Soldiers: Oklahoma National Guard.* Norman: University of Oklahoma Press, 1984.
Giangreco, D. M. *War in Korea, 1950–1953.* Navato, Calif.: Presidio, 1990.
Gugeler, Russell A. *Combat Actions in Korea.* Washington, D.C.: U.S. Government Printing Office, 1987.
Hackworth, David B. *About Face: The Odyssey of an American Warrior.* New York, London, Toronto, Sydney, Tokyo, Singapore: Simon and Schuster, 1989.
Hammel, Eric. *Chosin: Heroic Ideal of the Korean War.* Navato, Calif.: Presidio, 1990.
Hastings, Max. *The Korean War.* New York: Simon and Schuster, 1987.
Hermes, Walter G. *U.S. Army in the Korean War: The Ebb and Flow.* Washington, D.C.: U.S. Government Printing Office, 1992.
———. *U.S. Army in the Korean War: Truce Tent and Fighting Front.* Washington, D.C.: U.S. Government Printing Office, 1966.
Higgins, Marguerite. *War in Korea.* New York: Lion Books, 1951.
Hinshaw, Arned L. *Heartbreak Ridge.* New York: Praeger, 1989.
Hoyt, Edwin P. *The Bloody Road to Panmunjom.* New York: Military Heritage, 1985.
———. *The Pusan Perimeter.* New York: Stein and Day, 1984.
Knox, Donald, with addition text by Alfred Coppel. *The Korean War: Uncertain Victory.* New York: Harcourt Brace Jovanovich, 1988.
Mossman, Billy C. *Ebb and Flow, November 1950—July 1951.* Washington, D.C.: U.S. Government Printing Office, 1990.

Paik, Sun-yup. *From Pusan to Panmunjom.* New York: Brassey's, 1992.

Republic of Korea. *History of U.N. Forces in the Korean War.* 6 vols. Seoul, 1972.

Slater, Michael. *Hills of Sacrifice.* Paducah, Ky.: Turner, 2000.

Stokesbury, James L. *A Short History of the Korean War.* New York: William Morrow, 1988.

Sumers, Harry G. *Korean War Almanac.* Facts On File, 1990.

Toland, John. *In Mortal Combat: Korea, 1950–1953.* New York: William Morrow, 1991.

Tomed, Rudy. *No Bugles, No Drums: An Oral History of the Korean War.* New York: Wiley, 1993.

Varhola, Michael J. *Fire & Ice: The Korean War, 1950–1953.* Mason City: Savas, 2000.

Westhover, John G. *Combat Support in Korea.* Washington, D.C.: U.S. Government Printing Office, 1987.

INDEX

ABOUT THE EDITOR

Louis Baldovi served in the U.S. Army with the 45th Infantry Division as a rifleman during the Korean War. Following his reenlistment in 1953, Baldovi was assigned to the Hawaiian Infantry Training Center at Schofield Barracks, Hawaii, where he served as an instructor and drill sergeant.

Following his discharge from the army, Baldovi attended the University of Hawaii, where he majored in secondary education. He retired from the Department of Education after twenty-seven years of service as a teacher and principal.

He has served on several state veteran boards and committees and was instrumental in organizing Korean War veteran organizations in Hawaii.

Baldovi, his wife Valerie, and their four adult children live in Honolulu, Hawaii.